BRAZILIAN RHYTHMS *for the* DRUMSET

Bossa Nova and Samba
by Henrique C. De Almeida

CARL FISCHER®

65 Bleecker Street, New York, NY 10012

DRM119

ISBN 0-8258-5658-2

AF400674

Dedication

I dedicate this book to my father Dr. Gilberto Lobo de Almeida, and my mother, Maria da Conceicao Duperron Cavalcanti de Almeida.

A very special thanks to Ignacio Berroa, for the incredible support, encouragement, and long, deep conversations that directly inspired me to write this book.

Thank you Sandy Feldstein for being so patient, for teaching me about the publishing world and for working so hard with me on this project.

Thank you notes

I would also like to thank: My father and my mother; Leonardo de Almeida, Elizabete de Almeida, Leandro de Almeida, Jill Miller de Almeida, Joan Miller, Michelle Tennesen, Dawn Miller, Maureen Miller, Airto Moreira and Flora Purim, Nando Lauria, Alceu Valenca, Gary Chaffee, John Ramsay, Alan Dawson, Bob Moses, Lenny Nelson, Nana Vasconcelos, Don Um Romao, Adelson Pereira, Zezinho, Kelly Burns, Jeff Jenkins, Bill Kopper, Kim Stone, Scott Griess, Todd Steincamp at Brazilian Drums.com; David McAllister and Steve Nigohosian at LP percussion; Mile High Studios, Jennifer Corder, Rhonda Scocos, Graner Music; Nicholas Hopkins, Alex Teploff, Lola Kavonic of Carl Fischer Music; and The Berklee College of Music.

Henrique De Almeida & The Brazilian Jazz Project is:

Henrique De Almeida: drums, percussion and vocals

KIM STONE: bass

JEFF JENKINS: piano and keyboards

BILL KOPPER: acoustic and electric guitars

SCOTT GRIESS: sound engineer

Technical Info

Henrique plays Zildjian Cymbals, Yamaha drums, LP percussion, Remo drum heads, Vic Firth sticks and mallets.

TABLE OF CONTENTS

PREFACE

Welcome! I like to think of *Brazilian Rhythms for the Drumset* as a complete system of how to orchestrate authentic Samba rhythms on the drumset. My primary intent in writing this book is to show how Brazilian music can be applied to the drumset. Thus, no emphasis is placed on the technical aspects of hand drumming in Brazilian percussion music.

Each of the seventeen sections has been divided into subsections to aid in the learning process. Here is a brief synopsis of these sections:

Section 1

One of the most popular Brazilian music styles outside Brazil is the Bossa Nova, which is derived from Samba. I chose to begin with Bossa Nova because it is the least complicated rhythm executed by professional drummers on the drumset. You will also note that I have included a historical background of the Bossa Nova plus examples of the most useful patterns.

Section 2

Section 2 offers a historical background of Carnival, Brazilian culture, and the social and cultural impact of Samba in the Brazilian society. I then introduce the most popular Samba percussion instruments. The drumset performer will learn what the Samba percussion instruments sound and look like and will understand their intended musical function in the Samba ensemble. A listening example is given along with a score analysis for your study.

Sections 3–16

In Sections 3–16, I cover the system in depth, and I will demonstrate how you can create your own authentic Samba rhythms on the drumset. Note that in many instances I will give you examples of different patterns in a given style, simply to give you a starting point of reference that will hopefully inspire you. I encourage you to read carefully the instructions on how to create your own examples.

In *Drumset Samba Grooves: Performance Concepts* (Section 3, p. 60), as well as in other parts of the book, I offer suggestions on how to practice and create original parts. I encourage you not to ignore these sections because your work will eventually become a collection of your own interpretation of Samba, which, by the way, is exactly how musicians play in Brazil. For example, if you were to ask ten different drummers to play a Samba rhythm, you would hear many variations between all the drummers, yet the same core accents and orchestration.

Section 17

Finally, Section 17 addresses odd meters. Since the popularity of Brazilian music has increased among jazz musicians these days, I feel you would benefit from a basic knowledge and set of skills that would enable you to perform different styles of Samba in odd meters; this will be a wise investment of your time during your practice routines. Note that live performance and recorded examples are included for each style and play-along versions of the material are included throughout the book. You may find that they are fun to play with; in my opinion, they will help you develop a better feel for the music. I much prefer this way of learning to practicing with a click track or metronome.

If you know a little bit more about Brazil, Samba, and Carnival by the end of your studies with this book, if you can recognize and audibly differentiate the sounds of the most popular Samba percussion instruments, then I have accomplished my mission. The next step will be for you to create authentic parts and play some of the styles on your own.

Have fun, thank you so much for your interest in Brazilian music, and good luck with your drumming.

—Henrique De Almeida

ABOUT HENRIQUE DE ALMEIDA

Mr. Henrique De Almeida holds a Masters Degree in Music Performance, and is a graduate of The Berklee College of Music with a degree in Jazz Composition. He has performed, toured and or recorded with Nat Adderley, Nelson Rangel, Jeff Narell, Ira Sullivan, Tiger Okoshy, Victor Mendonza, Danilo Perez, Phil Wilson, Baron Brown, Matt Garrison, Kim Stone, Steve Hunt, Dave Valentin, Bill Summers, Hilton Ruiz, Betty Carter, Willie Williams, Nando Lauria, Alceu Valenca, Gilberto Gill, Greg Hopkins, Bill Cosby, Brian Lynch, Ronnie Matthews, David Williams, Luciana Souza, Katy Webster, and Oscar Kartaia among others.

His career includes performances, touring, T.V. appearances and recording through Europe, South America, North America and Central America. Some of his performance venues include New York City's Carnegie Hall, The Paris Olympia, The New York City Lincoln Center, The Kool Jazz Festival, The St. Louis Blues & Jazz Festival, The New Orleans Jazz & Heritage Festival, The Montreaux Jazz Festival, The Breckenridge Jazz Festival, The Aspen Jazz Festival, The Boston Globe Jazz Festival and The Hattiesburg Jazz Festival.

He was a long-time student of legendary jazz masters Mr. Allan Dawson, and Mr. Gary Chaffee while living in Boston, Massachusetts.

He is the leader of his own group "Henry De Almeida & The Brazilian Jazz Project". The group plays a mixture of Brazilian music and Jazz. The band has a new record to be released in the Fall of 2005. Mr. De Almeida is also the co-leader of the Colorado-based modern Jazz band, "Cornerstone", with bassist Kim Stone (Spyro Gyra/The Remington's), and the Jazz Fusion group "Deux" with Jazz bassist virtuoso Kirwan Brown.

SECTION 1: BOSSA NOVA
Introduction • Part 1

The sensuous Bossa Nova is characterized by a unique rhythmic pattern. Heavily influenced by the "Cool Jazz" of the 1950s and 1960s, Bossa is usually played with a light touch, in slow to medium tempos. It is known for harmonic sophistication and improvisation. Jazz combos blend the sounds of the acoustic piano, acoustic bass, acoustic nylon-string guitar, soft drumset and percussion. Sometimes the flute or the vibraphone enhances Bossa melodies.

There are three ways to begin to understand the right feel of the Bossa Nova:

- I strongly recommend listening to recordings of Brazilian artists. Examples are Tom Jobin, João Gilberto, Luiz Essa, Nara Leao, Carlos Lira, Johnny Alf, Chico Boarque, and Francis Hime. (I had the pleasure of touring with Hime in Brazil for a couple of years.)
- I also recommend going to live performances of Brazilian musicians. This is the best way to visualize how certain things are executed on different instruments, especially drumset and percussion.
- Finally, I recommend sitting in with Brazilian musicians as they play the Bossa Nova or playing with people who have experience with that music idiom.

Here are a few things to keep in mind when playing Bossa Nova on the drumset with a Brazilian Jazz combo:

- Always remember, the Bossa should be very sensual. It has a Jazz-ballad quality to it.
- Legato is the name of the game here. Keep it simple and suave. Play it softly. Brushes are welcome. A nice flat ride or even a cymbal with rivets goes well when playing Bossa.
- Remember to keep your Bossa interpretation distinct from other Brazilian styles such as the Samba. For example, I either play the Bossa clave or stay very close to it.

The clave pattern must be adapted to the contour of the song's melodic structure when you perform with a band. Listen to the melody. Make adjustments on your clave pattern to avoid rhythmic clashes.

Now let's take a look at some examples of Bossa Nova rhythmic patterns.

NOTATION KEY:

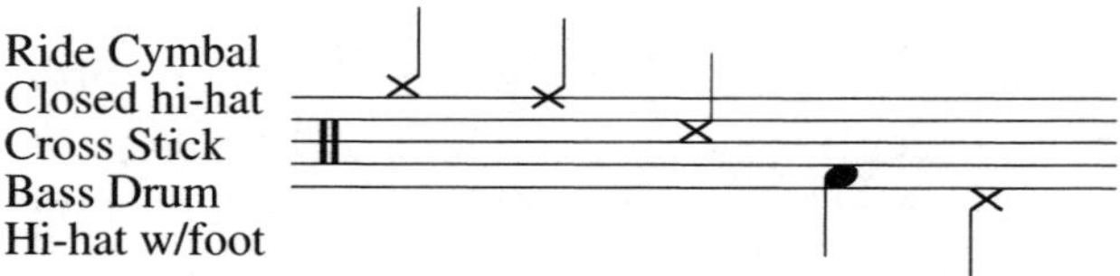

This is one of the most used Bossa Nova grooves, using the closed hi-hat and cross stick 3/2 clave. **NOTE:** Multiple examples are included on individual tracks.

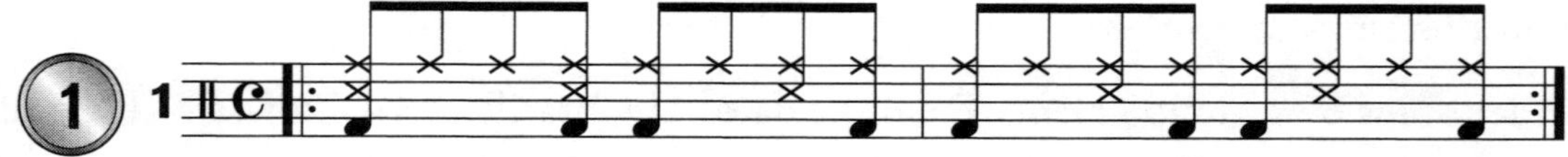

Now, in 2/3 clave.

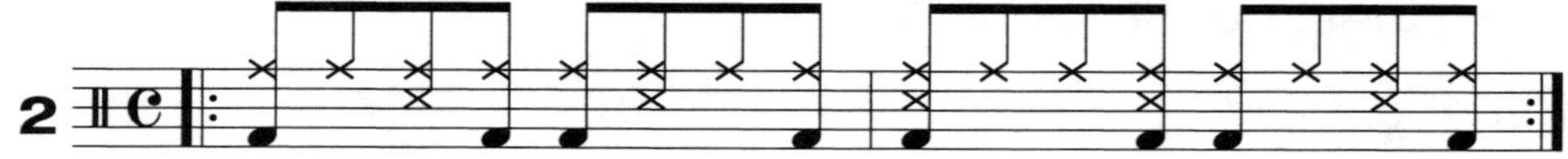

This example uses the ride cymbal; cross stick plays 3/2 clave.

Now, in 2/3 clave.

Right-hand Brush Strokes • Part 2

In this section the hi-hat and bass-drum feet ostinatos will be the same as in the previous section. While the left hand continues to play the Bossa clave in 3/2 and 2/3 with the cross stick, the right hand will be playing different patterns on the snare drum with brushes.

In 3/2 clave.

In 2/3 clave.

While keeping the hi-hat/bass-drum ostinato and the cross stick 3/2 or 2/3 clave, practice the following patterns. The right hand uses brushes on the snare drum.

Take a look at the following examples.

Right hand taps eighth notes with brushes on the snare drum. Left hand plays cross stick 3/2 clave.

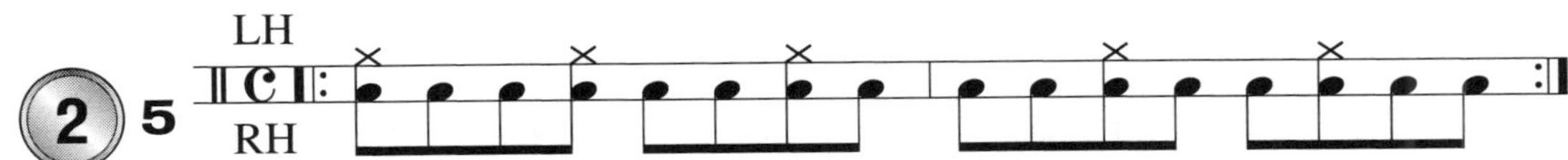

Right hand taps eighth notes with brushes on the snare drum. Left hand plays cross stick 2/3 clave.

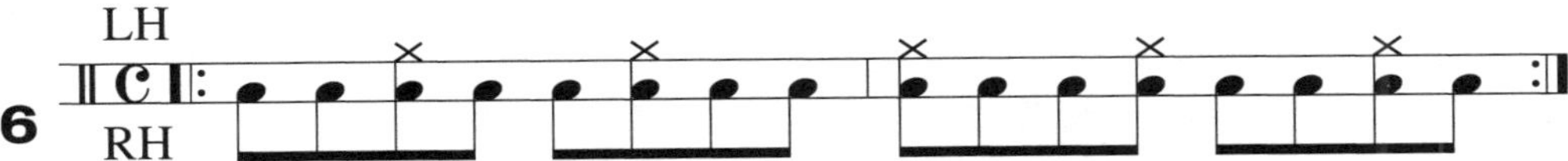

Right hand swishes side to side in eighth notes with brushes (**Sliding Staccato Sweeps) on the snare drum. Left hand plays cross stick 3/2 clave.

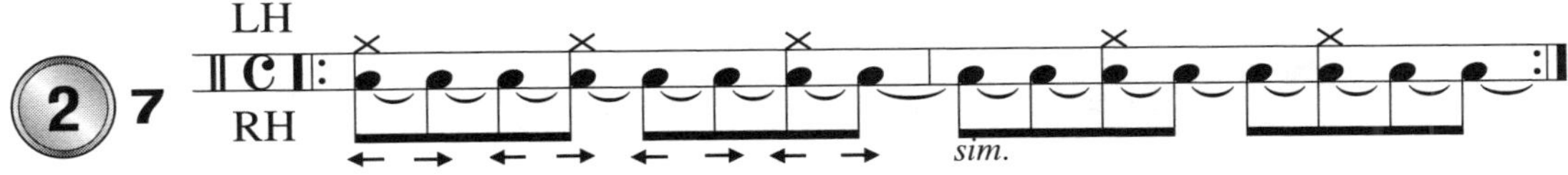

** Notation principles and terms used for brush playing are from *Brushworks, The New Language for Playing Brushes* by Clayton Cameron [Published by Carl Fischer Music, catalog number DRM105]

Right hand swishes side to side in eighth notes with brushes (**Sliding Staccato Sweeps) on the snare drum. Left hand plays cross stick 3/2 clave.

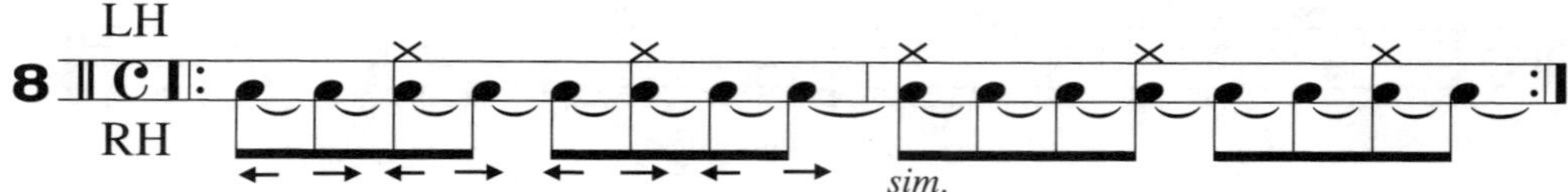

Right hand swishes in circles in quarter notes with brushes (**Quarter-Note Legato Sweeps) on the snare drum. Left hand plays cross stick 2/3 clave.

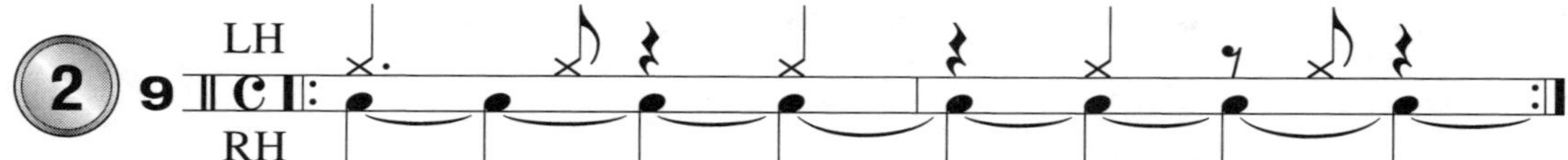

Right hand swishes in circles in quarter notes with brushes (**Quarter-Note Legato Sweeps) on the snare drum. Left hand plays cross stick 2/3 clave.

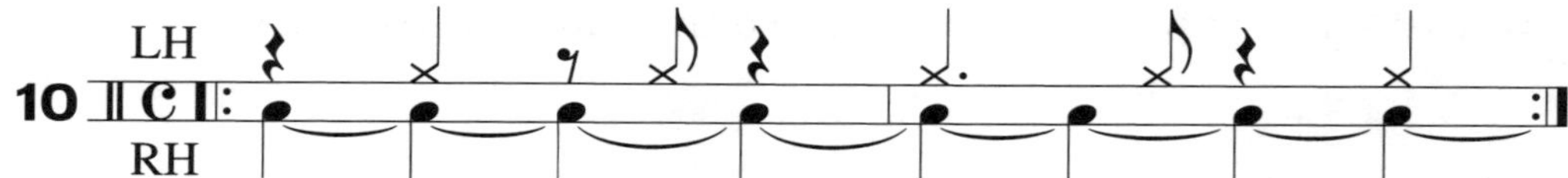

NOTE: When playing the circle brush pattern (**Legato Sweeps), the brush never leaves the drum head.

Right hand swishes in circles in half notes with brushes (**Half-Note Legato Sweeps) on the snare drum. Left hand plays cross stick 3/2 clave.

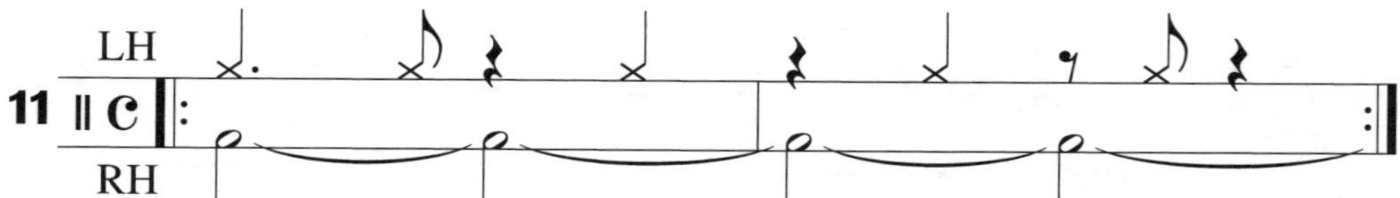

Right hand swishes in circles in half notes with brushes (**Half-Note Legato Sweeps) on the snare drum. Left hand plays cross stick 2/3 clave.

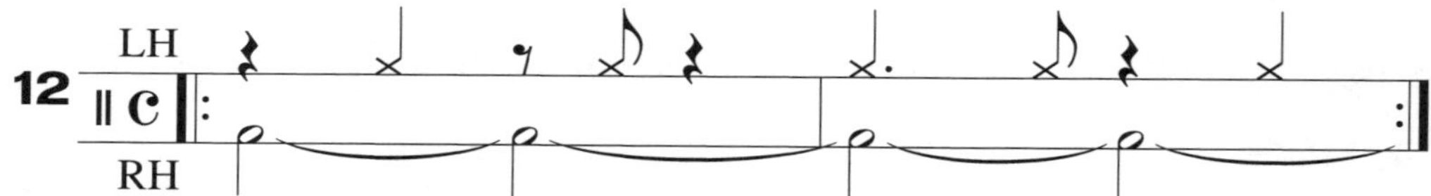

Right hand swishes side to side with brushes in sixteenth notes on the snare drum. Left hand plays cross stick 3/2 clave.

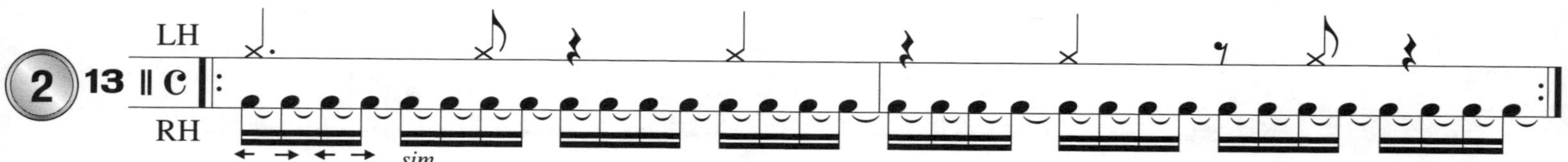

Right hand swishes side to side with brushes in sixteenth notes (**Sliding Staccato Sweeps) on the snare drum. Left hand plays cross stick 2/3 clave.

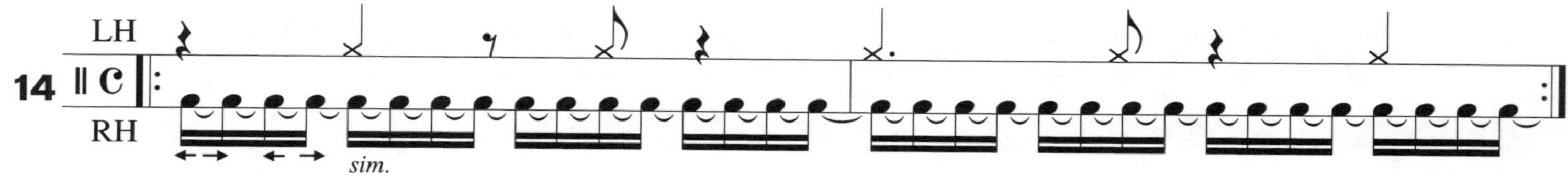

Right- and Left-hand Brush Strokes • Part 3

In this part both hands will play with brushes on the snare drum. The same hi-hat/bass-drum ostinato that was used in the Parts 1 and 2 will be used here as well.

Play the hi-hat/bass drum ostinato with all the examples in this section.

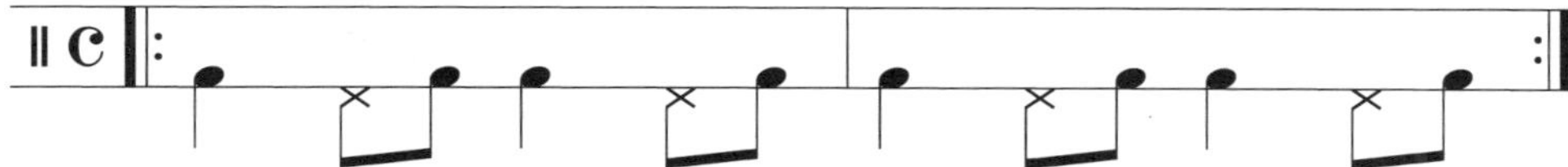

Right hand taps eighth notes, accenting the 3/2 clave. Left hand swishes side to side in eighth notes (**Sliding Staccato Sweeps) imitating a shaker sound.

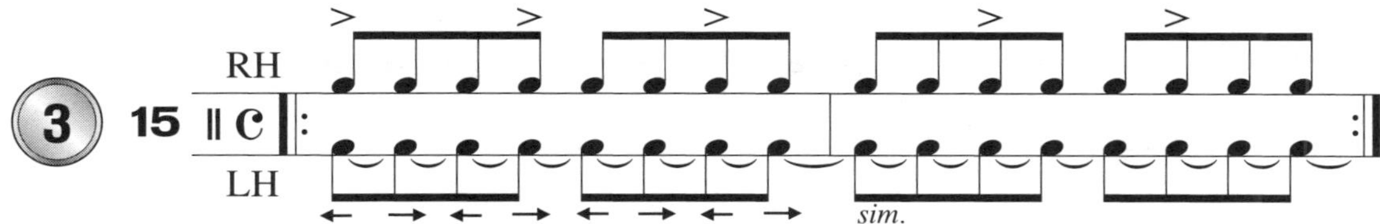

Right hand taps eighth notes, accenting the 2/3 clave. Left hand swishes side to side in eighth notes (**Sliding Staccato Sweeps) imitating a shaker sound.

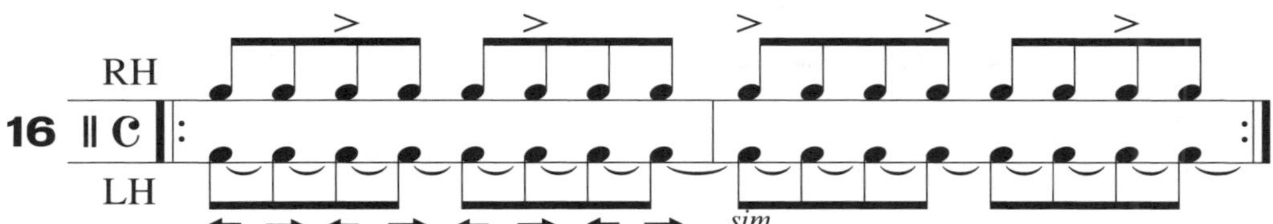

Right hand taps eighth notes accenting the 3/2 clave. Left hand circles in quarter notes (**Quarter-Note Legato Sweeps).

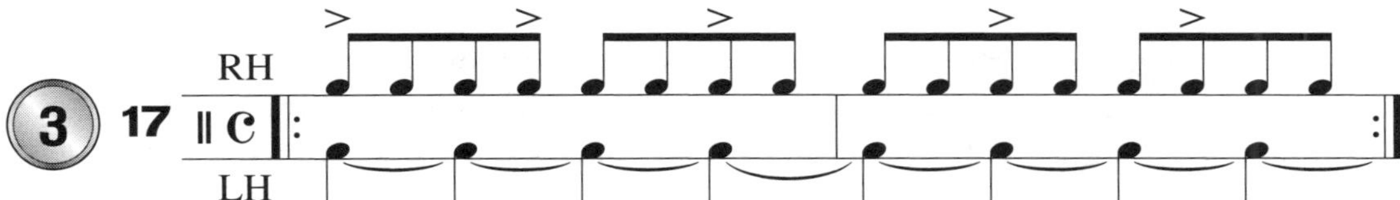

Right hand taps eighth notes accenting the 2/3 clave. Left hand circles in quarter notes (**Quarter-Note Legato Sweeps).

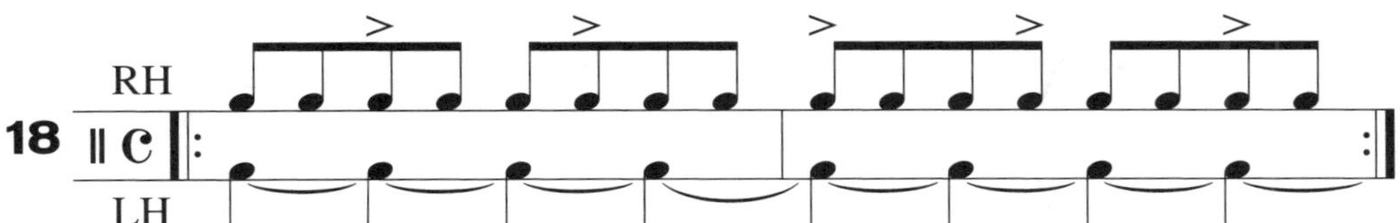

Right hand taps eighth notes accenting the 3/2 clave. Left hand circles in quarter notes (**Quarter-Note Legato Sweeps), accenting beats 2 and 4 by pressing the brush harder on the snare-drum head on those counts.

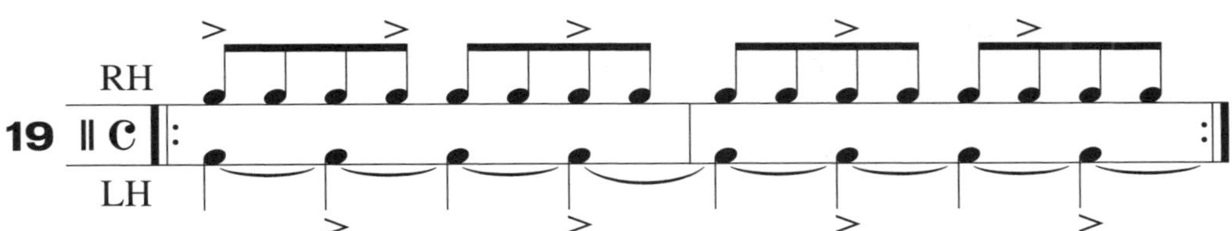

Right hand taps eighth notes accenting the 2/3 clave. Left hand circles in quarter notes (**Quarter-Note Legato Sweeps), accenting beats 2 and 4 by pressing the brush harder on the snare-drum head on those counts.

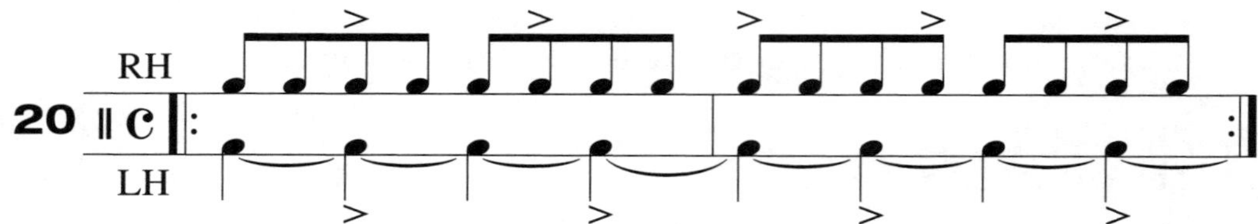

Right hand taps eighth notes accenting the 3/2 clave. Left hand circles in half notes (**Half-Note Legato Sweeps).

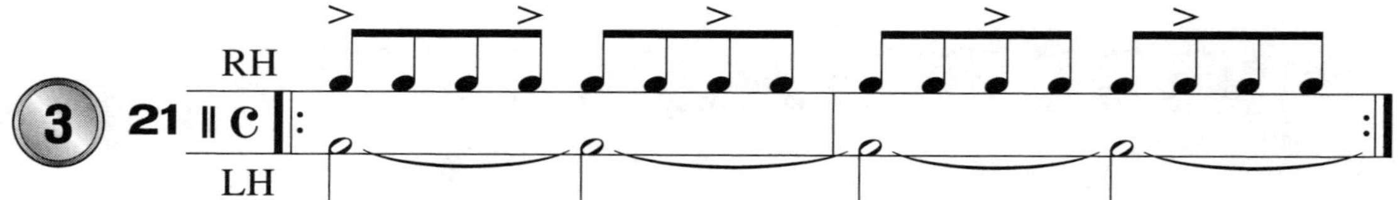

Right hand taps eighth notes accenting the 2/3 clave. Left hand circles in half notes (**Half-Note Legato Sweeps).

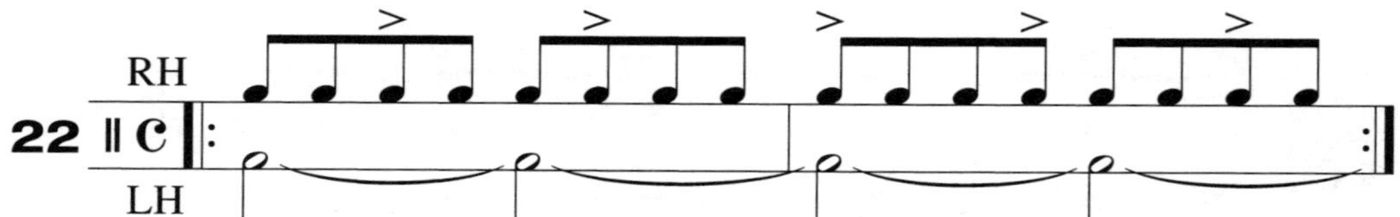

The Funny 2 Pattern

The Funny 2 Pattern is a right-hand brush diagram in the shape of a "2" or, for a more staccato sound, in the shape of the letter "Z."

Here are the moves. 1) Begin from the top of the number 2, and move clockwise on counts "one and", sliding to the right with a horizontal brush sidestroke. 2) Move to the bottom of the number 2 on the count "two". 3) End with five sliding side-to-side brush strokes (left-right-left-right-left) on counts "and three and four and". The right-hand brush should be on the left side on the bottom of the diagram. Be ready to start the next measure.

The motion of the right-hand brush "A" pattern should look something like this.

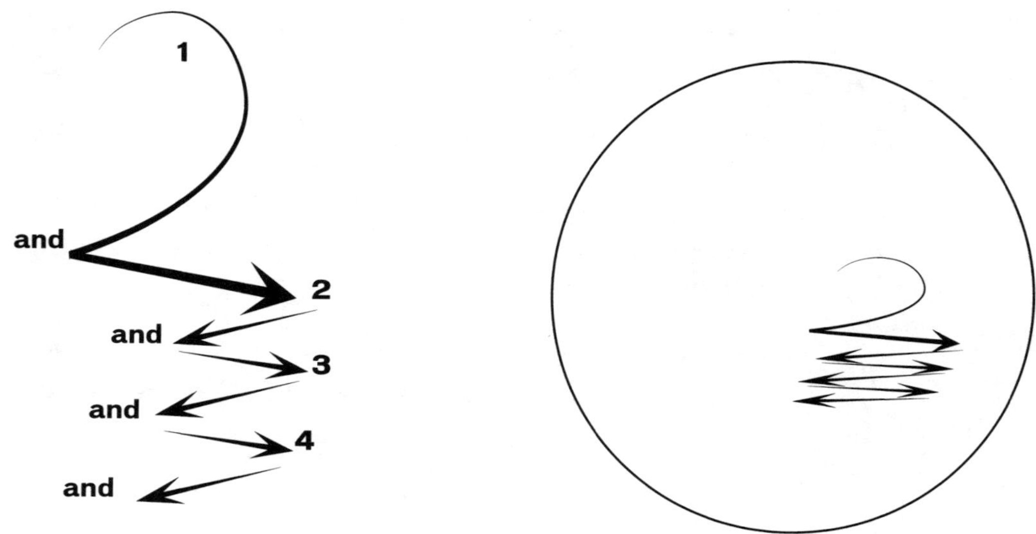

Showing the right-hand Funny 2 Pattern with notation:

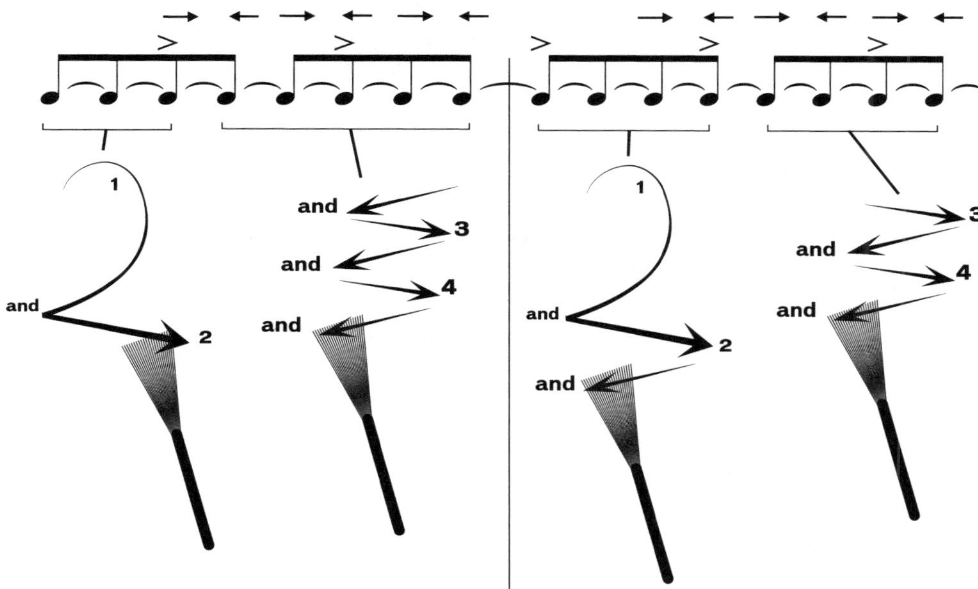

The next two examples use the Funny 2 Pattern in the right hand, along with Half-Note Legato Sweeps in the left hand.

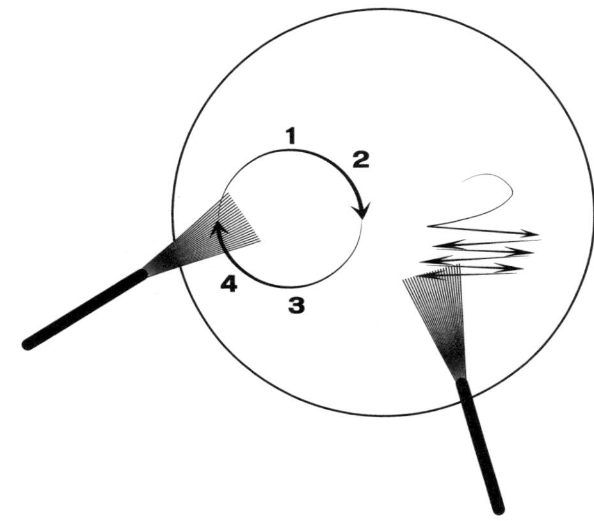

Right hand plays the Funny 2 pattern, swishing the counts "one and", accenting the 2/3 clave with side-to-side swish strokes. Left hand circles in half notes (Half-Note Legato Sweeps).

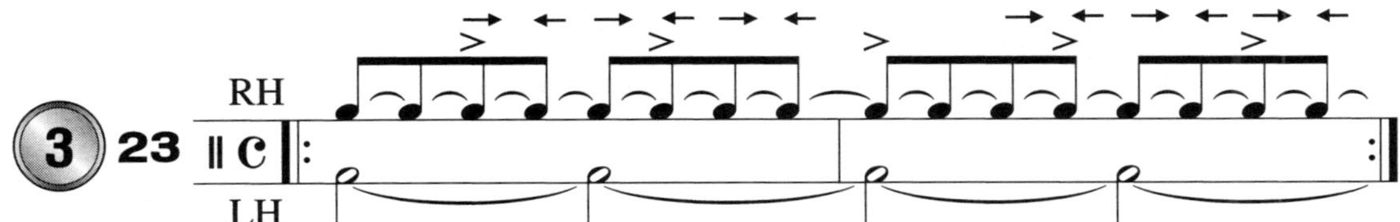

Right hand plays the Funny 2 pattern. (Accenting the 3/3 clave) Left hand circles in half notes (Half-Note Legato Sweeps).

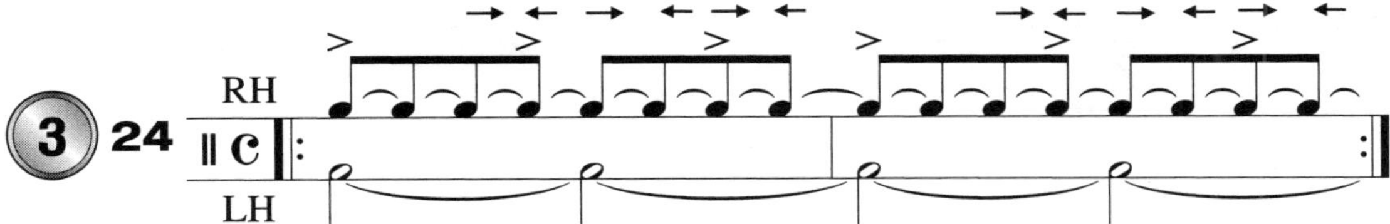

In examples of 25 and 26, we have right hand swishes side to side in sixteenth notes (Sliding Staccato Sweeps), imitating a shaker sound, while accenting the 3/2 clave. Left hands circles in half notes (Half-Note Legato Sweeps). This example implies a double-time feel and should be used only if the music calls for it. I find it appropriate to use this type of sixteenth-note pattern only in extremely slow tempos.

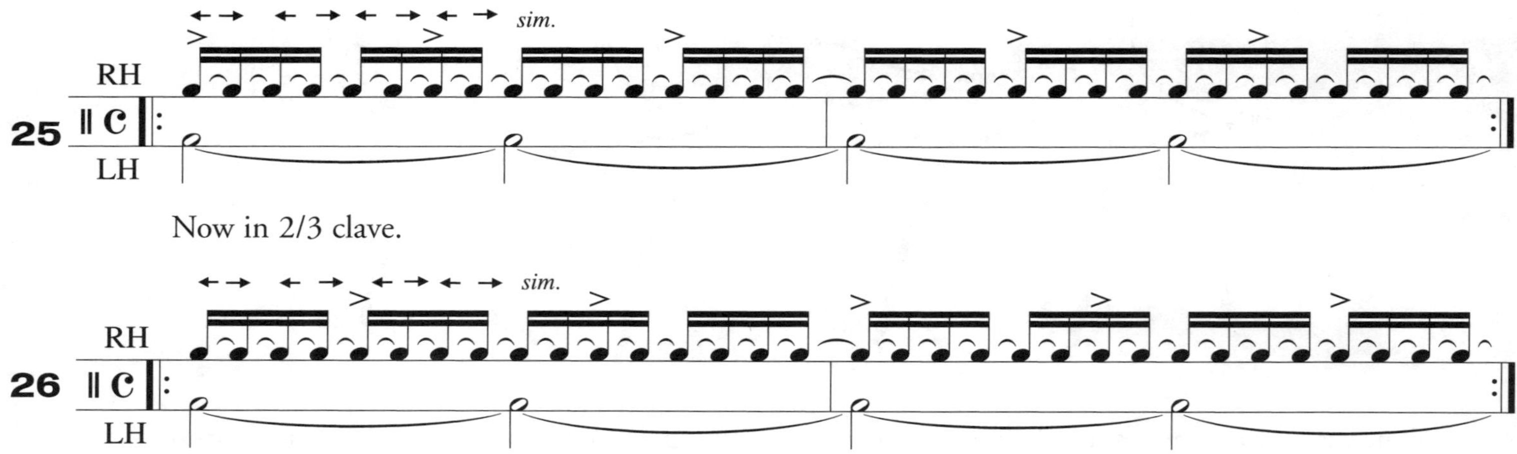

Now in 2/3 clave.

Right Hand Plays Shaker

Brazilian drummers and percussionists sometimes add color to eighth notes and sixteenth notes by playing shakers in one hand and the Bossa Nova rhythm on the drumset. The following examples substitute the shaker for the hi-hat, ride cymbal or brushes.

Left hand plays 3/2 Bossa clave. Right hand plays shaker in eighth notes.

Now in 2/3.

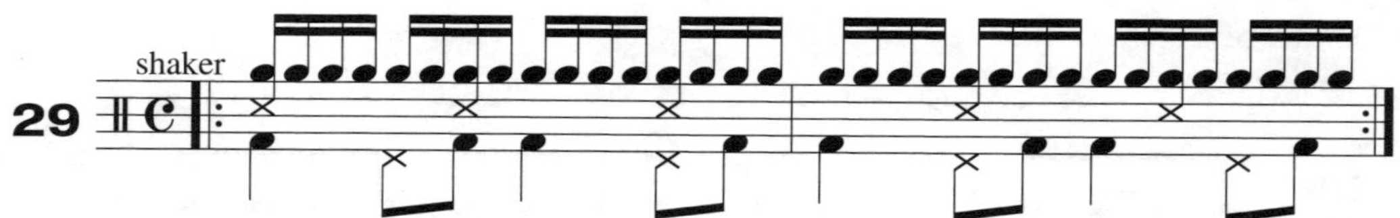

Left hand plays 3/2 Bossa clave. Left hand plays shaker in sixteenth notes.

Left hand plays 2/3 Bossa clave. Left hand plays shaker in sixteenth notes.

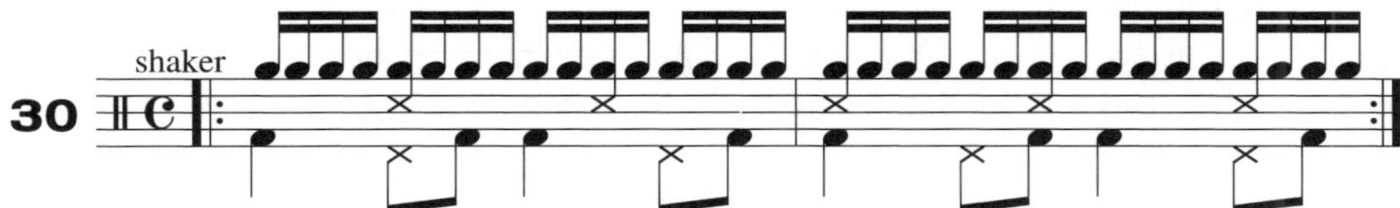

One-measure and Three-measure Phrases

One-measure Bossa Nova clave patterns can be very effective. Here are some ideas you should try by playing them with the previous examples. Try these examples with one-measure phrases.

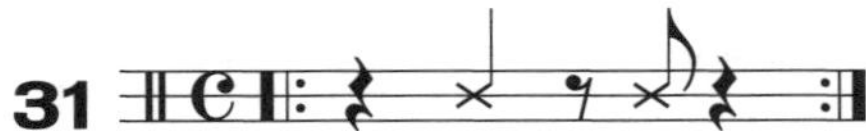

This is a three-measure phrase using the dotted quarter-note.

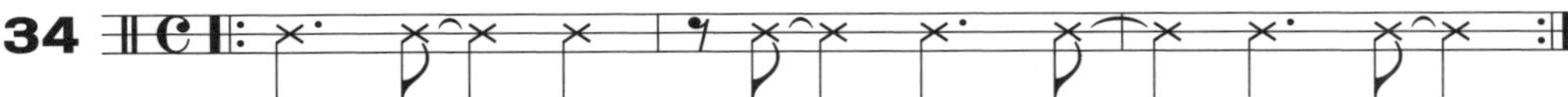

Hi-hat and Bass-Drum Ostinatos

Here are some hi-hat and bass-drum ostinatos. Try playing them with the previous examples.

Here is a reminder: Listen to recordings of Bossa Nova artists to get more ideas of hi-hat and bass-drum ostinatos.

Bossa Bolero

This is a Brazilian hybrid groove. It is not a Bossa, and it is not an authentic bolero, but rather a blend of both. If you listen to Gal Costa, Lulu Santos or many others, you will hear singers expressing the Bossa Bolero grooves. They usually have slow tempos.

NOTATION KEY:

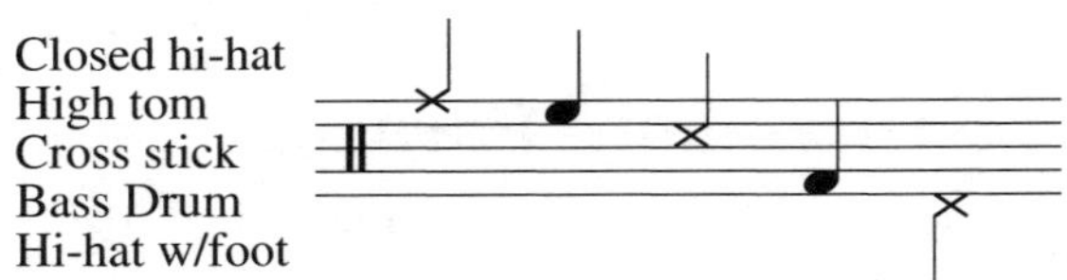

In 3/2 clave.

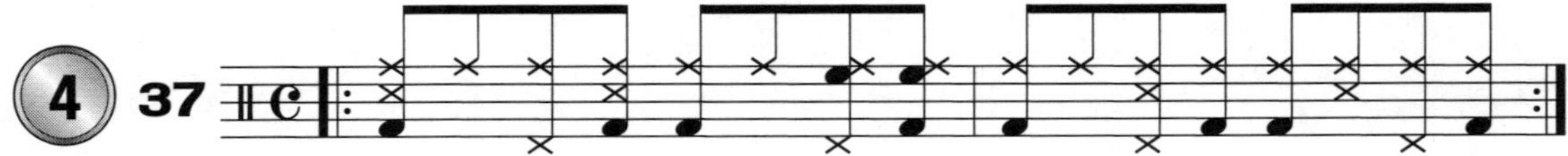

In 2/3 clave.

In 3/2 clave.

In 2/3 clave.

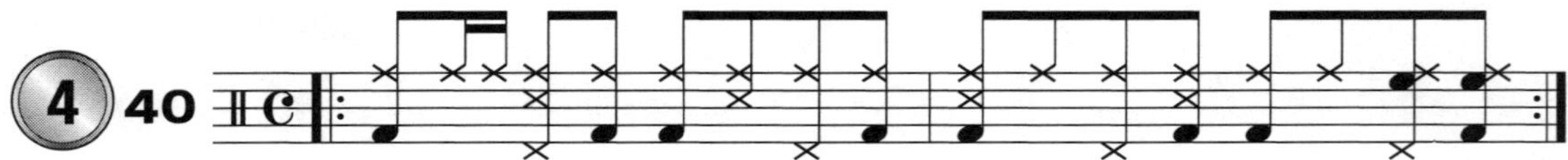

Here, the "feel" of 2/3 clave is implied, although some parts of the clave are omitted.

Here again, we imply a 3/2 clave.

Playing the second note of the 2/3 clave on beat 3 allows more time for the left hand to move from the snare-drum cross stick to the tom-tom.

The concept is similar here, implying the 3/2 clave.

NOTE: Once you are familiar with the Bossa Bolero patterns, try playing them as a four- or eight-measure phrases. Play four or eight measures as written in the examples. Then, without stopping, switch the right hand from the hi-hat to the ride cymbal. Continue playing the same parts on the rest of the drumset. (The left foot will be playing 2 and 4 on the hi-hat.) The change will usually occur during the B-section or the bridge of a song.

I recommend alternating back and forth from the hi-hat to the ride cymbal until you are comfortable doing this. Your goal is to be able to shift from the hi-hat to the ride cymbal without affecting the sound of the other parts of the pattern.

Contemporary Bossa Nova Grooves

As you mature as a musician, you will develop your own vocabulary of grooves, concepts, and other musical tools. You will incorporate what you have learned from as many different styles of music as possible. Once you have researched, studied, and learned how to play authentic patterns of a certain styles of music, it will be equally important for you to adapt to the contemporary musical situation for which you are performing.

Sometimes, playing in an "authentic" way will not seem comfortable or suitable for a venue. Knowledge of various authentic styles permits you to call on your own mental database filled with what you have absorbed as a listener and a performer. Your logical next step will be to experiment by mixing and combining styles in a hybrid way.

Mixing and combining styles is commonly known today as "Fusion." With a respect for various music styles and where they came from, always be sensitive to where it is appropriate to play in Fusion style and where it is not. When I adapt Bossa Nova patterns in a contemporary style, I think of the great drummers who successfully incorporate in their playing American Jazz and Rock concepts with the Brazilian feel. A good example is the approach used by drummers Danny Gottlieb and Paul Wertico.

The following Bossa Nova-based grooves are fused with elements of Jazz and Rock. I personally use these grooves successfully when playing "Brazilian Jazz" tunes, or when I play songs that have Brazilian flavor. While I keep the Bossa Nova feel, I give more elasticity to the beat. I stretch the pattern to improvise with less restriction than the authentic style. My Bossa clave rhythm will be embellished. The ride ostinatos are a little more involved than the ones in previous Bossa Nova examples.

Fusion Bossa Grooves

Here are grooves suggesting a fusion, double-time feel. Notice the two extra notes embellishing a Bossa clave. The two notes are play right after the clave note, making the clave rhythm longer and more elastic. These grooves also include Rock/Pop ride-cymbal ostinatos.

In 3/2 clave.

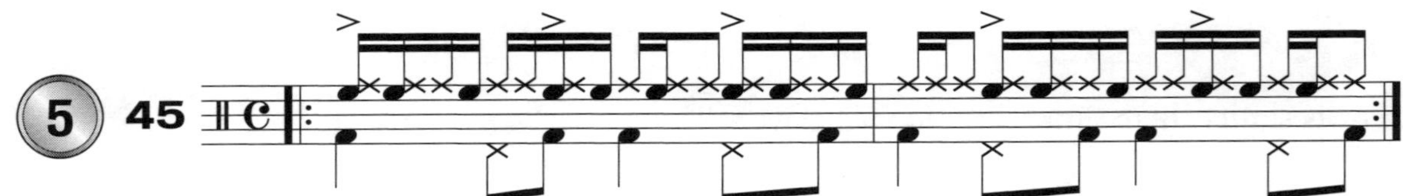

In 2/3 clave.

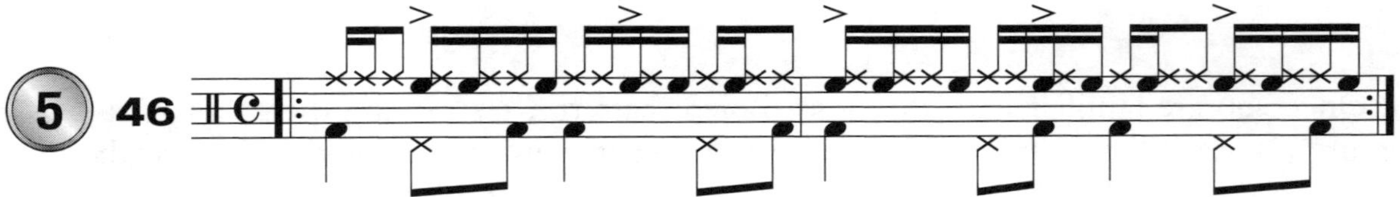

In 3/2 clave with another cymbal ostinato.

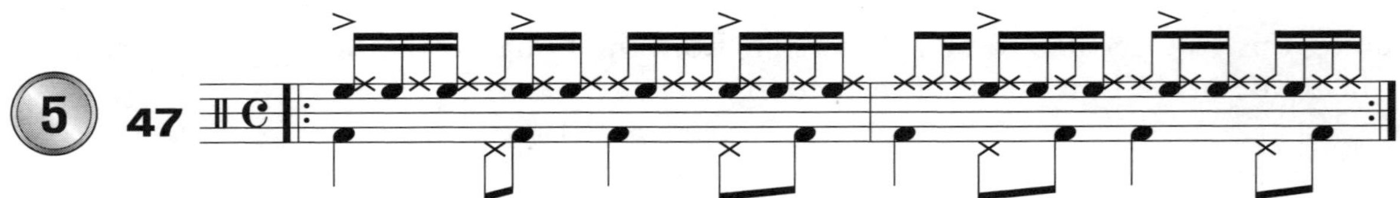

In 2/3 clave.

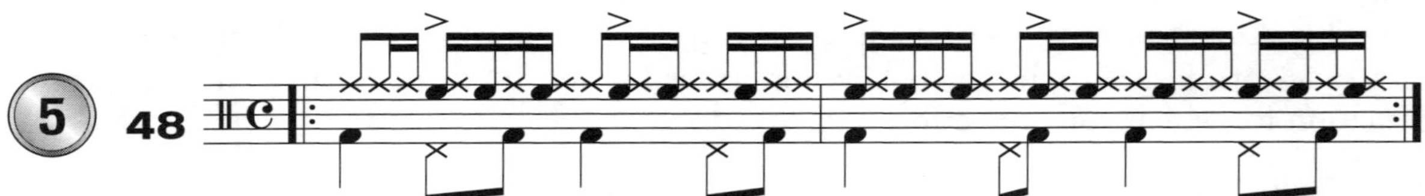

Here we use the eighth-note ride-cymbal ostinato. The clave is 3/2.

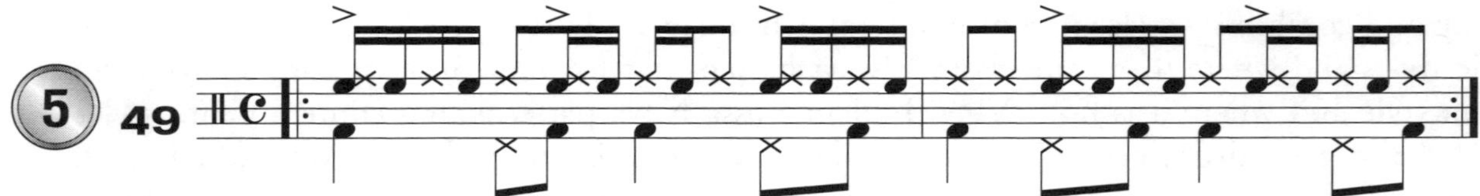

Now in 2/3 clave.

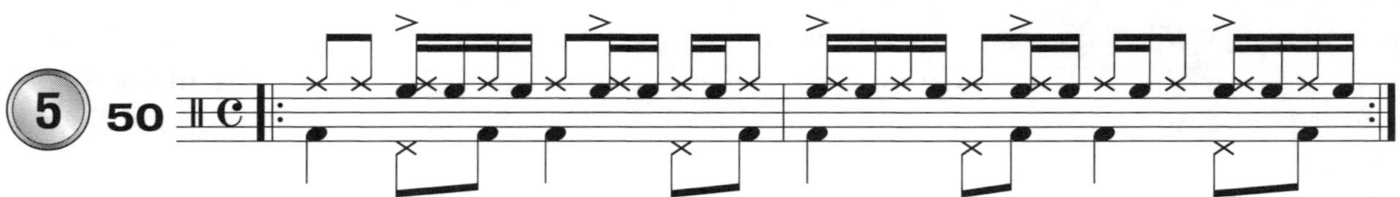

In this example, the ride cymbal plays sixteenth notes. This is a nice pattern for slow tempos. The clave phrasing is in 3/2.

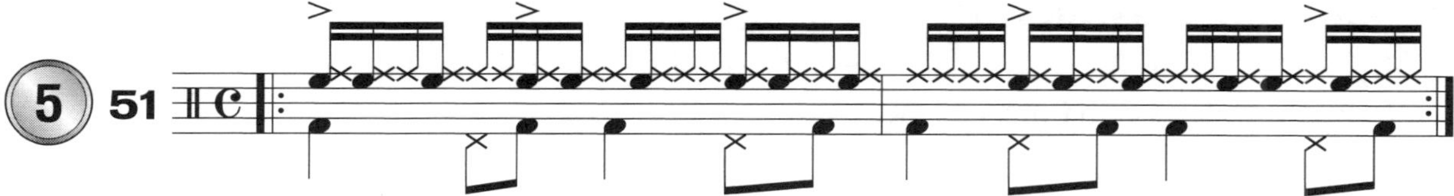

Now in 2/3 clave.

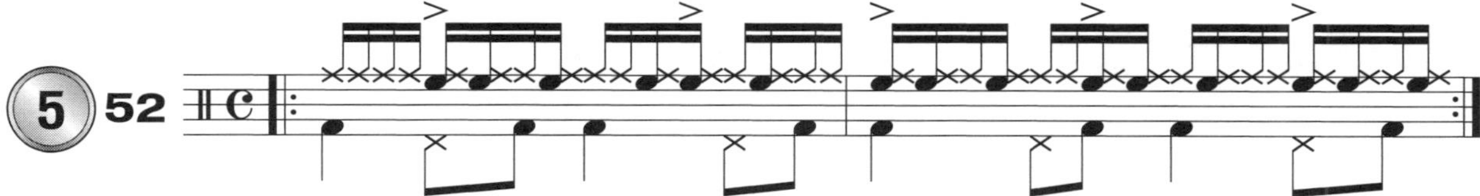

Pop/Bossa Grooves (One-measure phrases)

In these one-measure phrases, the Bossa Nova feel is represented only by hi-hat/bass-drum ostinatos and the second part of the 3/2 Bossa clave. Ostinatos with the eighth and sixteenth notes will be used here. Either one gives an elastic feel to the backbeat on the snare drum, which should be played pretty strongly.

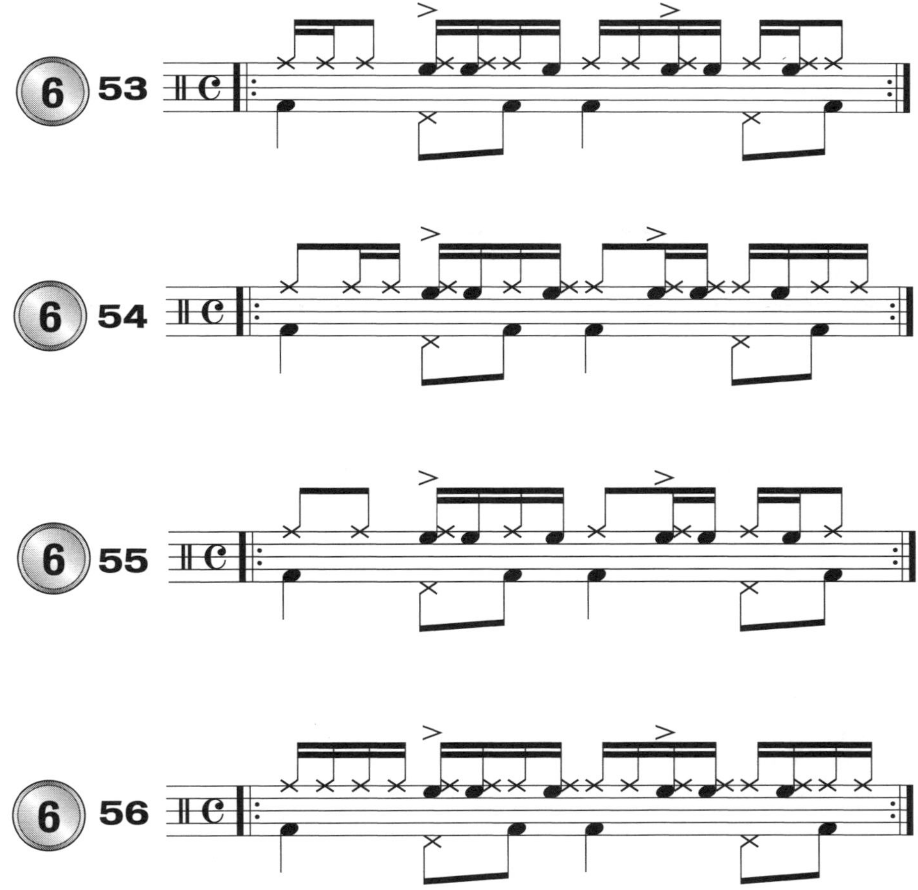

This track ends with an improvised solo demonstration.

NOTE: after you practice these examples, try to move some of the beats around. Start the pattern on different parts of the measure, for instance, on beat 3.

Hi-hat Ostinato Variations

Now play these examples of hi-hat ostinatos over the previous examples of Fusion/Pop/Bossa patterns. The bass-drum parts remain the same.

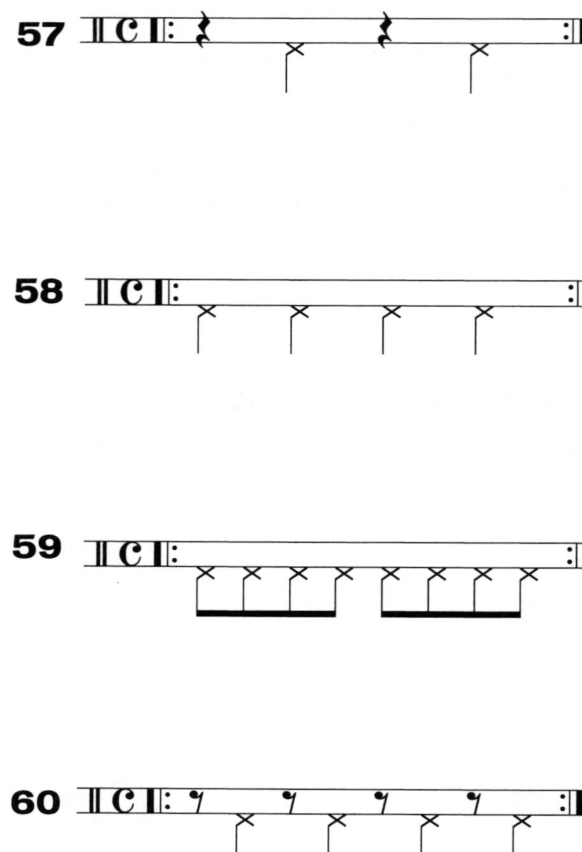

Autumn Tale on page 148 in the Play-along Section (Disk 2, Track 2, without drums on Track 9) incorporates the Bossa Nova and Contemporary Bossa Nova grooves presented in the text. Have fun playing this chart.

SECTION 2: SAMBA

Introduction

Historical Background

It is generally understood that Portugal colonized what we know today as Brazil. But cultural customs from many parts of the world came to Brazil, especially from Africa. Culinary tastes, religion, music, and dance came with the large numbers of African slaves brought to South America. The "seeds" of what we call Samba music style and dance probably arrived in Brazil with those slaves as early as the 1500s.

The word Samba, as with many Brazilian music styles, actually came to mean a combination of activities: music, dance, and a celebration of some sort. The same can be said of many Brazilian traditions with musical expressions. Two examples are Candoble (an Afro-Brazilian religion that combines Catholicism with old African traditions) and Maracatu, combining music, dance and procession in Pernambuco, a state in northeastern Brazil.

We must recognize that Samba styles we hear today were **NOT** originally popular across all Brazilian social and economic classes. When Africans were brought to Brazil as slaves, they adapted their native religious ceremonies, folkloric celebrations, music and dance to meet new, harsh situations. For example, various Afro-Brazilian religious and folkloric celebrations included rhythmic patterns played only by clapping of hands.

Syncopated hand-clapping rhythms from Afro-Brazilian rituals such as the Capoeira (a martial art with music and dance) can still be heard today in some of the Samba styles such as the Samba de Roda. Those types of clave-oriented, hand-clapping rhythms will often be heard in the music styles coming from northeastern Brazil. Although they may still be performed by hand, many are now played on drums and other percussion instruments.

Early twentieth-century technology spread awareness of the Samba to descendents of European settlers. The recording industry began to distribute Samba performances to the wider Brazilian population around 1917. As more and more homes had access to radio, middle and upper social classes enjoyed the music in the comfort of their homes, at social gatherings and clubs. Eventually, the Samba was incorporated into Carnival festivities, enjoyed across all Brazilian society.

The Samba Culture

Samba has a profound influence on the people in the complex Brazilian society. Nowhere is it more evident than in music and dance. The Samba has had an impact on most of Brazil's music genres, including the more sophisticated Bossa Nova, a favorite of the country's upper class.

But it has been the poorer, working-class people who have been the leading force behind the Samba. They created it, and they are the constant innovators of its stylistic development. They have every right to claim ownership of it.

That's not to say the upper social class of Brazil is not involved with Samba. Although they are appreciative, their claim to the music is both more passive as consumers of the genre, and more modest by contrast to the passionate involvement of lower-income, working class Brazilians. The development of the Samba in Brazil can be compared to the way the Blues culture developed in the United States.

The Samba is a constant cultural companion to the Brazilian people. Its presence is felt in the daily affairs of Brazilians at social gatherings and sports events. It is heard at soccer matches as well as Carnival celebrations.

Soccer is Brazil's most popular sport. Just about every state in the country has at least one huge soccer stadium as a home for its popular soccer team. Percussion ensembles will be present at the most important soccer matches, usually played on Sundays. Each ensemble is a micro version of a Samba school Bateria (also known as Charangas). Its job is to cheer up the team players and the audience as well.

The style of Samba played by the Charangas is usually Afro-Samba (no melodic/harmonic instruments). It is usually Batucada style, meaning that the ensemble is relatively small when compared to a huge Samba school Bateria. The Charanga will usually not have doubling instruments because there are typically fewer than ten people in the ensemble. On rare occasions, a trombonist who plays for a ballroom style ensemble, a Gafieira may sit in with the Charangas.

The Carnival

Carnival celebration, held in February of each year, is one of Brazil's largest events. It is a very profitable business for promoters of the tourist industry as well. Carnival keeps the Samba alive and well, because it involves all social classes, especially the impresarios. Although the modern demands of event promoters and tourist guidelines have their influences, the Samba is the heart of Carnival. And the Samba remains in the hands of hard-working Brazilian Sambistas.

The Samba Schools

Many Brazilian scholars believe that the first Samba school was an organization named *Deixa Falar*. When the name translates from Portuguese to English, it reads something like "Don't worry about gossip" or "Let them talk." African-Brazilians from Bahia, in the Northeast part of the country, brought the organization to the city of Rio de Janeiro around 1928.

Since then, Samba schools have become much like today's neighborhood associations. They are clubs. The primary activity of members is to prepare for the yearly Carnival parade competition. These larger Samba schools will take an entire year to prepare for the next Carnival celebration. Members of each Samba school do all their necessary pre-production activities. For example, they compose their own music, make costumes, and build floats.

Today, there are more than forty Samba schools in Rio de Janeiro. Each school is made up of approximately 4,000 members. Schools are grouped into competitive performing divisions. About sixteen of the best Samba schools make up the prestigious top group known as *Grupo Especial*. The remaining schools are ranked into separate groups known as "A", "B", "C" and so forth.

Although we have discussed Rio's large Samba organizations, there are Samba schools all over Brazil. Some are small groups called Blocos. Each Bloco may have only twenty to fifty members. They are not as active throughout the year and do not have the same infrastructure of the larger Samba schools.

Rio de Janeiro is home to the largest Samba schools in Brazil. Each school has its own distinguishing traditions, symbolic colors, and flag. Each school scores a unique composition for each year's Carnival parade. Because each school behaves almost like a sports club, it has an individual history. Its own celebrities lead the front in a parade in one of the Samba school's most prestigious sections, the *Comissao de Frente*.

Samba schools are the primary source of Brazilian Samba music and Samba musicians in both quantity and quality. Some of the most popular Samba schools are Mangueira, Beija Flor, Mocidade, Salgueiro, Imperatriz, and Portela. Many of today's prominent Samba artists/musicians, or Sambistas, have become successfully involved in other music projects. They may record different Samba genres like the Pagode, or perform in other live musical and choreographic productions. But most of them were, at one time or another, members of Brazil's Samba schools.

Although known as Samba schools, they are not what we might think of as a normal school. Their approach is completely different from what we might expect in a typical classroom. It would be difficult to find a curriculum syllabus or to find the name of the principal. No diplomas are handed to Sambistas upon graduation. Instead, the entire school is competing to win a trophy.

There is systematic hierarchy in a Samba School with definite teaching and learning experiences. And there is a mission to be accomplished, namely to win the Carnival parade. Each school works hard to have the best percussion section, known as the Bateria. Each school will also build extravagant floats and design luxurious costumes (the "fantasias"). Each of these activities and all of them together are designed to become famous and win trophies.

Experienced people take on different positions of leadership with areas of responsibilities to match a Samba school's various pre-production activities. Numerous departments are necessary to make these unique and complex organizations work. Top leaders, known as the Nata or the Partido Alto usually direct the entire organization. They are people who understand the tradition of the school and have earned respect and status by working for years and years in areas of their expertise.

People who have typically reached the ranks of leaders are sometimes referred to as *velha Guarda* (the old guard). These older folks are held in respect and are usually easily recognized by all Samba school members. The *velha Guarda* are living proof of a school's tradition. They possess knowledge that has been passed on, usually by oral tradition, from generation to generation.

The *velha Guarda* possess the know-how about complex dance choreographies that are traceable to the old motherland, Africa. Some dances can be directly connected to the rituals of Umbanda, Candoble, or other Afro-Brazilian religious ceremonies and celebrations. The old guard is responsible for preserving important Samba school traditions such as the dance steps performed by the *Porta Bandeira* and the *Mestre Sala*.

Porta Bandeira is a very prestigious position given to a Samba school female member. She parades with the Samba school's flag. The *Mestre Sala* is a very skillful male dancer dressed in luxurious fourteenth-century court vestment costumes. He dances courteously around the *Porta Bandeira* as he escorts her along the entire parade.

The Bateria, made up of hundreds of drummers (sometimes as many as 300 people), is the percussion section of a Samba school. It is led by someone who has vast knowledge of the entire Samba percussion family, known as the *Mestre de Bateria* (Bateria Master). This highly ranked leader works directly with the composers, the Partido Alto and the Nata.

Each year the Samba composition for the next parade is selected by vote. It is known as the *Samba Enrredo*. It is the Bateria Master's responsibility to arrange all percussion parts around the selected song, much like aural music scoring.

The music-composition process, designing and constructing extravagant floats and luxurious costumes, endless rehearsals, and many other aspects of preparation for the yearly Carnival parade give purpose and direction to the lives of Samba school members. The Samba, the parade, a chance to be a King or Queen for a day at Carnival; for a Sambista, this is what Carnival is all about.

The Samba Enrredo/Samba De Avenida

Each year's Carnival is a highly publicized competition involving almost the entire city of Rio de Janeiro as well as the rest of Brazil. Like the Super Bowl, this parade attracts worldwide audiences. Every year, each Samba school carefully researches and comes up with its own thematic motif. The motif will be represented in the lyrics of the Samba Enrredo. It is also known as the Samba de Avenida (Avenue Samba style). Costumes, floats, and every aspect of a Samba school's parade performance will reflect its chosen theme. Samba de Avenida is the most energetic, powerful Samba style played in Brazil. It is performed by the largest percussion ensemble in the world, the Samba school's Bateria.

The Bateria

A Samba school's Bateria is a gigantic, vibrant and very energetic percussion ensemble. Its pulse and very well-rehearsed beats are the heart of the parade. It is a Samba school's "signature," if you will. The percussion arrangements function as a powerful rhythmic anchor to the harmony, melody, and especially to the lyrics of its organization's parade theme.

It is important to point out that the Bateria is exclusively a percussion ensemble. There are no harmonic or melodic instruments among its members. There are literally hundreds of percussionists with hundreds of percussion parts being doubled and played simultaneously. They dance and play their instruments at the same time thousands of people are singing.

During the parade, a podium is usually set up with a PA system. This is so everyone can hear the *puxador* (person singing lyrics through a sound system) with a small group of vocalists and a string ensemble. The string section may include a very small four-string guitar (the cavaquinho) and a seven-string guitar playing bass lines. Sometimes there are also six-string acoustic guitars and a few percussionists on the podium. This is changing little by little with wireless microphones and new technologies. In the near future we may see the group of *puxadores* mixed in with the rest of the floats.

The combination of as many as 4,000 Samba school members playing, singing, and dancing creates a massive groove attack with an infectious feel. Not only are the Samba school members dancing and singing, the entire audience goes into a homogeneous head bopping. Their combined effect defies description.

The endurance, technique, chops and time feel of Samba school percussionists (Batuqueriros) are superb and beyond belief. Pandeiristas (percussionists who play the pandeiro) often surround dancers, known as Passistas, who portray the many characters of the Samba school's annual theme. Not only are Pandeiristas masters of their instruments, they are also fantastic jugglers who demonstrate great showmanship during the parade.

The Baterias cause the ground to shake with their vibrant, explosive enthusiasm and thunderous drumming. Their performance has been carefully orchestrated during the entire year prior to the Carnival parade. Arduous, nightly rehearsals result in breathtaking, rapid contrasts of sound and rhythm.

One moment the full ensemble plays. The next, a sudden change of dynamics for the famous, traditional "tamborim breaks." Then, it is suddenly back to the full ensemble again. Dynamics go back and forth primarily to help shape the verse/chorus/refrain-type music form. This is all very well implemented in the writing of a Samba school's Samba Enrredo.

Samba Percussion Instruments

Although this book is devoted to performing Brazilian music styles on the drumset, it is important to have a basic knowledge of some of the most important Brazilian percussion instruments.

The goal is to give you a brief introduction to these instruments. You will see photos of them, learn their names and briefly learn how each one functions. Although we will mention some of the most used patterns for them, technical aspects of performance will be topics of a future work.

The Surdo

One or more surdos can be found in each Samba percussion ensemble. The largest Samba percussion ensemble of all, the Samba school bateria, will have as many as three surdo groups, each playing a different size surdo. Each surdo section in a Bateria will have a different musical function according to the size of the instrument (small, medium, or large). Smaller Samba groups, such as the Charanga, Batucada, or Pagode ensembles, may have only one surdo.

Surdos are barrel-shaped drums made of wood or metal, and are carried by means of a shoulder strap. The plastic or calfskins drumheads located on each end of the drum can vary in diameter from fourteen to twenty inches. The largest surdo will be twenty-eight inches tall or possibly taller.

The surdo is the heartbeat drum of the Samba. The largest surdo is known as maracanan (named for one of the world's largest soccer stadiums located in Rio de Janeiro) or *treme terra* (meaning ground shaker). It functions as a bass drum and is often referred to as a Brazilian "floor tom."

Musicial Function of the Surdos and the Surdo Part

THE LARGEST SURDO: THE MARACANAN

The part played by the largest surdo, the de *marcação* (meaning to mark the beat), never changes. In Portuguese the translation could also mean "from which everything else is built upon." It can be found in all Samba musical situations. A percussionist who plays only the largest surdo very rarely solos or deviates from the standard part.

The function of this lowest-pitched surdo is to play the downbeat. It is important to point out that the Samba downbeat is not the first beat of the measure; it is the **SECOND BEAT.** Samba is felt in $\frac{2}{4}$, in which case, the second beat is the downbeat. The largest and lowest surdo has a strong beat or pulse. The surdo passes beat 1 quietly, with a muffled stroke, and accents beat 2 with an open stroke. Throughout this book, this part refers to the surdo part.

The surdo part is the heartbeat of the Samba, the foundation, and its reference point. Everything else will be played against the important Samba surdo pulse, with its relaxed, and steady rhythmic foundation. This is the most important rhythm in the Samba percussion ensemble. Once the surdo "2" feel is established, all the other musicians will have this strong pulse to play anything they want against it. A Samba groove is only as good as the surdo part is steady.

I have seen Samba music notated in $\frac{2}{4}$ and $\frac{4}{4}$. Arrangers in the United States sometimes write Samba music charts in $\frac{4}{4}$. In those instances, the surdo part should have the accents for each measure on beats 2 and 4.

THE MEDIUM SURDO: SYNCOPATES

The medium surdo part only exists in an ensemble if more than two surdos are present. Then the medium surdo reinforces some of the main surdo part and at the same time superimposes another rhythmic figure. A good example is when the medium surdo commonly superimposes a rhythmic figure of a triplet feel against the eighth note and sixteenth notes played by large and small surdos.

THE SMALLEST SUDO: COUNTER SURDO PART

The musical function of the small surdo is to play against the main surdo part. In other words, the smallest surdo plays on non-accented parts of the measure. So, if we are in 2/4, the main surdo accents beat 2 of the measure, while the small surdo plays the opposite, accenting beat 1. The end result is a dialog of high-low-high-low, etc. Think of the combined rhythm as breathing, inhaling and exhaling.

Here are some examples of large, medium and small surdo parts.

The large surdo with the lowest pitch accents the second beat.

The small surdo with the highest pitch plays a counterpoint role, accenting beat one.

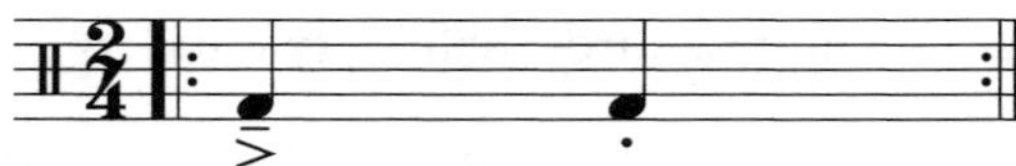

The third plays a part similar to this one.

There are many variations of the second and third surdo parts. We will look at them later in this section when we transfer them to the drumset bass drum.

The Third Surdo

The surdo beat is essential to any Samba percussion ensemble. The surdo beat may be referred to as the *marcação*.

Smaller Samba ensembles will usually have one surdo. Sometimes they play a combination of surdo-one parts with variations. If a small ensemble has only one surdo, it *may* play a mixture of surdo parts. A Samba school's large Bateria may play three or more coordinated surdo parts, but each individual surdo will usually play the one part assigned to its size.

Whether played by a large or small Samba ensemble, the largest surdo part (accented note on the 2 of the measure) will always be present. The 2 of any measure, if counted in $\frac{2}{4}$, will be the accent from which everything else in a Samba style will be built. Arguably, listeners will be able to identify the style known as Samba by hearing only the surdo part because it is that sound that will always be present as the foundation of a Samba.

Third Surdo Variations

The main surdo keeps the binary pulse in the Samba with a steady, unshakable foundation. The counter-surdo responds to beat 2 on the weaker beats of the measure by playing on the 1s. The third surdo plays a very important role, contributing to the signature of a particular Samba ensemble. It not only reinforces the main surdo, but it lends character to it by skating by the measure and "playing in the cracks."

Examples offered in this book portray just the basic concept of Samba third surdo variations. There are so many possible variations it would be impossible to notate all of them. Although third surdo variations are very syncopated, they do not clash with other percussion parts (especially the tamborim part).

The third surdo variations could be played (although rarely) by a second surdo if there are only two surdos in an ensemble. If there is *only* one surdo, the third surdo part may be played. Or it may not be played at all. However, it is uncommon to hear a very nice Samba groove being played without some simple variations, even if there is only one surdo in the group. It is important to notice that if three surdos are available, the largest surdo part should not have variations.

Here are some examples of third surdo variations played against a simple and basic Samba percussion ensemble groove.

VARIATIONS AGAINST A SAMBA GROOVE

This very simple Samba groove has not been written for a complete Samba percussion section. It is lightly orchestrated to place focus on the third-surdo part examples that will follow. As you listen to this groove, notice how changing a third-surdo part influences the entire mood of the groove.

Listen to the following examples of third-surdo variations being played against this Samba rhythm. Notice that although very syncopated rhythms are being played, they blend well together.

SAMBA VARIATIONS PATTERNS

Play with a muffled left-hand stroke where rhythms are noted with "X". Play regular notation with a mallet in the right hand using an open sound.

The CD example contains two measures of the underlying pattern, while the surdo rests, followed by two measures with the surdo.

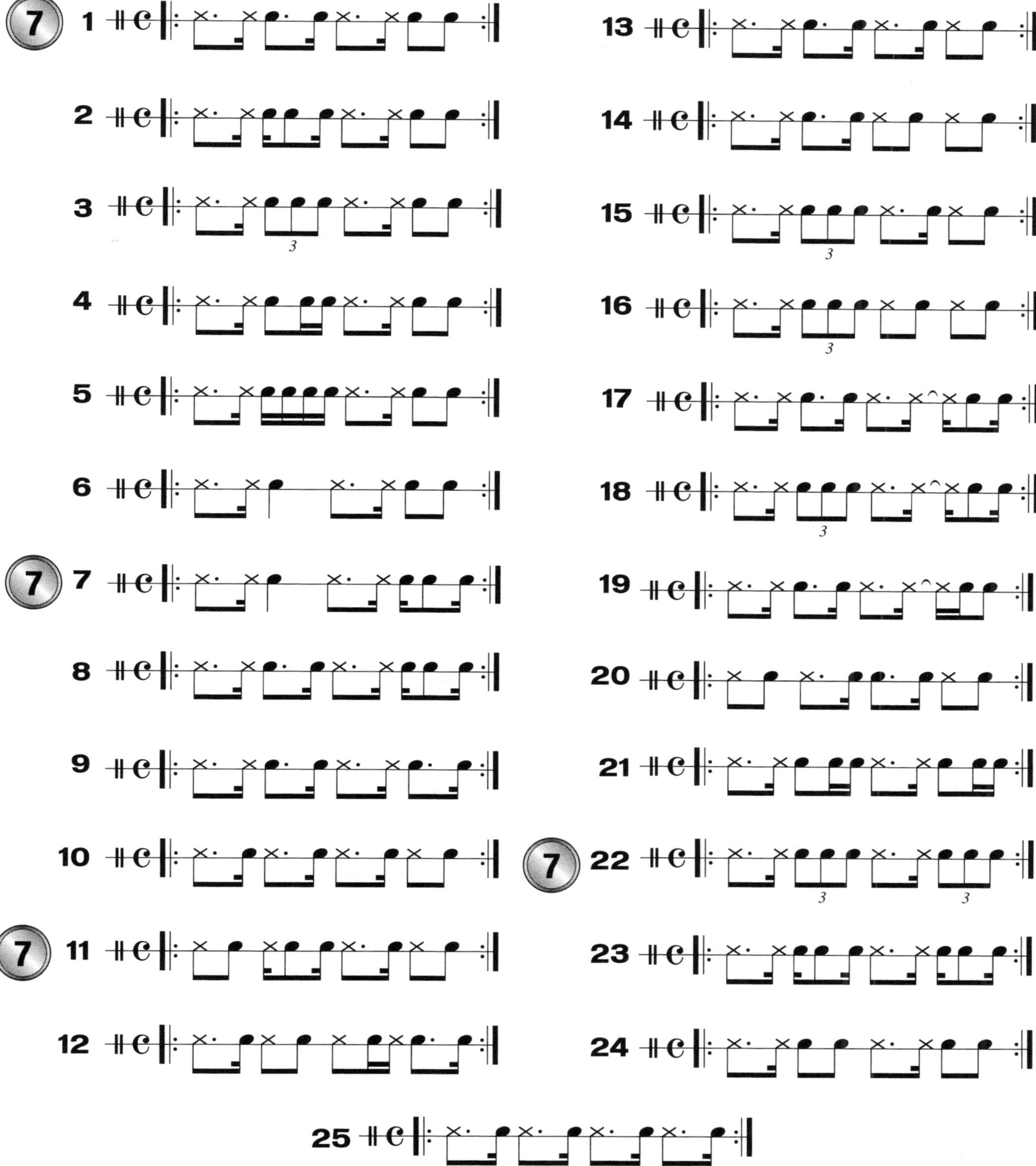

SAMBA VARIATION PATTERNS IN TWO-MEASURE PHRASES

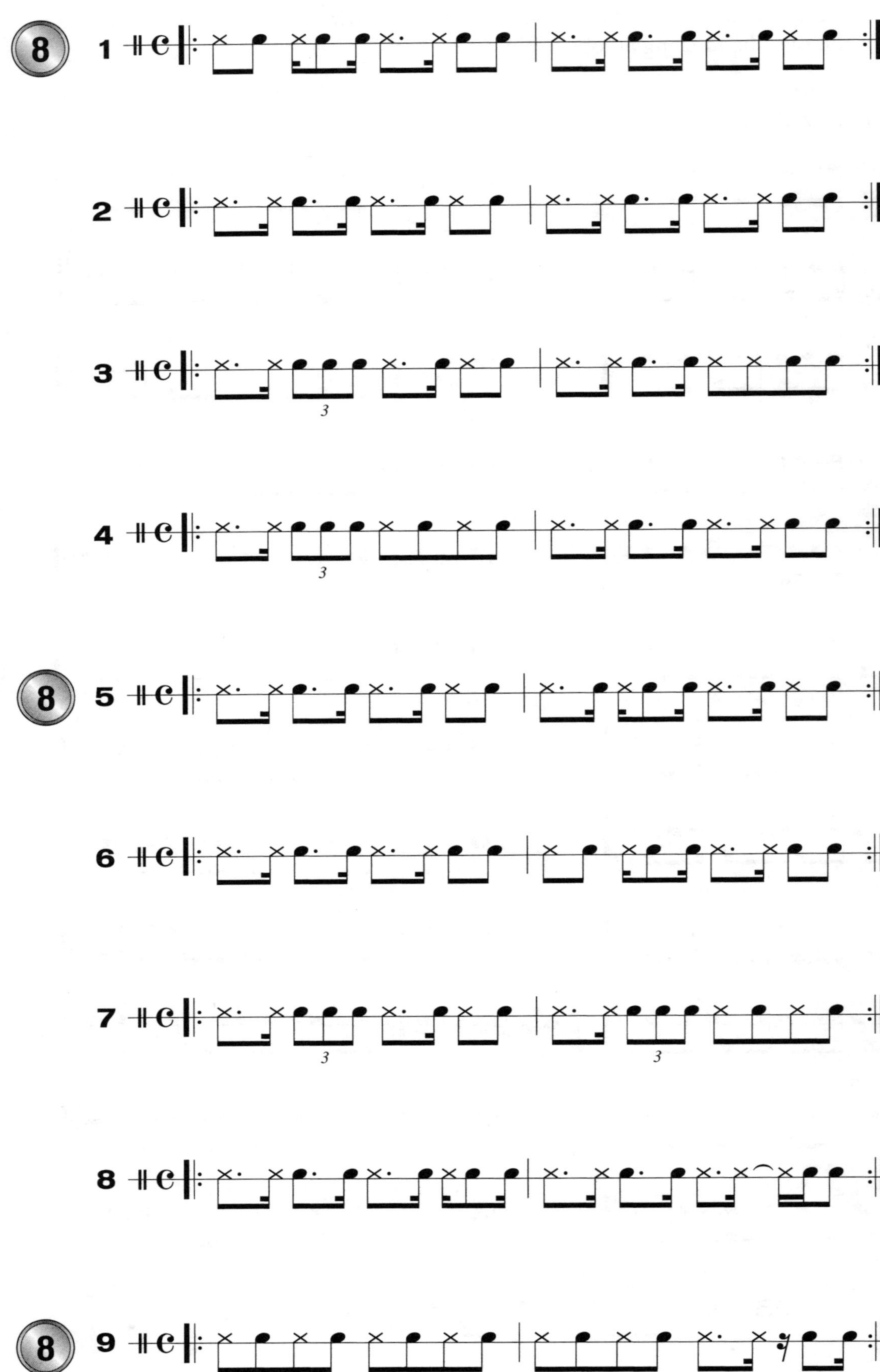

SAMBA VARIATION PATTERNS IN FOUR-MEASURE PHRASES

The Repinique

The role of the repinique in Samba styles is to improvise Samba rhythms, soloing on top of the rest of the percussion ensemble. Because the repinique can be heard so easily among the batucada, it can be used to give musical cues such as anticipating a break, changing the groove or fills (known as *viradas*).

The repinique drum looks like a drumset tom. Although there are various available sizes, the most common sizes are diameters of ten, thirteen and fourteen inches. Like most percussion instruments used for outdoors in parades or batucada jams, a shoulder strap is used to carry it. It may have calfskin or plastic heads on the top and bottom. Most outdoor performers prefer plastic heads, because they stand up against uncertain weather and have unsurpassed volume.

The repinique is usually tuned very high in pitch. It is played with longer and thinner-than-usual drumset sticks. Sometimes the drum will be played using sticks in both hands. When it is, the sound of the drum is loud, cutting through all other Samba percussion instruments in volume and clarity. A repinique can also be stroked with a wooden or plastic stick in one hand, while the other hand strokes the drum using various techniques to achieve open and closed tonalities, rim shots, etc.

REPINIQUE RHYTHMS: SAMBA EXAMPLES

Repinique rhythms are adaptable to many variations. Here are a few examples of what a repinique percussionist might play as the thematic basis for improvisation.

NOTATION KEY:

X = Left hand muffles the head, Right hand strikes with a stick.

Repinique Fills

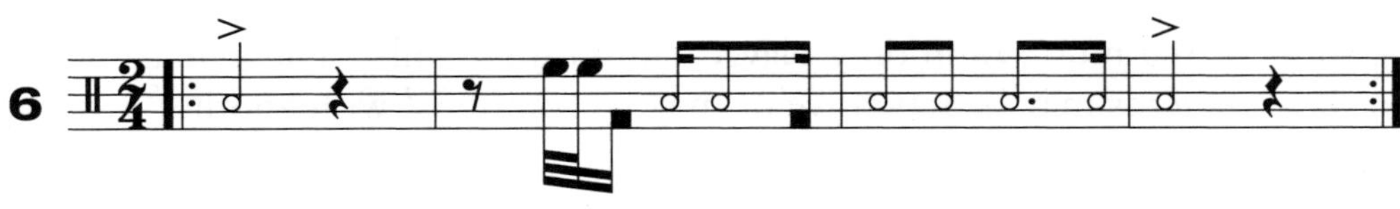

The Tamborim

The tamborim is one of the smallest drums found in the Brazilian percussion family, if not the smallest. Tamborims have various diameters and depths, but it is usually small, about six inches in diameter and one-inch in depth with calfskin or plastic drumheads. One hand holds the tamborim while the other uses a plastic or long wooden stick to achieve its medium high and somewhat dry tones. Pressing and releasing the fingers against the head will obtain open and closed tones.

The tamborim can be coasting and just keeping a pattern. Or it can be used in a way similar to the repinique, soloing over the Samba groove, giving cues and improvising Samba rhythms. Large Samba schools will use the tamborim unlike the repinique. Tamborims will perform in very large sections in parade performances. Hundreds of highly organized tamborim drums will play well-orchestrated parts in unison with counterpoint, syncopated rhythms against the verse and chorus of the Samba Enrredo. The effect may be like the horn section in a funk band or swing big band, in musical conversations responding and answering to the vocals.

In smaller Samba ensembles, the tamborim solo is played in a more subdued way. It will embellish its own parts, repeating over and over in a way common to Samba styles. The pattern is almost like a clave because it becomes the important secondary sound after the surdo part. If a surdo part is being played along with one of the common tamborim Samba parts, the combination can be heard as a bona- fide Samba groove.

Tamborim patterns can be orchestrated for the drumset snare drum, as we could do for the repinique. Here are some commonly used tamborim patterns.

TAMBORIM EXAMPLES

Here we have some of the most commonly played tamborim, Samba-style percussion rhythms. Keep in mind these patterns may be repetitive or may be combined with another pattern to create larger phrases.

Samba rhythms are in $\frac{2}{4}$ and are usually notated that way. I show the rhythms below in $\frac{4}{4}$, making them easier to read and allowing clear visual recognition of where the patterns resolve rhythmically.

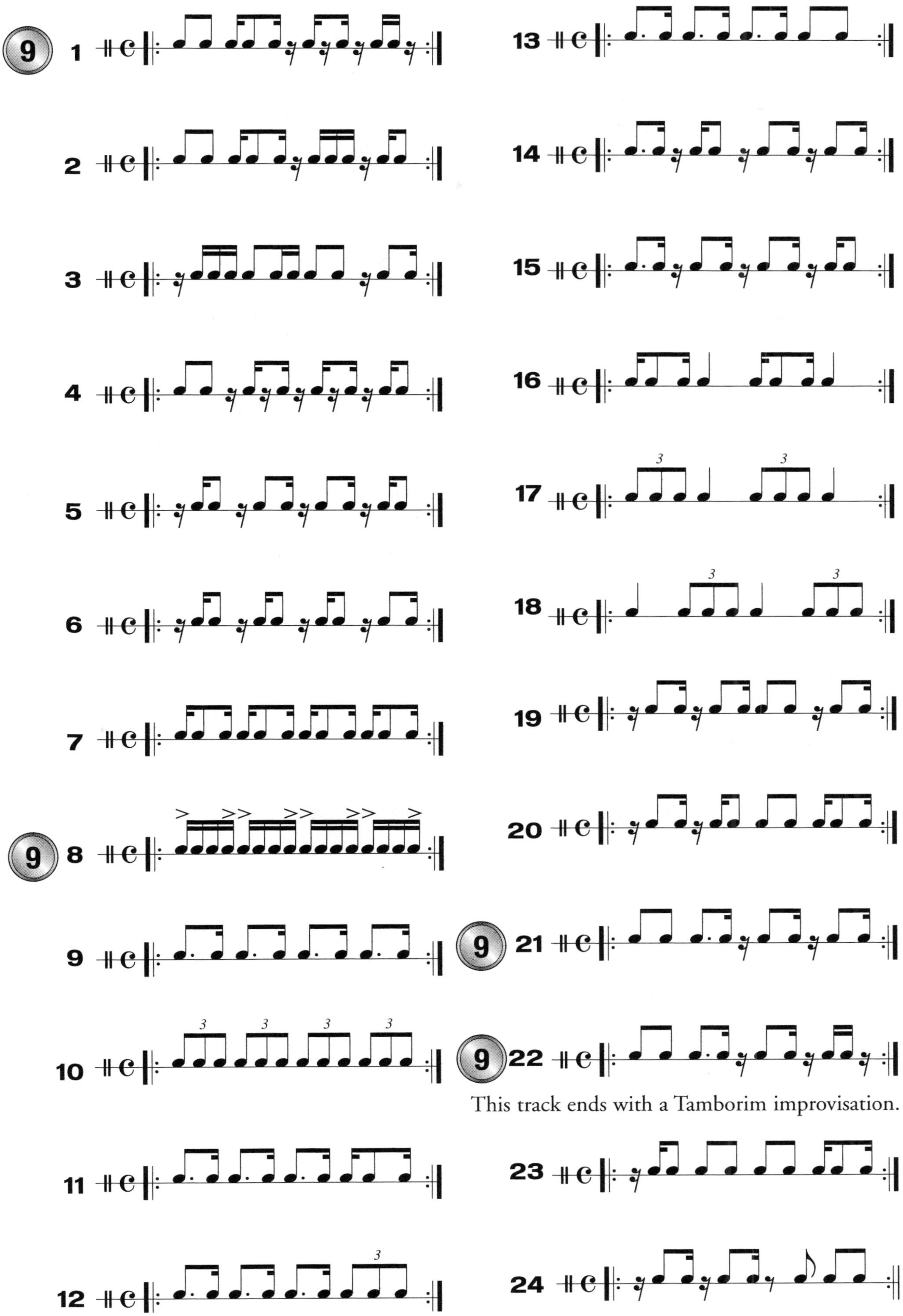

This track ends with a Tamborim improvisation.

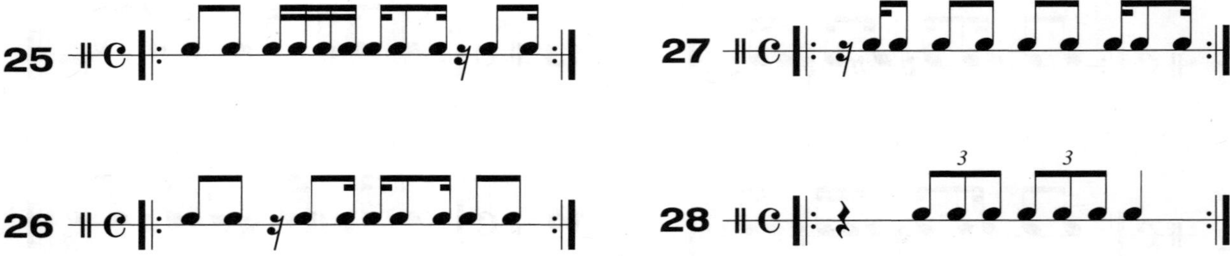

TAMBORIM EXAMPLES WITH SAMBA DE AVENIDA (PARADE SAMBA) VOCALS

The following examples illustrate the type of phrasing/fills performed by Samba schools when the tamborim section interacts with Samba de Avenida vocals. These rhythmic phrases are usually placed carefully in between vocal rests or for emphasizing musical statements. Notice the difference between the first series of tamborim examples and these. The earlier sectional patterns were shorter, but these are longer and more likely to be repetitive, not improvised.

TWO-MEASURE PHRASES/FILLS

FOUR-MEASURE PHRASES/FILLS

TAMBORIM SECTIONAL SOLO

Sometimes small Samba ensembles will have three of four tamborim players who have rehearsed unison parts/solos to play on top of the Samba groove performed by the larger group. Here is an example of a tamborim section in "solo-question-answer" style. It usually sounds as if they are playing flams.

The Pandeiro

A tambourine with jingles, the pandeiro is one of the most technically demanding percussion instruments. Usually shallow in depth, pandeiros vary in diameter. Ten, twelve, thirteen and fourteen inches are very popular among Sambistas.

Play the pandeiro by holding and shaking it with one hand. The other hand will strike the drum using different stroke techniques and hand positions.

The musical function of the pandeiro will vary in the Samba ensemble. In a medium-to-large Samba ensemble, the Pandeiristas (percussionists who play the pandeiro) will generally play consecutive sixteenth notes that mimic the surdo, shaker, and caixa parts.

Many of the Samba percussion instruments can be reproduced with the pandeiro by applying different techniques and strokes simultaneously.

PANDEIRO EXAMPLES

I will not go in depth on the technical aspects of this demanding Brazilian percussion instrument because our focus here is on the drumset. The example of the rhythm and accents below gives you only a simple idea of what a pandeiro percussionist plays in a Samba-style performance.

The Cuica

The cuica is an unusual instrument because it is played by applying friction. Typically made of metal, the cuica looks like a tom-tom, because it has an animal skin on one end while the other end is open. A very thin wooden stick is attached to the inside and center of the skin.

A wet, small cloth/fabric covers the thumb and the first finger of one hand as the percussionist slides it forward and backward, pressing the cloth against the thin stick inside the cuica. By controlling the amount of pressure that is applied, the percussionist can achieve a roaring sound. The other hand holds the instrument, adjusting pressure on the skin from the outside of the drum. More pressure produces a higher pitch; less pressure produces a lower pitch.

By controlling the amount of pressure, a roaring sound is achieved. Playing the cuica requires both hands pressing and releasing the skin and the stick. Good Cuiqueirios (percussionists that play the cuica) can make sounds that range from a human voice to animals growling.

The cuica role in a Samba ensemble is that of a soloist improvising and playing variations of Samba rhythms. The cuica adds very nice color to an ensemble; it certainly adds excitement. The very melodic phrasing of the cuica parts and variations can be interpreted at the drumset.

CUICA PATTERNS

The cuica pitch range is made of more than two tones. I will focus only on low and high tones for your purposes. Here are some rhythmic examples of what a cuica player might play in a Samba ensemble performance.

Notation Key: lower notes are low pitch; upper notes are high pitch.

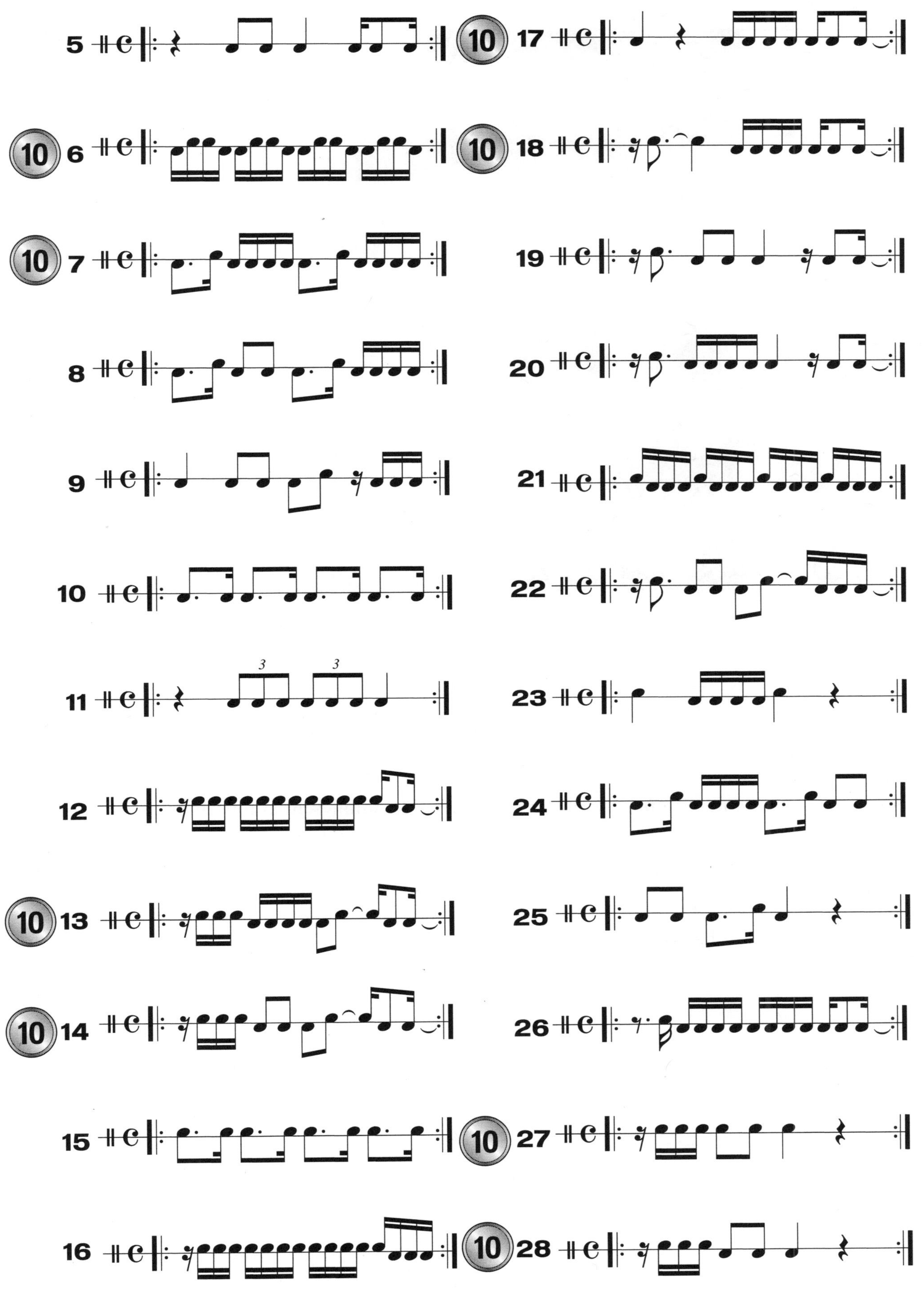

5
10 6
10 7
8
9
10
11
12
10 13
10 14
15
16
10 17
10 18
19
20
21
22
23
24
25
26
10 27
10 28

The Caixa

The caixa is a Brazilian version of the snare drum. It's made of wood or metal and, like the snare drum, is played using two sticks. However, a caixa does not have a sophisticated snare mechanism system.

As it is found in most Samba ensembles in Brazil, the caixa has a very simple mechanism producing a sound similar to a snare drum that has not been tightly tuned. This makes the snares resonate loosely, allowing and favoring the execution of buzz rolls and similar techniques.

The role of the caixa in the Samba ensemble is to provide a "cushion" with a constant pulse of sixteenth notes. The caixa, like the Surdo, provides an essential element of the Samba.

In a small Samba ensemble, the caixa incorporates accents similar to the repinique and sometimes the tamborim to spice things up a little.

Another Portuguese word for snare drum is *tarol*.

CAIXA SAMBA PATTERNS

Here are examples of very common caixa Samba patterns. Notation key: "X" = rim shot.

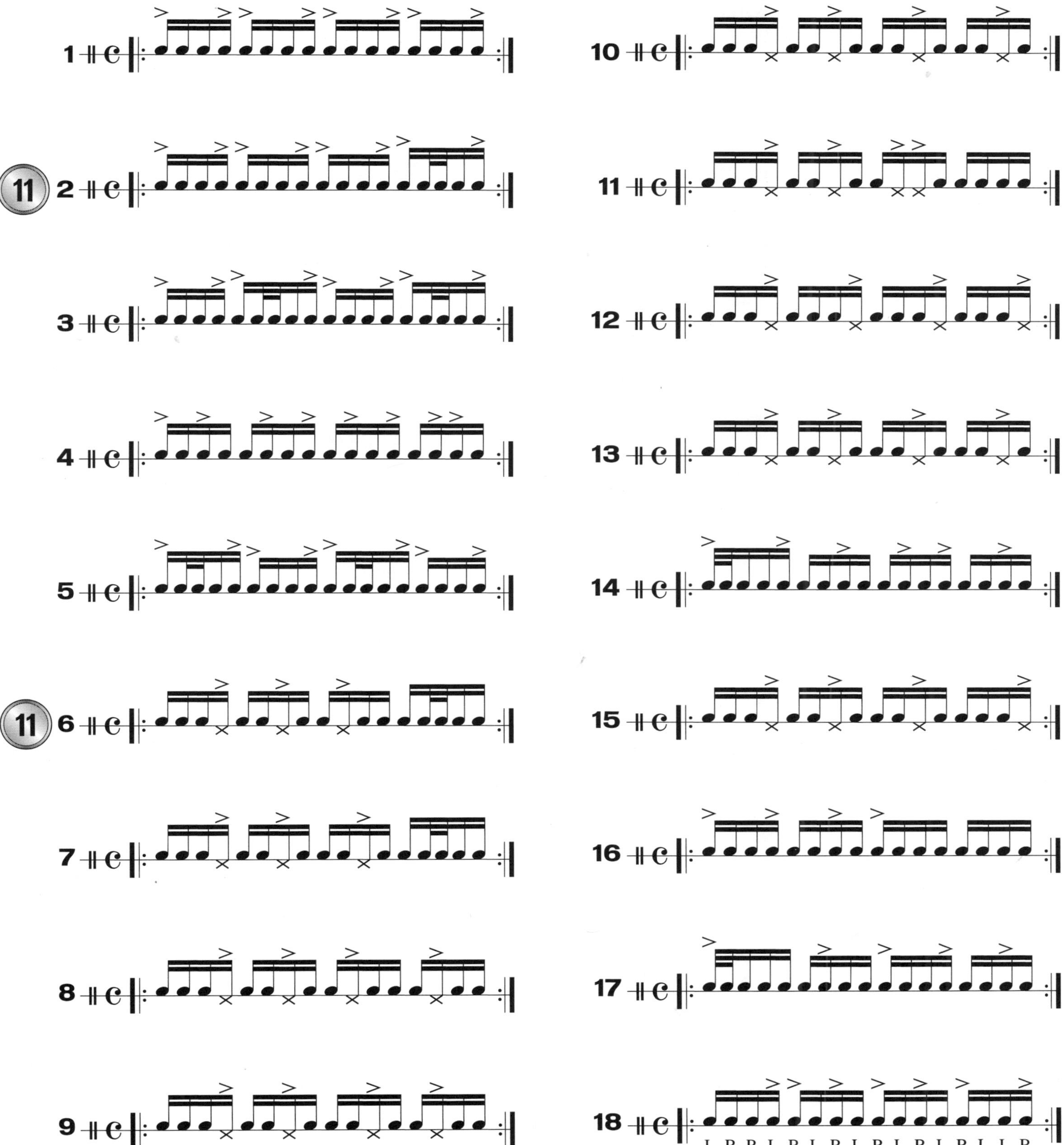

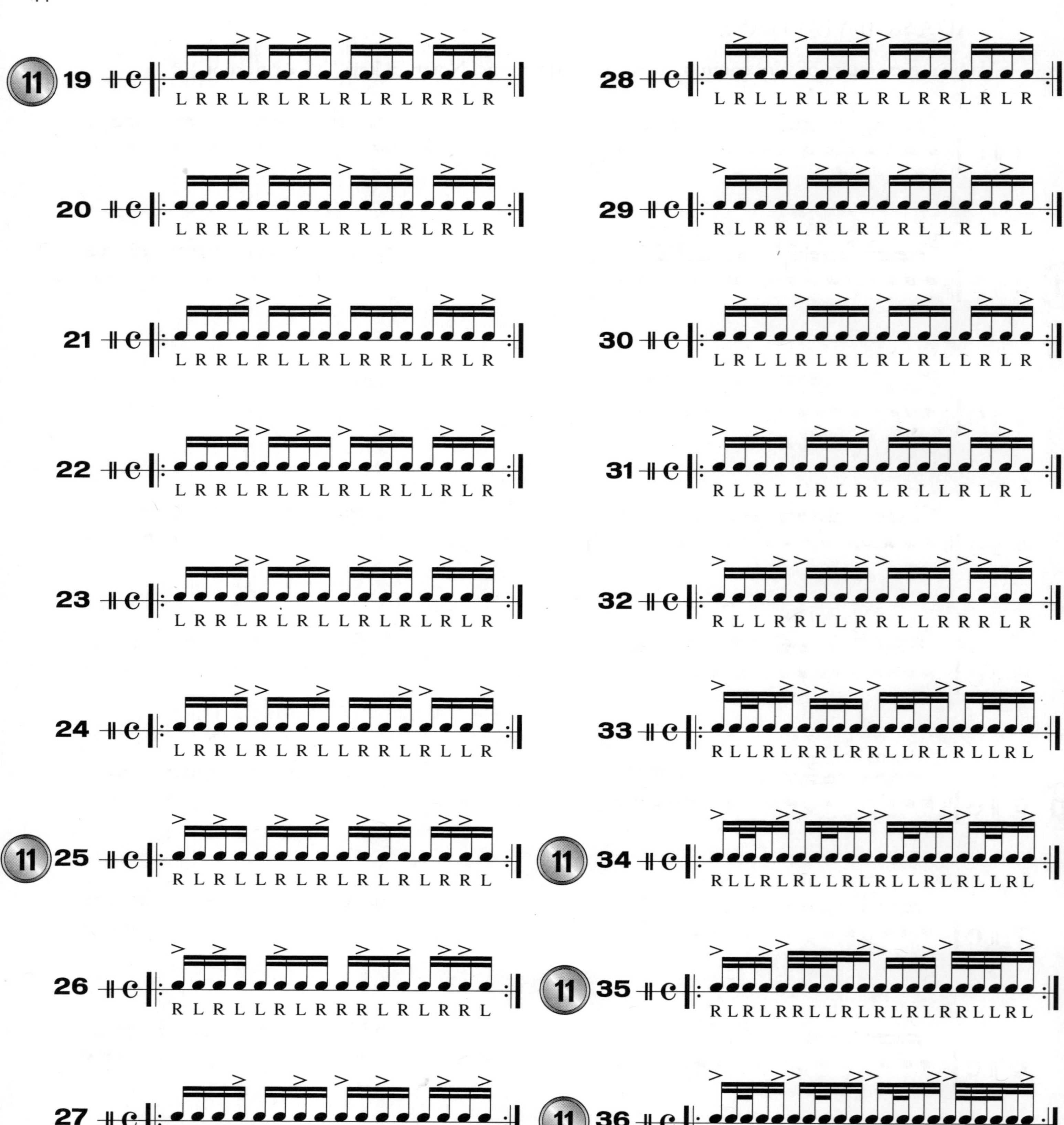

The Ganza/Chucalho

Ganza and chucalhos are Brazilian equivalent of shakers, and have similar rhythmic functions. Ganzas are usually made of metal in cylindrical shapes. They will have some sort of beads or grains inside of them, making a shaker sound when played.

Chucalhos, however, produce a somewhat different sound because there have no beads inside. Instead, they are open instruments with small jingles connected by thin metal rods. Chucalhos are designed to play for outdoor performances where the percussionist needs loud volume instruments.

The ganza and chucalho function to play ostinatos, usually in sixteenth notes, in the Samba. If their patterns are played on the drumset, they are ideal for the hi-hat or ride cymbal.

Here are some basic Samba shaker patterns:

The Agogo

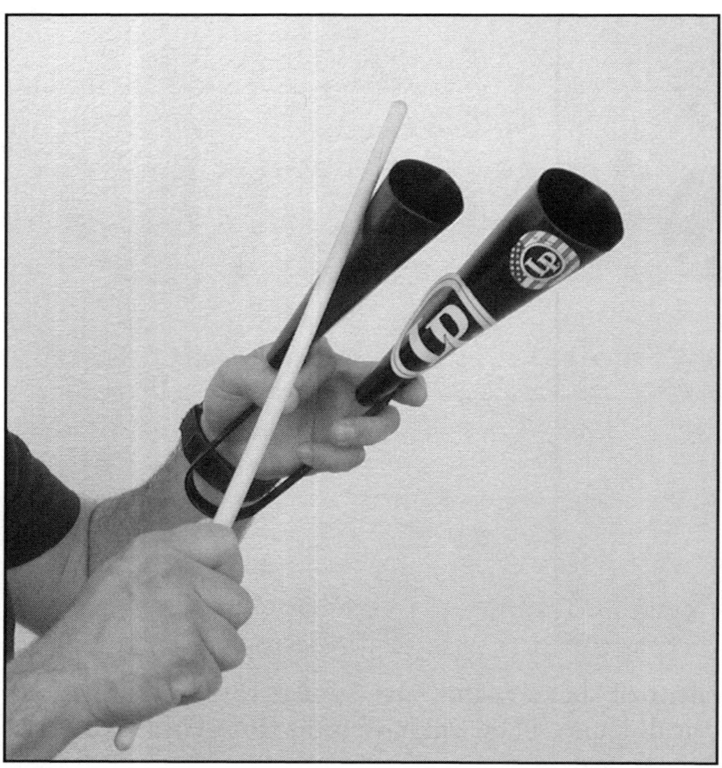

The agogo is a percussion instrument with three basic sounds: low, high, and muffled. A flexible steel rod connects two bells, each of which has a different pitch.

The larger bell, with the lower pitch, is on the bottom. The top bell, which is smaller and has a higher pitch, is situated above and farther back. The percussionist plays back and forth, between the low and high bells, by striking them with a stick or mallet. The percussionist can bend the rod so the bells actually touch each other. When the two bells touch, a muffled sound can be achieved.

Agogo parts are unlike the parts for the snare, surdo, or shakers. Those instruments usually play a series of sixteenth notes, closely together, creating a very dense rhythm. The role of the agogo in the Samba ensemble is similar to the cuica.

Although an agogo part can sometimes be very busy, it usually is played with a lot of syncopation and space between notes. There is usually a somewhat melodic motif involving two tonalities. Think of agogo parts as good sources for drumset interpretations.

AGOGO SAMBA PATTERNS

Here we have some of the commonly used agogo Samba patterns. While it is possible to create many different sound characteristics and tonalities with the agogo bells by pressing the rod and muffling the sound, the focus below is on the two basic sound: high and low pitches.

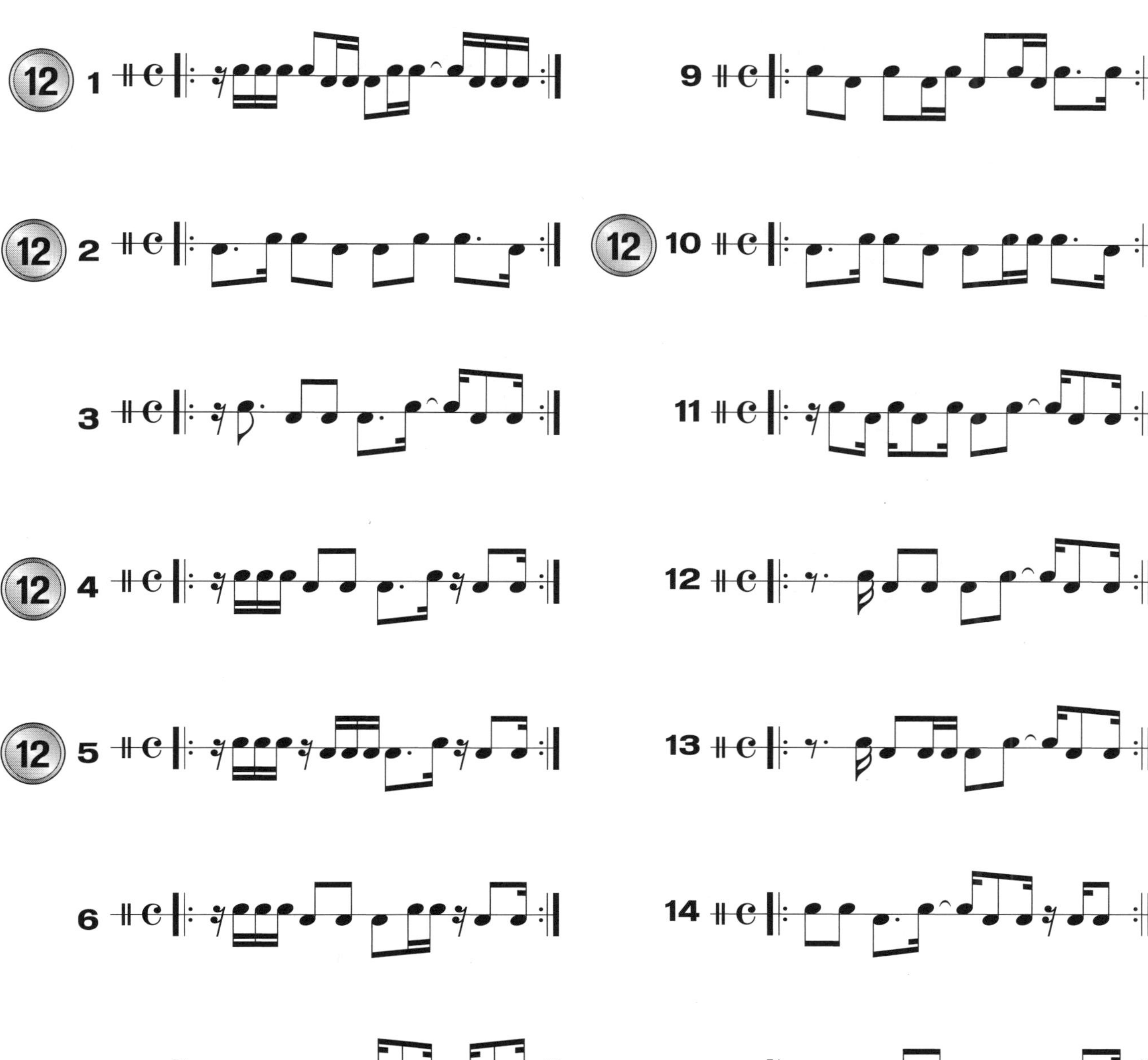

48

The Reco-reco

The reco-reco is a "scraper" instrument, Brazil's version of a guiro. It may be made of wood for indoor use or of metal for outdoor use.

Samba school percussionists usually play cylindrical-shaped, metal reco-recos that are half-opened with metal springs that run between both ends. The percussionist uses a thin metal mallet (similar to a triangle beater) to scrape the springs with up and down strokes. reco-reco patterns are very similar to chucalho and shaker Samba rhythms.

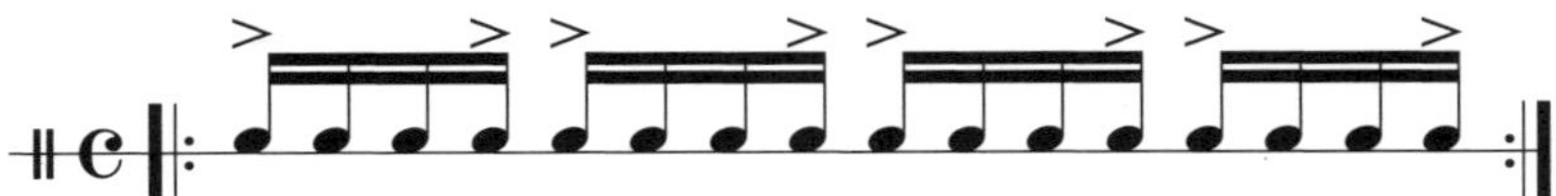

The Apito

The apito is a whistle used in the Samba and other forms of Brazilian music. Its principal function is to give cues to the Samba school's musicians in the Bateria. The *Mestre de Bateria* (Percussion Section Master) plays the apito to signal all sorts of changes in the music being played along a Carnival route.

In a smaller Samba group setting, known as a *batucada,* the apito will be given a rhythmic part to play, different from Bateria cues. Rhythms can be played on the apito similar to agogo and cuica parts. The Samba whistle has three pitch tones.

The apito pitches can be played to produce "Samba Calls." They are brief melodic riffs sporadically introduced in a performance. The apito calls "spice" things up a bit.

APITO SAMBA CALLS

Apito calls come and go quickly. They are relatively short when compared to other Samba percussion instruments. The apito will not be heard continuously in a Samba performance. It has long rests, but it will definitely be heard.

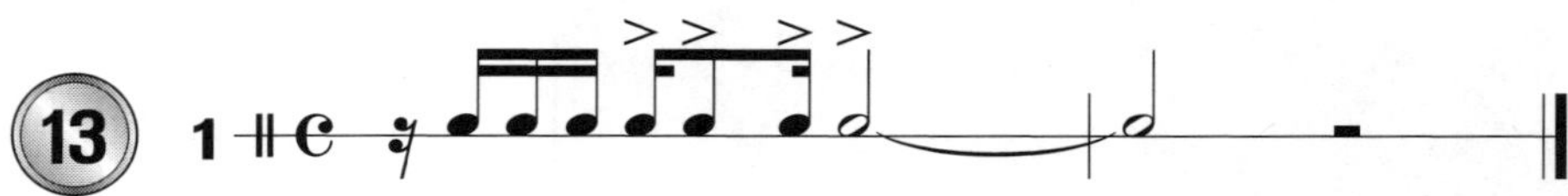

Bateria/Charanga/Batucada: Example of a Score

Now it is time to give an example of a Samba percussion ensemble. This example blends the playing styles of Samba school Bateria and smaller Samba Charangas groups. The score includes some of the concepts that were presented in earlier sections in this chapter.

First, I will present a brief analysis of the percussion score beginning with the introduction.

Introduction

The first measure has the apito cueing up the ensemble with a one-measure phrase. It is a typical apito call to initiate the *batuque* (percussion groove). This is also known as a "call and response" progressing from the second part of the first measure to the second measure. The apito calls the riff, and the entire ensemble responds to it.

In the third measure the apito plays something new, creating an AAB call. The third measure becomes like a second cue-type of riff, directed to the repinique. At this point, the rest of the ensemble is silent. They yield for a response that is made only by the repinique.

The repinique responds on the fourth measure. This is not only a response to the apito. The repinique itself cues the rest of the ensemble to begin a Samba groove. The entire ensemble responds in m. 4. In doing so, the ensemble goes into a Samba groove vamp.

Once the vamp is established, all instruments are free to "say" what they want, as long that they don't clash with the rest of the parts of the overall arrangement.

Measure 9 of the score shows an "On Cue Apito Entrance." Another apito call tells the tamborim section and the rest of the ensemble to get ready for a tamborim solo. In an expanded version of the call and response concept, the apito phrase starts at m. 9. The rest of the ensemble responds at m. 12 with a unison part. It involves the apito, repinique, cuica, agogo, tamborim, and pandeiro sections.

Measure Thirteen

A tamborim solo begins in m. 13. In this way we see and hear an example of tamborim "section solo" in a musical situation. The tamborim section plays a four-measure phrase four times, doubled by the cuica and agogo sections.

Measure Seventeen

While the tamborim phrase continues in m. 17, it culminates as another unison section comes in on m. 19. This begins another very good example of call and response, starting at m. 20 and continuing to the end of the piece.

14 Batucada One

HENRIQUE C. De ALMEIDA

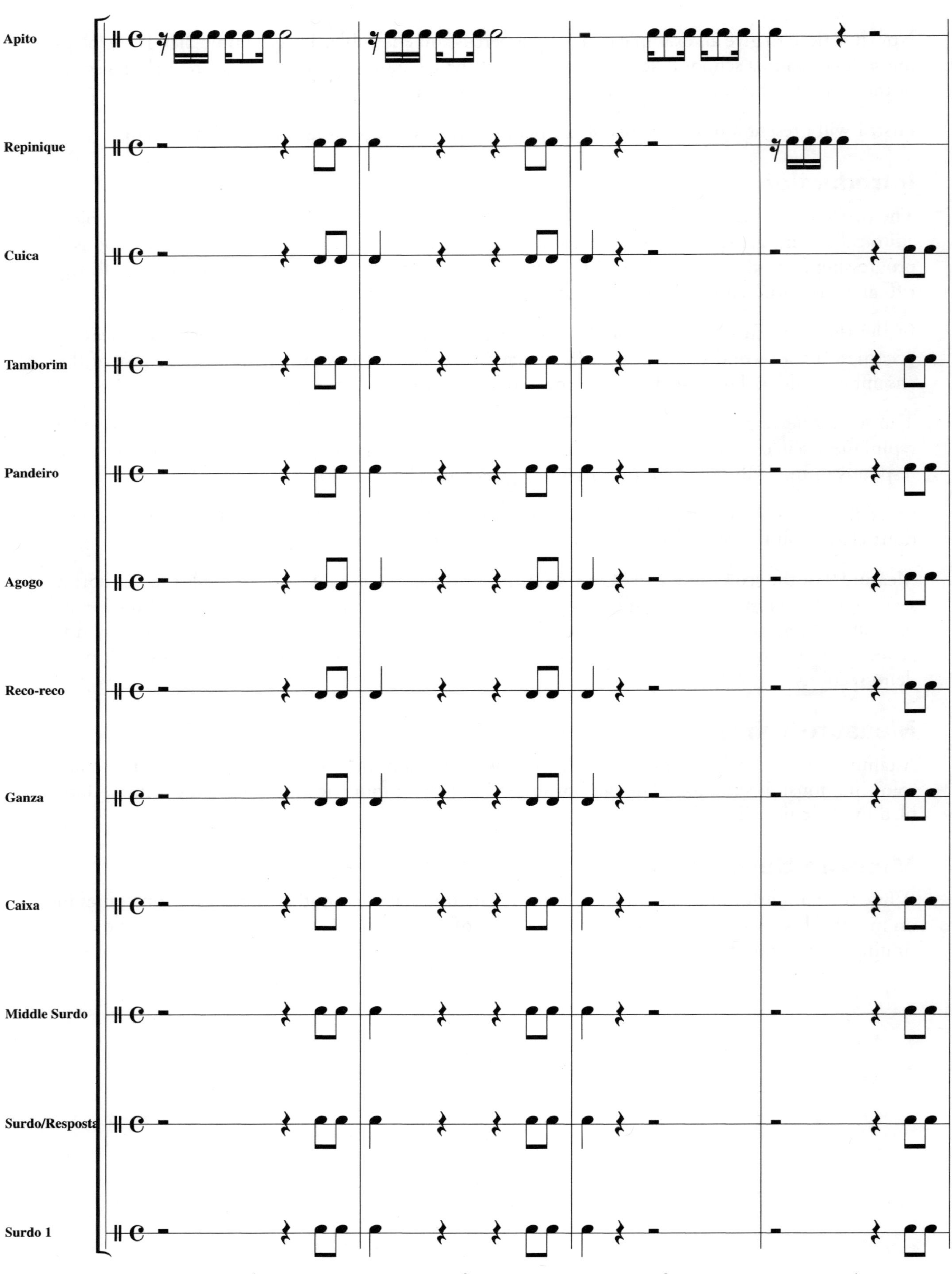

Play repeat 4x's

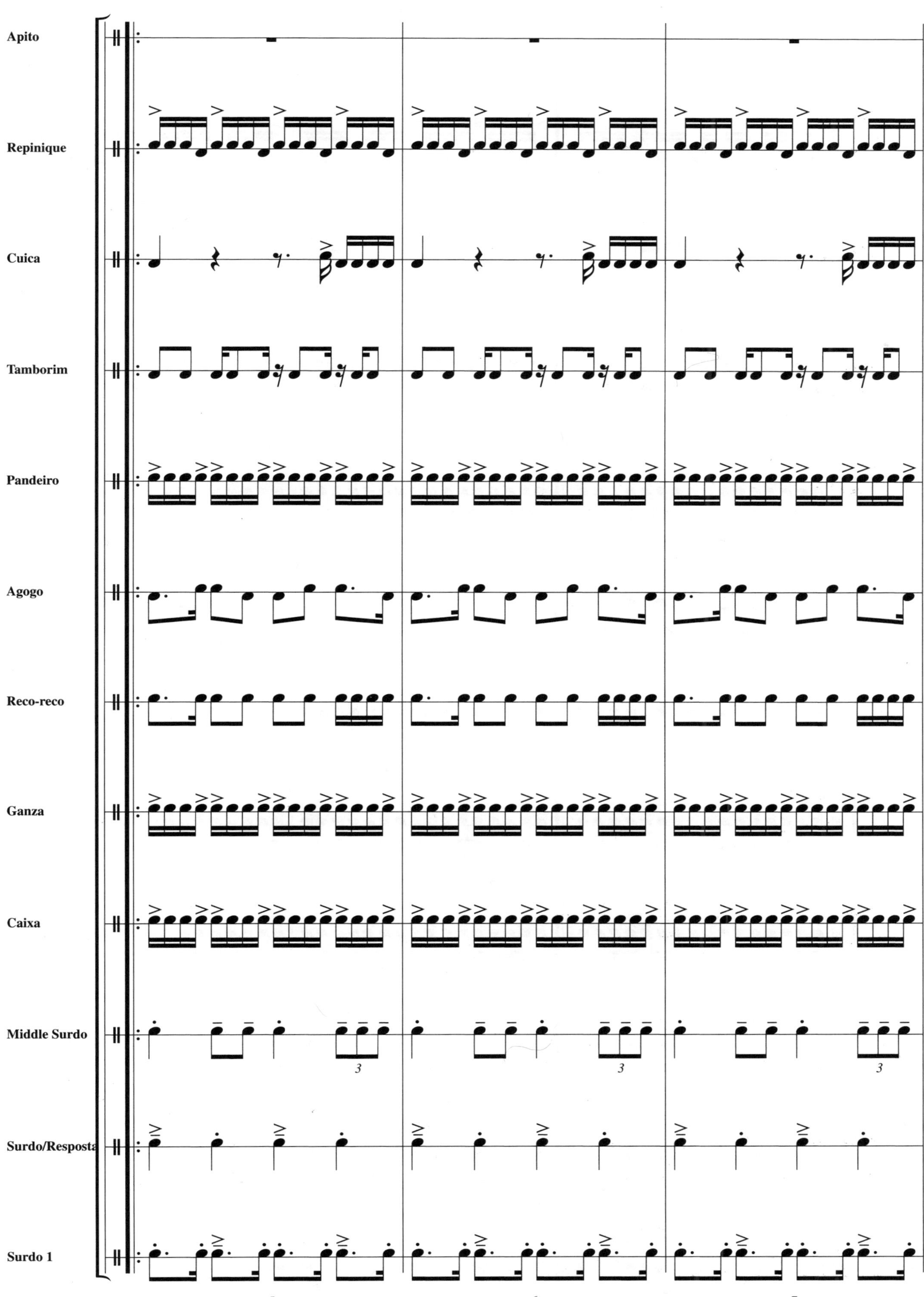

DRM119

**Apito entrance on cue,
play 4 measures and go on to the next section**

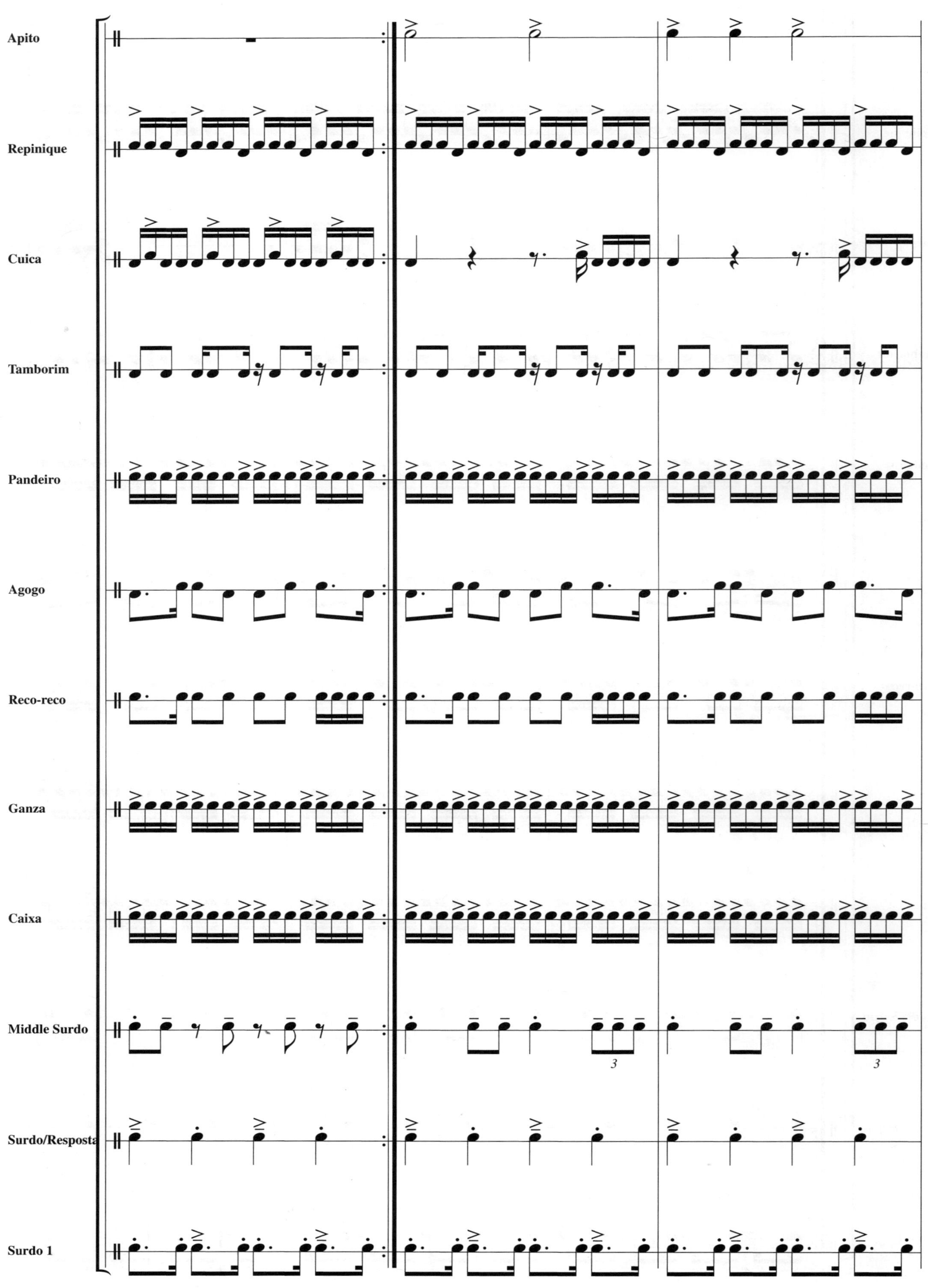

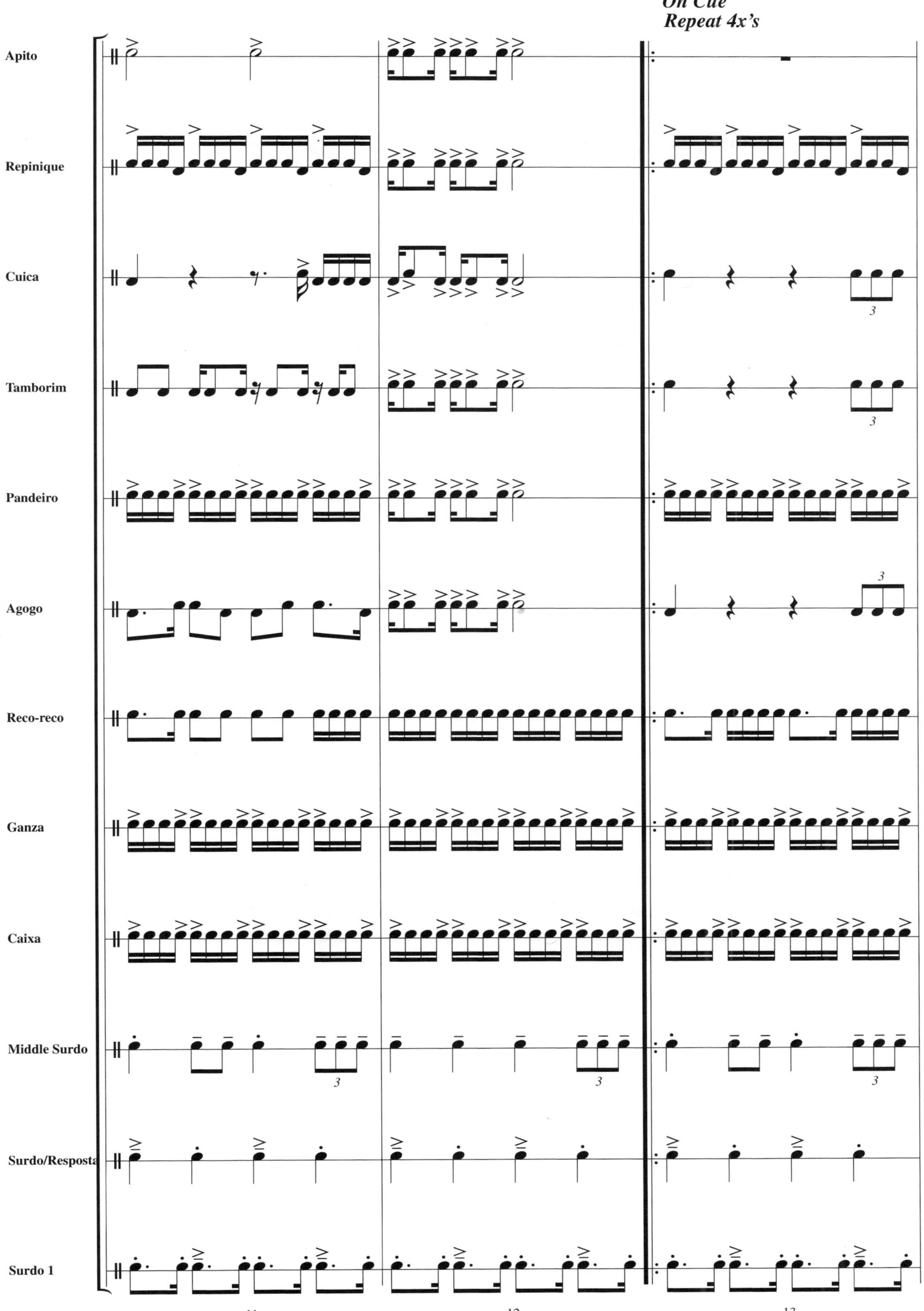

DRM119

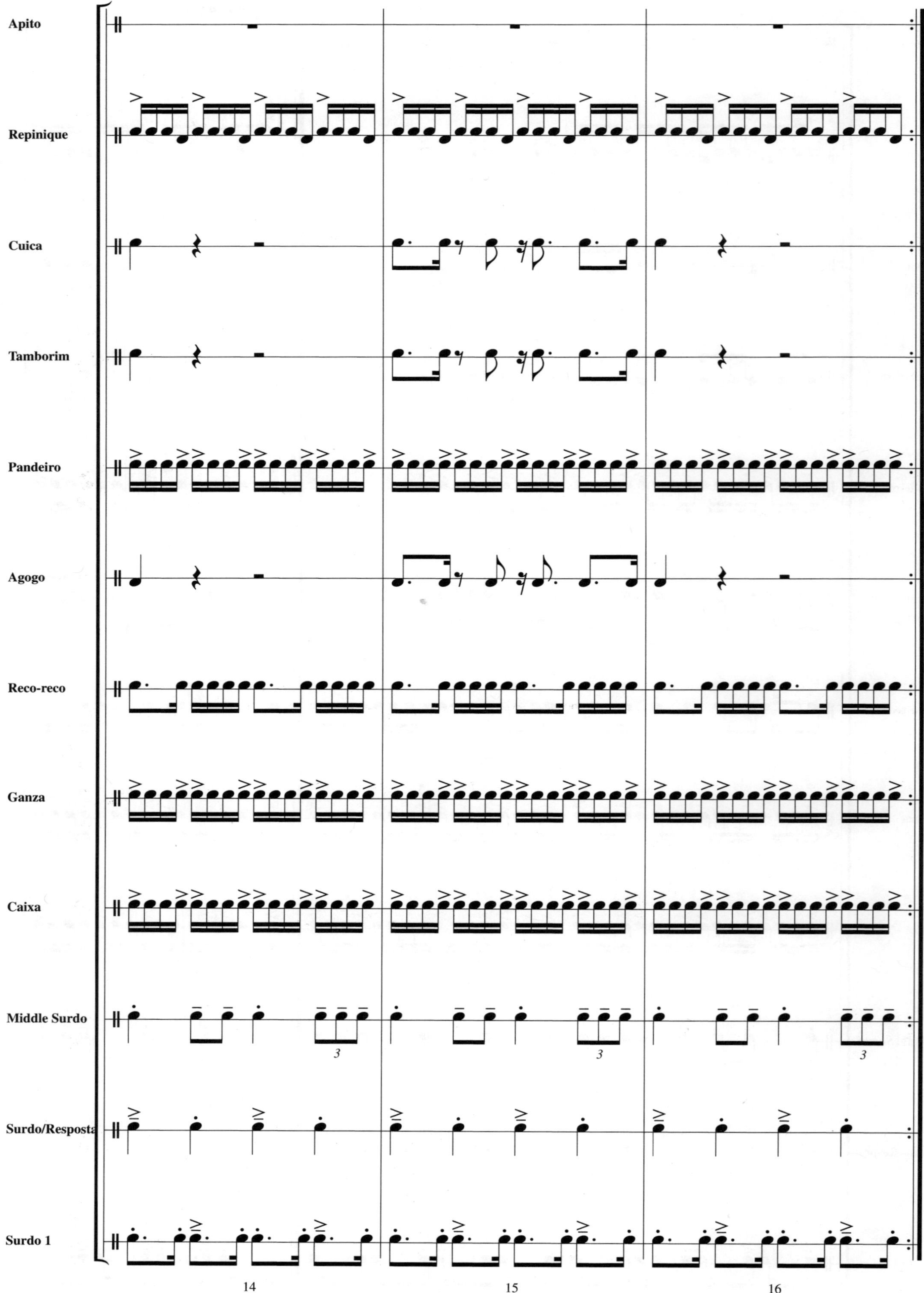

Apito
Repinique
Cuica
Tamborim
Pandeiro
Agogo
Reco-reco
Ganza
Caixa
Middle Surdo
Surdo/Resposta
Surdo 1
3
3
3
14
15
16

Apito
Repinique
Cuica
Tamborim
Pandeiro
Agogo
Reco-reco
Ganza
Caixa
Middle Surdo
Surdo/Resposta
Surdo 1
17
18
19
20

Apito
Repinique
Cuica
Tamborim
Pandeiro
Agogo
Reco-reco
Ganza
Caixa
Middle Surdo
Surdo/Resposta
Surdo 1
21
22
23
24

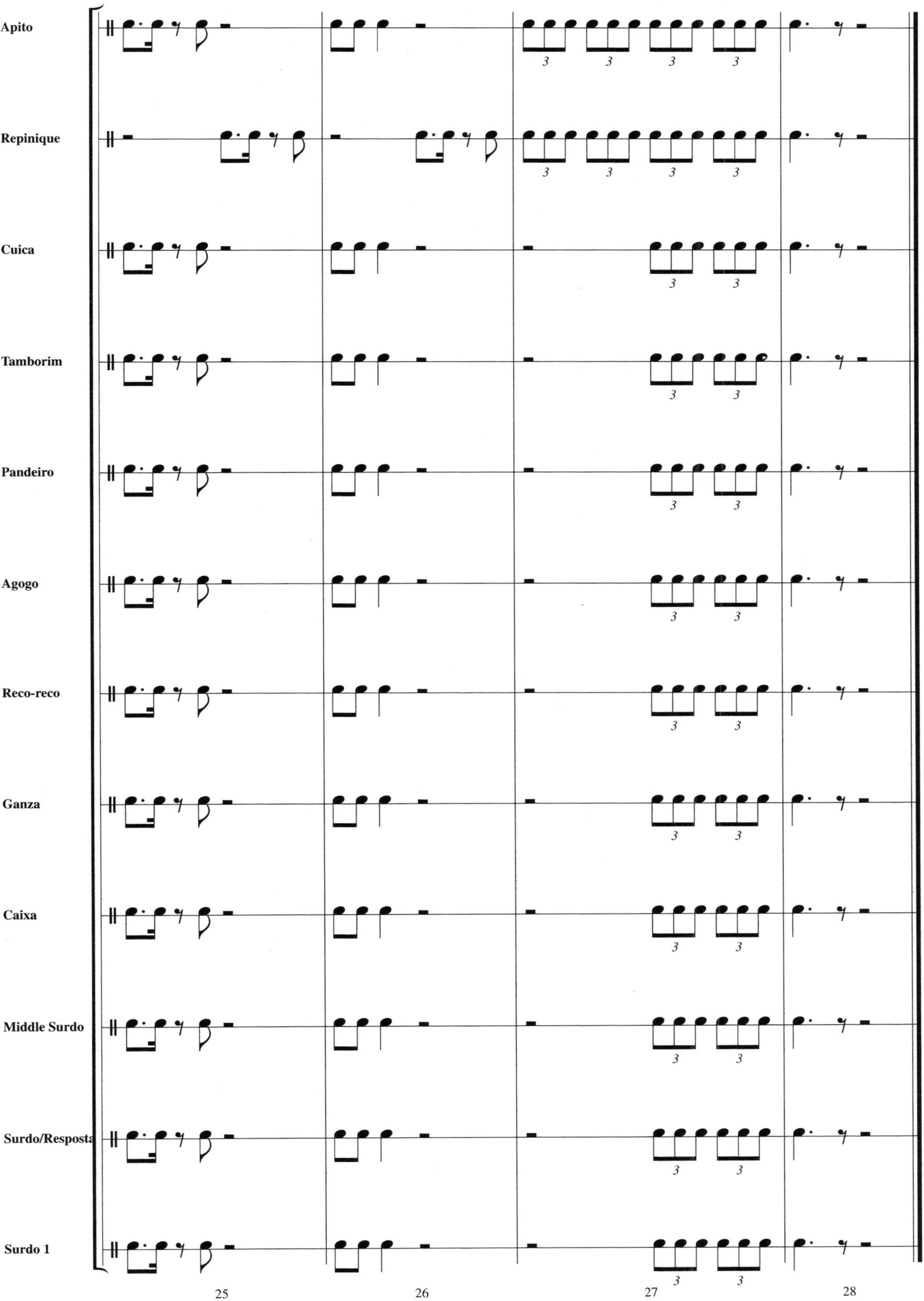

SECTION 3: DRUMSET SAMBA GROOVES

We have presented a review of Samba percussion instruments and how they are played. Understanding this will enable the percussionist to play Samba on the drumset. The different ways to perform Samba on the drumset will be determined by the amount of knowledge, creative imagination, and practice one has had.

The drumset can be adapted to replicate three basic ways to play Samba rhythms. This section will discuss a) Afro Samba/Batucada, b) Samba de Prato, using cymbals, and c) Samba Fusion. Practice exercises will build your knowledge of them. As we move to the drumset, we begin with a general discussion of performance concepts.

Performance Concepts

The most obvious way to play Samba on the drumset is to reproduce some Samba-school percussion parts played by the Bateria on the drumset. To do so, it is important to review Section 2, where Samba school percussion parts were explained. Pay special attention to the examples of the rhythms played on the surdo, pandeiro, caixa, tamborim, agogo, repenique, cuica and ganza.

There are endless ways to reproduce the sounds of a Bateria using a standard drumset configuration. Here are some of them:

- The floor tom can duplicate the surdo sound.
- The snare drum can reproduce caixa sound.
- The snare drum, with snares off, can imitate the repinique sound.
- The snare drum can mimic a tamborim sound by playing with a cross stick or playing on the drumhead with a stick while the other hand muffles the head.
- The closed hi-hat can easily duplicate the sounds of a shaker.

High- and low-sound melodies are played on percussion instruments that use different pitches. For example, the sounds of tom-toms are not exactly like the sounds of the cuica, agogo, or the Samba whistle. But the toms can be played effectively and easily to approximate the two- or three-note melodies of those instruments.

Replicating Three Basic Ways
To Play Samba Rhythms

There are three basic ways to perform Samba on the drumset. It is important to be very familiar with them, because you will apply them to many variations.

1) Afro-Samba

Brazilian music scholars identify a form as an Afro-Samba style, when an ensemble is made of percussion instruments only, and when no melodic or harmonic instruments are present, with the exception of the human voice. There are many variations of Afro-Samba styles that can be interpreted on the drumset. Two of the more popular styles are the "Samba Cruzado" and the "Samba de Batucada."

It is very important to note this distinction. The drumset imitates the sounds of an Afro-Samba bateria, but typically does so as part of a group that will also include melodic and harmonic instruments. When we refer to Afro-Samba on the *drumset*, we are referring to the style drummers use to recreate the sounds of a percussion group, such as the batucada ensemble, the Charanga or the Bloco. Sonically speaking, that means the drummer will focus on imitating sounds of instruments such as the surdo, caixa, repinique, tamborim, or ganza. There is little emphasis on the ride, crash and hi-hat cymbals, because there are no cymbals in an authentic Samba percussion ensemble.

An Afro-Samba ensemble in the authentic forms is wholly made up of percussion instruments. In Portuguese, the term Batucada is used to mean the same thing as Afro-Samba. When a Brazilian drummer is asked to play a Batucada on the drumset, the sound of a Samba percussion section will be duplicated.

The drumset Afro-Samba style is usually used when a thicker sound texture is desired. It is especially effective during an introduction to a song, a drum solo, fade-outs, or parts of a music arrangement where the drums need to be a little more pronounced. Arrangers will sometimes use a percussion batucada/solo with Samba breaks in the middle of a song as a highlight of an arrangement.

Technically, one of the most effective ways to manage that is to play bass drum and hi-hat ostinatos with the feet, while the hands move around the snare drum, tom-toms, and floor toms. Cymbals are seldom played; if they are, they are used only for accents. The orientation of Afro-Samba is drum-heavy.

The main thing to remember when playing an Afro-Samba style on the drumset is to try to sound like a group of people playing percussion instruments together. The best way to imitate the style and sounds of a bateria or batucada ensemble is to put most of the focus on the snare drums, tom-toms, and floor toms.

SOUND SOURCES

Sound sources for Afro-Samba playing ideas on the drumset are taken from percussion parts of the surdo, caixa, repinique, and other instruments in the Samba percussion family.

The entire drumset is played with a thick, massive sound when it recreates the Batucada/Afro-Samba style. It does not leave a lot of musical "space" for other instruments to participate actively in a musical dialog. The Batucada way of playing may create a very excited feeling, but drummers have had to come up with other ways to create a Samba feel on the drumset that was more supportive during other parts of a song.

Whenever a thinner orchestration is desired, it is essential to maintain the Samba energy and still leave space and dynamics for other instruments to build upon. The Samba de Prato style was introduced because it is ideal for those purposes.

2) Samba De Prato/Ensemble Samba

Samba de Prato is the most popular way of interpreting Samba on the drumset. The drummer does not recreate a percussion-ensemble sound. Instead, the drumset supports an ensemble that might include a bass, piano, guitar, sax, and vocals. The drummer focuses on interpreting a Samba feel with lighter orchestration using fewer drums. Put emphasis on the ride and hi-hat cymbals to create a "forward motion."

Brazilians refer to the ensemble Samba as the Samba de Prato. It is played by leading with the hi-hat or ride-cymbal ostinatos (for example from ganza/shaker parts), a hi-hat/bass-drum accompaniment (usually from a surdo part), and improvised left-hand patterns (usually from tamborim parts) on the snare drums, toms, or other available sound sources.

Samba de Prato leaves a lot of sonic space. It is a more ensemble-friendly way of executing a Samba feel. Fewer notes are played on the drums, and more notes are played on the ride/hi-hat cymbals to create a lighter feel.

SOUND SOURCES

The right hand will play hi-hat/ride-cymbal ostinatos that are repetitive, producing a sound similar to the ganza/shakers sound. The left hand usually plays rhythms taken from parts played by the cuica, agogo, or, most frequently, from tamborim parts.

The Samba de Prato is adaptable to many different Samba styles and musical situations. It can certainly be used to keep time, solo, and play fills.

3) Samba Fusion

Samba Fusion mixes both Afro-Samba and Samba de Prato techniques. It usually involves the execution of feet ostinatos while the hands are playing in a more linear or semi-linear fashion, moving from the cymbals/hi-hat to the snare drum and tom-toms, and back and forth.

When we discussed Afro-Samba and Samba de Prato, cymbals functioned as ostinatos or accents. Hand ostinatos might still be played in Samba Fusion, but they will be more fragmented. They are usually orchestrated among different parts of the kit.

The stick work is more involved. It is also often distributed equally between the two hands rather than stationary right-hand lead ride patterns played in a Samba de Prato. Feet ostinatos are, however, often used. The hi-hat will usually keep time, while the foot plays the bass drum in figures taken from different surdo parts.

SOUND SOURCES

Sound sources for Samba Fusion can vary considerably. Percussion parts from the Samba percussion family are certainly sources for rhythmic ideas. But the guitar, bass, and other ensemble instruments present additional possibilities to perform parts. One good example is to incorporate rhythms played by a guitar in the drumset groove. Orchestration among the drumset, with different sticking combinations of left- and right-hand accented and non-accented notes, is one of the most useful tools in the execution of that style.

Syncopated rhythmic textures are more desirable for a Samba Fusion style. A section of a song may call for an "implied" surdo. For example, the accent can be played on the "2" of the measure without completely going over to a Batucada style. It is possible to produce a "surdo feel" at the same time, keeping some sort of ride going on the cymbal.

Breaking up the ride pattern to incorporate tom-tom accents is one of the characteristics of Samba Fusion. This becomes literally a mixture of Samba de Prato and Batucada thus creating a fusion of the Samba styles.

SECTION 4: AFRO-SAMBA (PART 1)

Concept

As mentioned earlier, the main idea when playing Afro-Samba on the drumset is to reproduce the sounds played by a Samba percussion ensemble. There are many ways to accomplish this. One of the basic ways is to match the sounds of Samba percussion instruments with what is available to you on your drumset. Here are some examples of matches:

Surdo	Bass drum/floor tom
Caixa	Snare drum
Tamborim	Snare drum cross stick
Shakers	Closed hi-hats/ride cymbal
Repinique	Ringing edge of the snare drum with snares on or off
Cuica	Hi tom-tom, low tom-tom

The key to success is starting simple. First start to explore possible rhythmic patterns by using hi-hat/bass-drum ostinatos against a snare-drum part. Using this concept makes it possible to come up with some very interesting Afro-Samba grooves.

Practice Procedures

Practice using the following sequence to help you develop coordination and necessary confidence.

1. Pick a caixa pattern.
2. Play it along with foot hi-hat ostinatos.
3. Play it along with foot bass-drum ostinatos.
4. Play it along with hi-hat/bass-drum ostinatos.

Take a look at some feet-ostinato possibilities.

Hi-hat Ostinatos

Bass-Drum Ostinatos

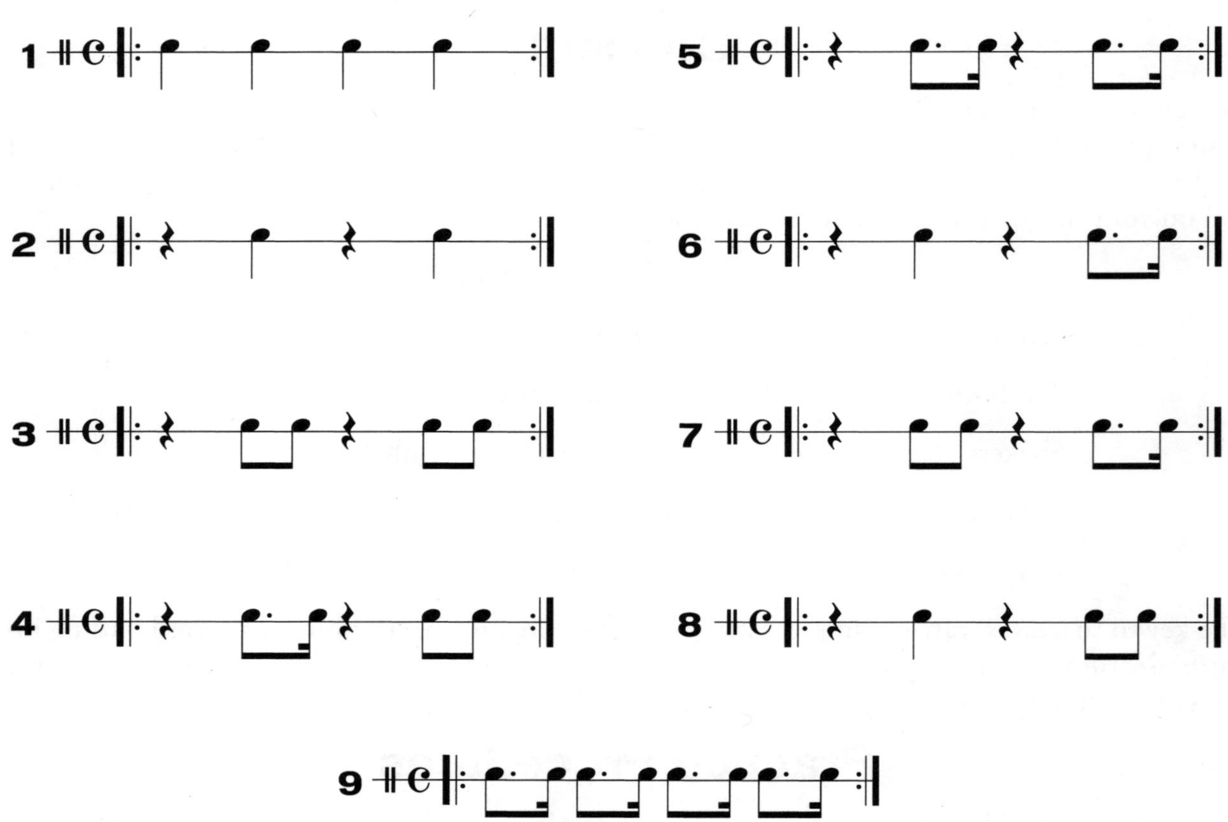

Hi-hat and Bass-Drum Ostinatos

Pick a caixa pattern.

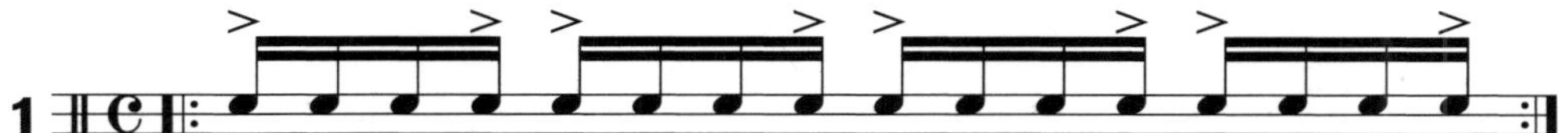

Play the caixa pattern with the hi-hat foot ostinatos.

Then play the same caixa pattern, now with the bass-drum ostinatos.

After practicing with the hi-hat foot ostinatos and the bass-drum ostinatos, play the caixa pattern along with the hi-hat/bass-drum ostinatos.

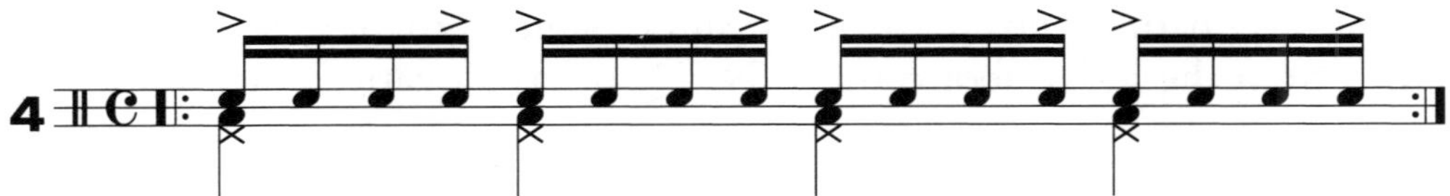

Here are a few grooves that can result from the caixa exercises.

Practicing the entire section of caixa patterns against the feet ostinatos will give many groove options. The following practice procedures present further explorations and possibilities of bass-drum ostinatos.

Pick a caixa pattern that you like and play it along with the third surdo Samba variation patterns shown earlier. "X" notes mean a hand-muffled stroke on the surdo, and regular note heads indicate an open tone.

Play the open tone with the bass drum and the "X" notes with the hi-hat. You can also play the open tone with the bass drum without any hi-hat at all. Or if you want to play a simple hi-hat, refer to the hi-hat foot ostinatos. First, pick your choice of hi-hat ostinatos. Then, run the third surdo examples along with it.

Here are some examples of third surdo Samba variation patterns from the book, against a caixa pattern. First, we have caixa Samba pattern No. 1 from page 43 notated on the snare drum. The hi-hat and bass-drum parts were taken from the third surdo Samba variation example No. 1 from page 29. A muffled tone indicates hi-hat; an open tone indicates bass drum.

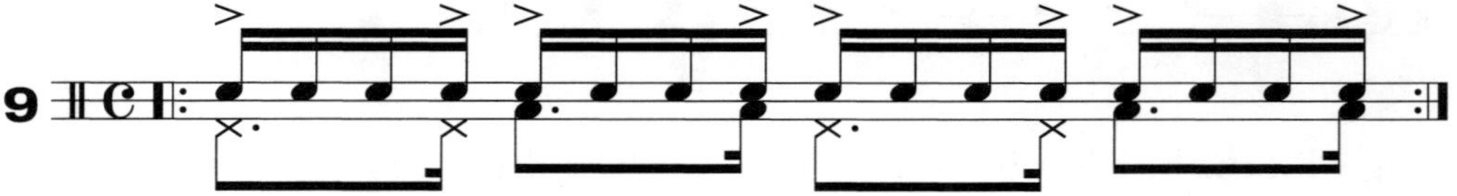

Second, we have caixa pattern No. 1 with third surdo Samba variation No. 20. Notice that the hi-hat pattern is from the hi-hat foot ostinato No. 1. It has a quarter note on each beat of the measure.

Finally, we have caixa pattern No. 1 with a surdo part on the bass drum taken from the third surdo Samba variations in two-measure phrases No. 1, first measure. The hi-hat plays quarter notes.

It is important to understand a process of building simple Afro-Samba grooves that will both sound authentic and will work with given music. A student can develop unique grooves by choosing caixa, surdo, hi-hat, and bass-drum ostinatos from the examples demonstrated here and then putting them together. The grooves, although original, will still sound very authentic because their parts were taken from original, authentic Samba percussion parts as the source.

SECTION 5: AFRO-SAMBA (PART 2)

Moving Caixa Parts between the Floor Tom and Tom-toms

Exercises in the previous section gave ideas of how to develop skills to play Afro-Samba rhythms using the snare drum with hi-hat and bass-drum ostinatos. Once you are comfortable with those methods, it's time to move on.

The next step is to play the same feet ostinatos against caixa patterns. However in this section, the hands will move around the tom-toms and floor tom. This approach will result in producing a very thick Batucada sound.

Remember where the strong accents are in this style: the "2" in $\frac{2}{4}$ and the "2" and "4" in $\frac{4}{4}$.

Here are the steps to follow:

1. Pick a caixa pattern.
2. Pick a hi-hat/bass-drum ostinato.
3. Play them together.
4. Move some of the caixa pattern's right-hand notes to the floor tom.
5. Move some of the caixa pattern's right-hand notes to the floor tom and high tom.
6. Move some of the caixa pattern's right-hand notes to the floor tom, high tom, and middle tom.
7. Move some of the left hand notes to toms.
8. Move some of the right and left-hand notes among all of the toms.

Note: When moving around the tom-toms and floor tom, try to keep in mind where the different surdo parts would fit. Try placing the right sound in the correct place for the right "feel."

Afro-Samba Groove Examples

Take a look at the following examples to help you practice the Batucada Afro-Samba style. Pay attention to sticking, accents, and orchestration as you try to understand the concept. Remember that the rhythmic materials demonstrated in this section are caixa patterns being played between the snare drum and tom-toms. Practice them and try also to come up with your own versions of Afro-Samba by using the same concept.

The examples shown below should be played with different feet ostinatos. Here are the suggested practice procedures.

1. Choose one feet ostinato, either hi-hat, bass-drum ostinato or hi-hat and bass drum ostinato from earlier examples.
2. Run through the examples below while keeping the same feet ostinato throughout.

Note: Use alternate stickings: RLRL etc., except when indicated otherwise. Fill examples are usually played not more than two times. They are good for indicating the end of phrases.

NOTATION KEY:

68

Here is an example of a very popular hi-hat and bass-drum ostinato.

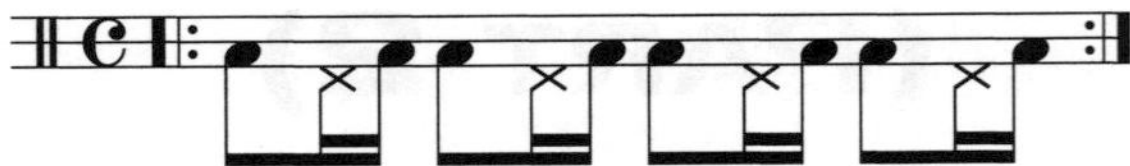

The following examples will involve the use of high tom and low tom.

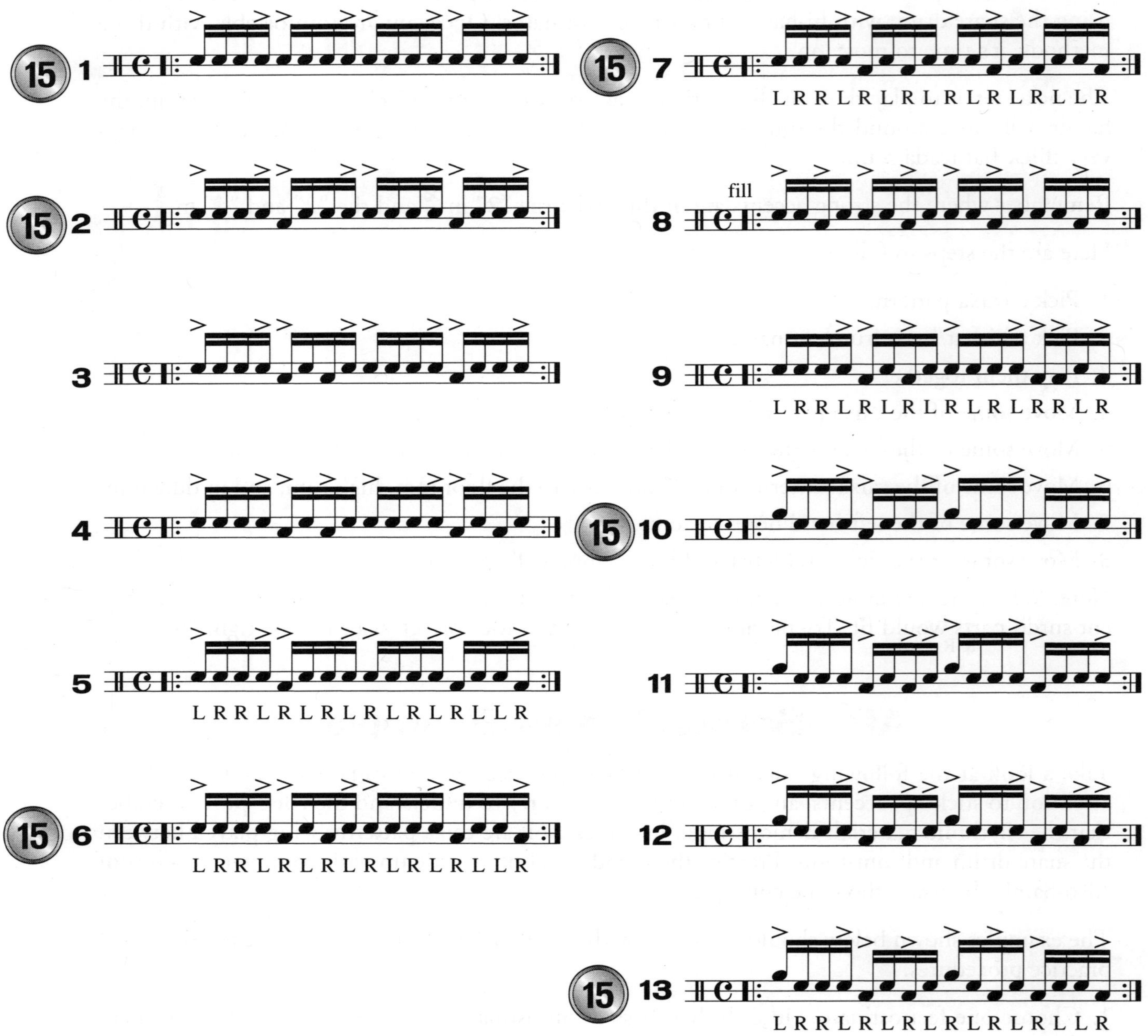

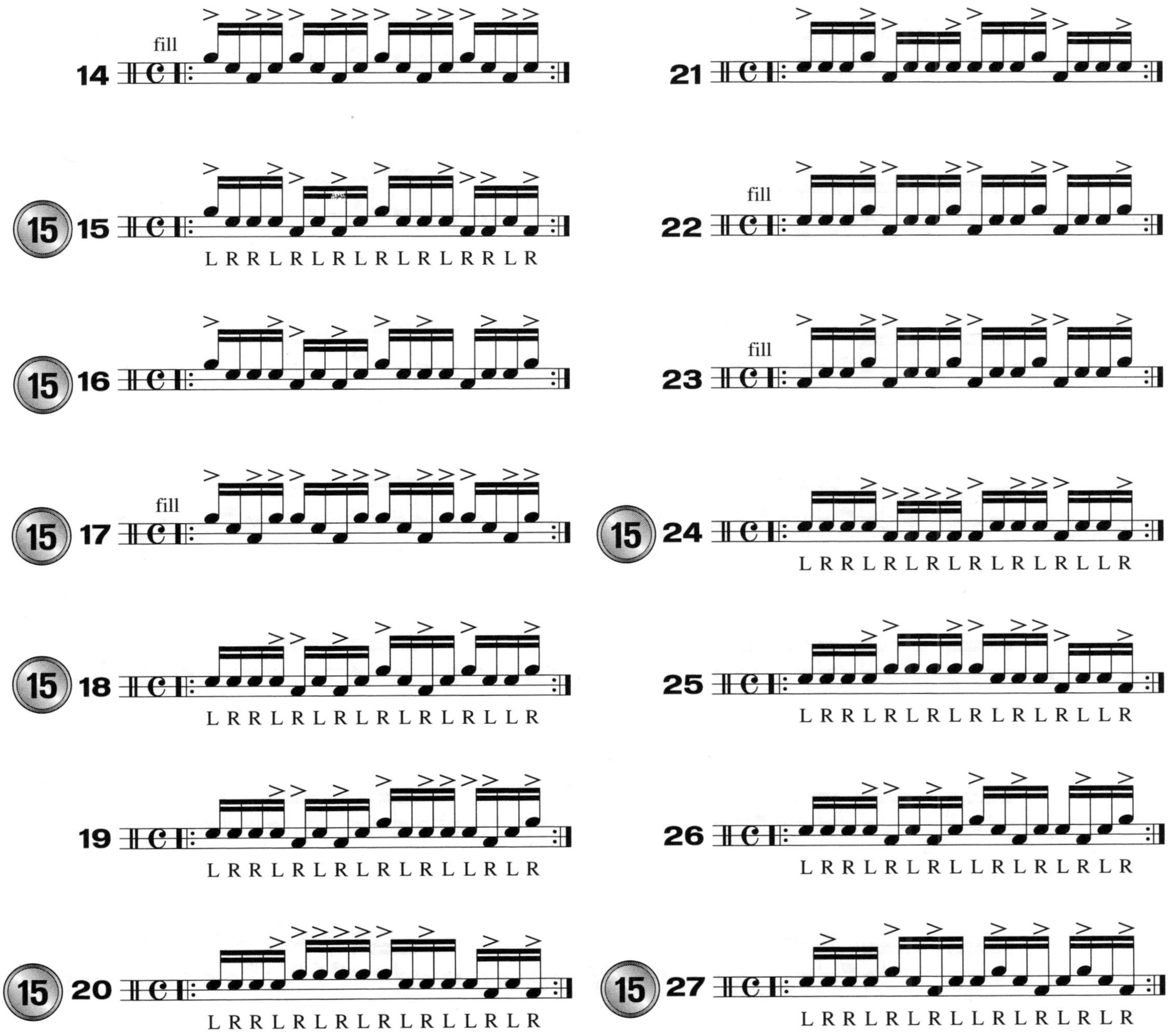

The following examples will involve the use of high tom, low tom, and floor tom.

NOTATION KEY:

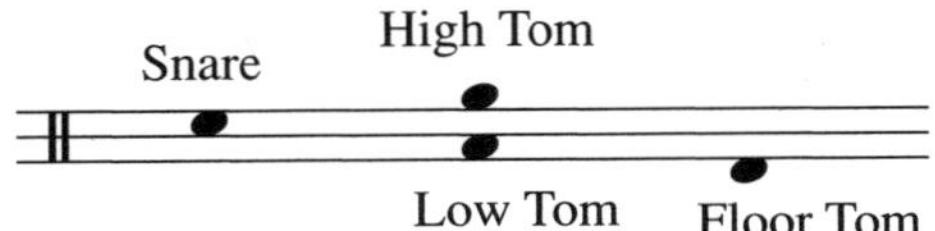

70

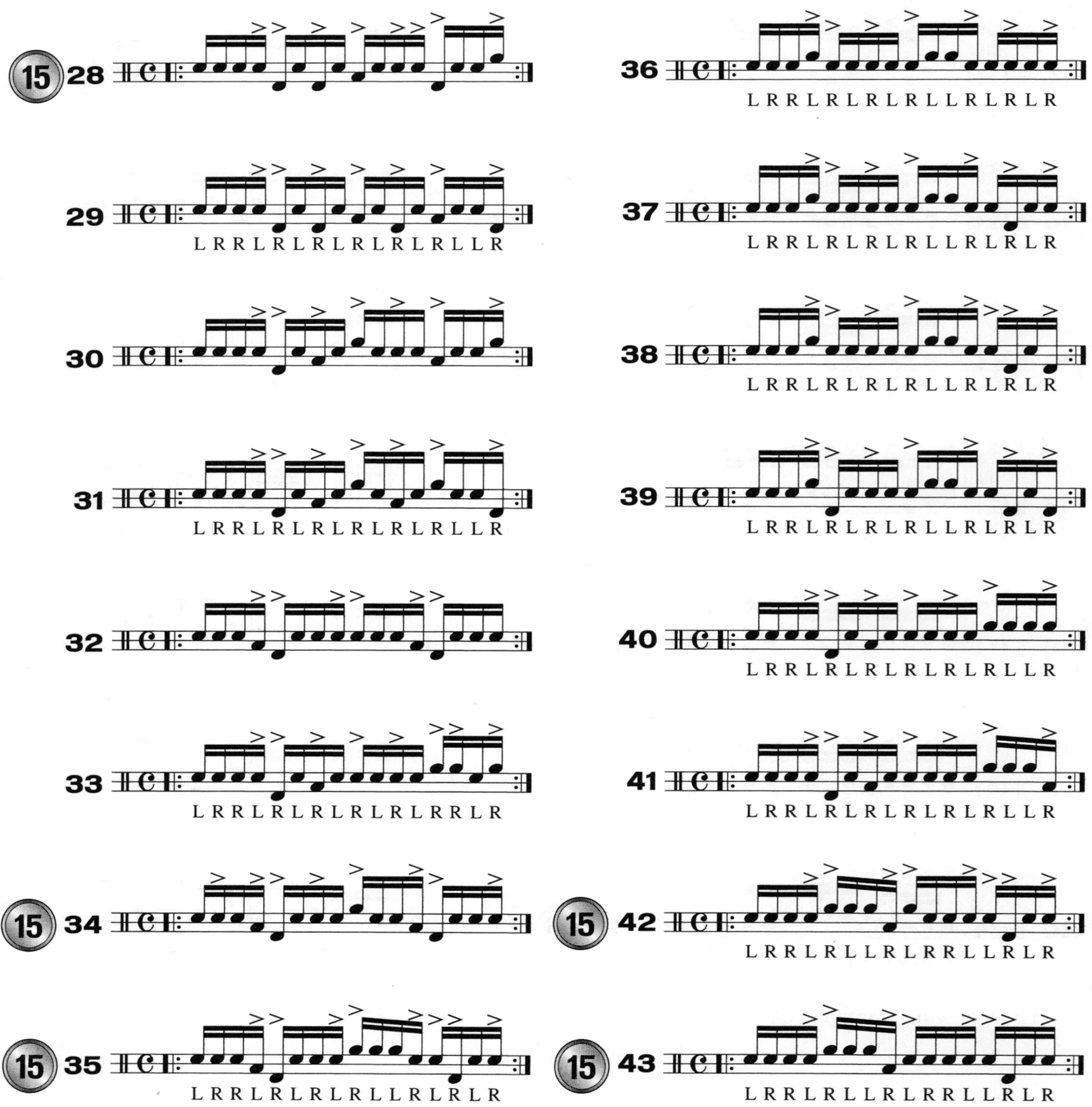

DRM119

SECTION 6: AFRO-SAMBA (PART 3)

Embellishment and Orchestration

In the previous section we saw two ways of playing Afro-Samba on the drumset:

1. Snare drum against feet ostinatos.
2. Snare drum and tom-toms against feet ostinatos.

We began first by simply playing caixa patterns on the snare drum while playing different hi-hat and bass-drum ostinatos. Second, we played the feet ostinatos and played caixa patterns on the snare drum, high tom, low tom, and floor tom.

The examples were based on very simple caixa patterns without any rolls. When composing your own grooves, explore caixa patterns that contain rolls. They will add a different sound and feel.

Here is a list of things that could also be done with this material:

1. Double some of the snare-drum notes, from sixteenth notes to thirty-second notes, making a double-stroke roll instead of a single-stroke roll.
2. Move some of the right-hand notes to the hi-hat. Open or closed sounds could be used.
3. Move some of the left-hand notes to the hi-hat. Open or closed sounds could be used.
4. Experiment with "cross-over". This means crossing the right hand over the left, or crossing the left hand over the right. This simple concept will create new sound possibilities.

Let's take a look at example No. 22 from the caixa patterns on page 44.

Basic pattern:

Doubling some of the notes:

Moving some of the notes to the hi-hat:

Opening the hi-hat in some of the notes:

A little solo demonstrating concepts described above is given on page 72.

Note: The caixa pattern sticking LRRL RLRL RLRL LRLR will be the only sticking used for this entire Etude. Note how a simple Afro-Samba groove can be transformed into a Samba-Fusion style by incorporating the hi-hat cymbal.

The feet ostinato will be:

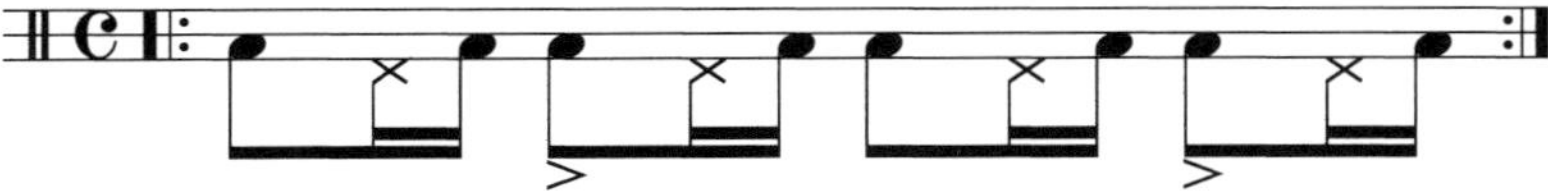

Afro-Samba Solo with Embellishments

16

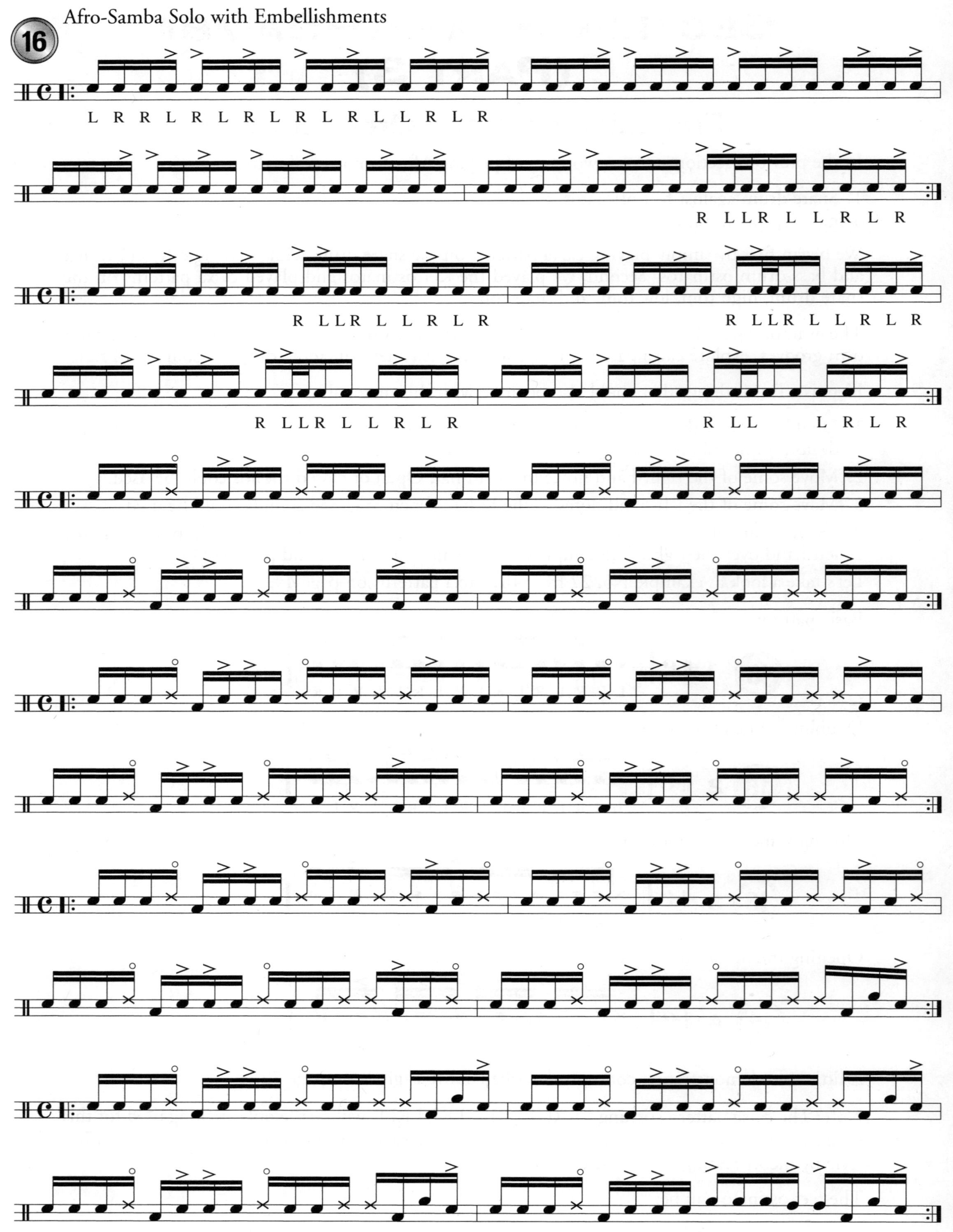

SECTION 7: AFRO-SAMBA (PART 4)

Cruzado

Samba Cruzado

Samba Cruzado is another way to perform Afro-Samba on the drumset. Traditionally speaking the Samba Cruzado is played primarily on the snare drum and tom-toms against Samba hi-hat/bass-drum ostinatos. The right hand plays consecutive sixteenth notes on the snare drum using rhythmic ideas from caixa, tamborim, and repinique patterns. The left hand crosses over the right and plays different surdo parts between the tom-toms and floor toms.

Snare-drum Parts

The key factors to producing a dynamic Samba Cruzado are how the accented notes and non-accented notes are played with the right hand on the snare drum. Playing the snare drum "flat" without any accents will make this type of groove very static.

Non-accented notes should be played very softly on the drumhead. Accented notes should be played with a rim shot on the very edge of the snare drum to produce a ringing sound.

Having a specific rhythm idea for accented notes, such as those of the tamborim parts, will give the snare drum a very good rhythmic motive to be developed. Usually phrases that are of one measure in length are ideal for this situation. Here is an example of how to come up with Samba Cruzado snare parts.

Flat snare-drum part:

Clave idea:

Snare part plays a clave-type rhythm, filling out the rest of the measure using sixteenth notes.

Come up with your own ideas as you use this concept. Tamborim parts demonstrated in an earlier part of this book are among many good sources for accent possibilities.

NOTATION KEY:

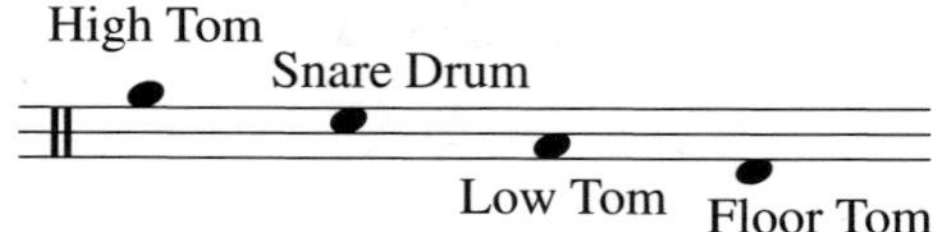

Left-hand Examples

13

20

14

21

(17) 15

22

16

(17) 23

(17) 17

(17) 24

18

25

19

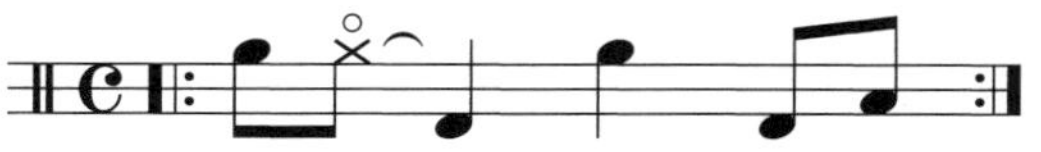

NOTE: Also try the examples above with different snare accents such as this:

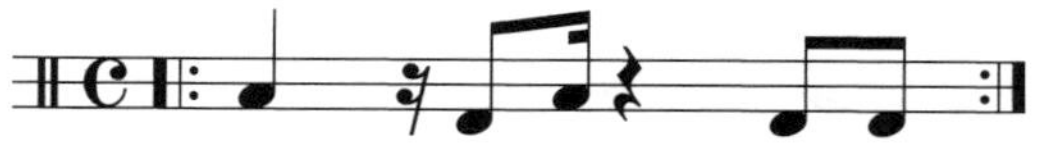

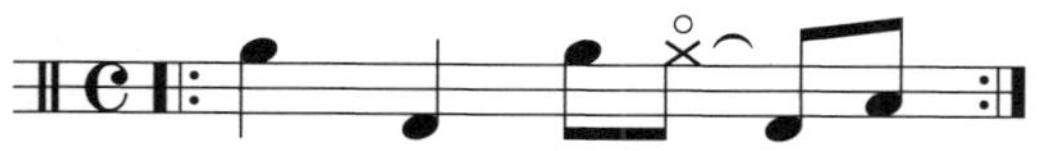

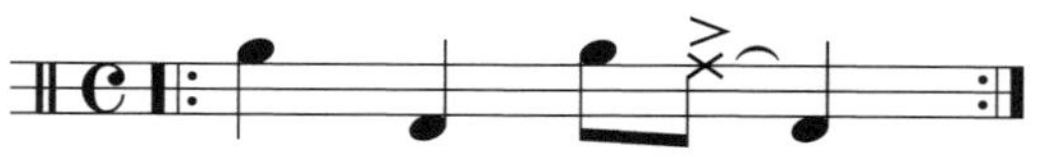

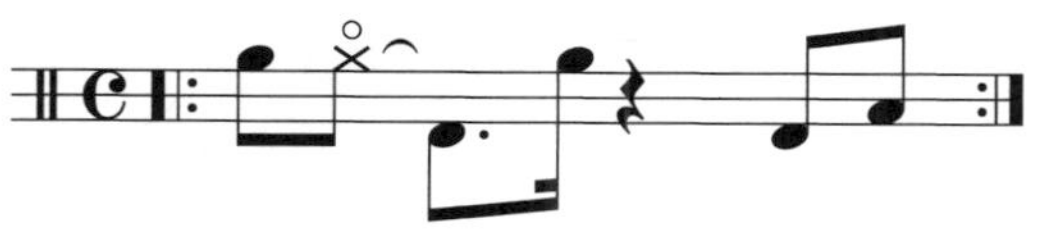

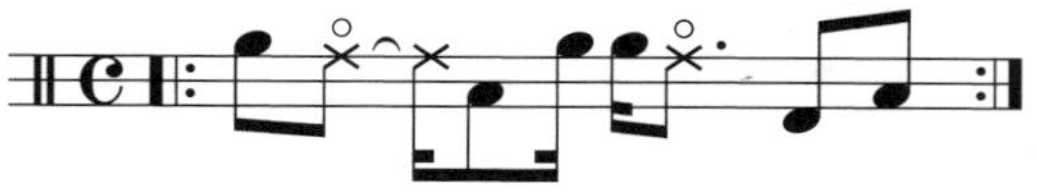

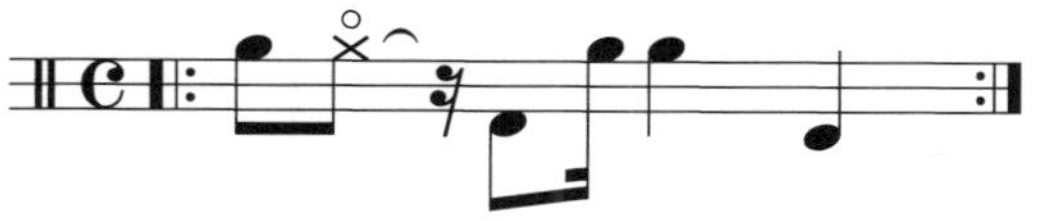

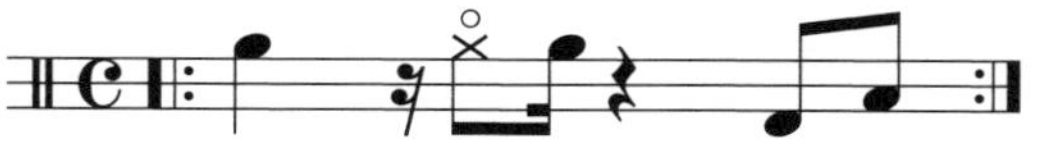

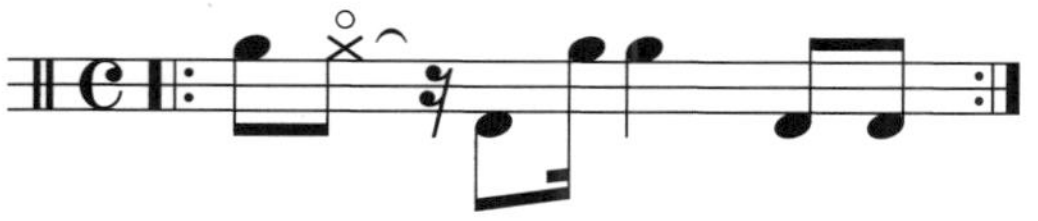

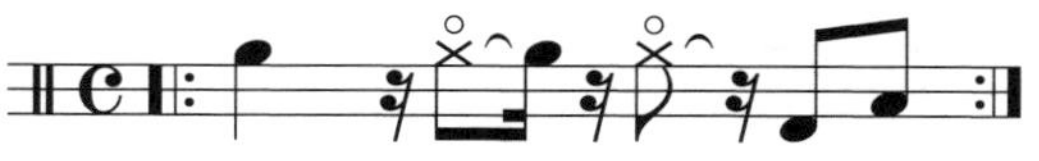

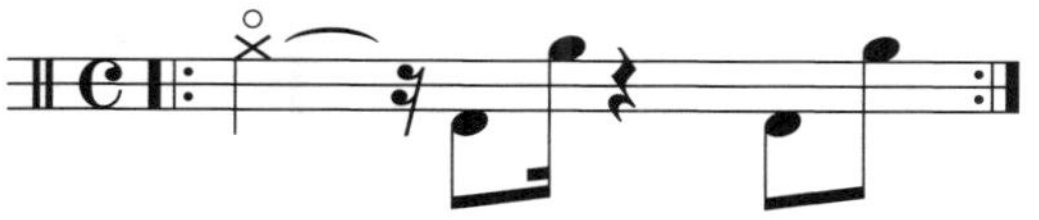

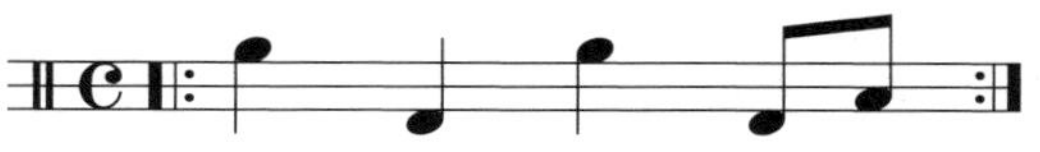

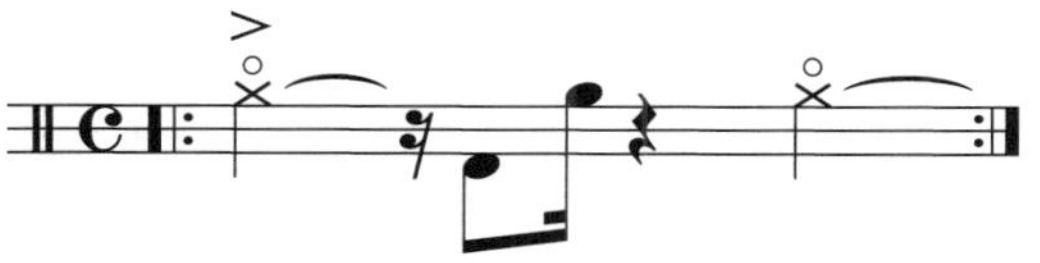

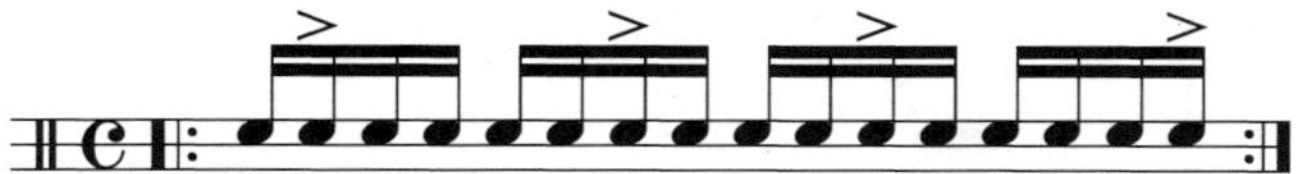

Here is a group of Samba Cruzado examples with different snare-drum accents. First, play the snare part, then add the hi-hat/bass-drum ostinato. Finally, add the tom-toms and hi-hat, playing with sticks.

Snare Drum
Bass Drum/Hi-hat

(17) 26

Tom-toms/Hi-hat

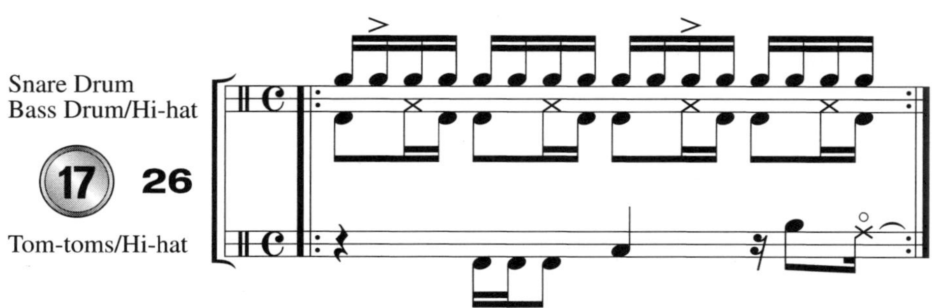

27
28
29
30
17 31

Try a different method to embellish the last two examples. A "hit-and-stepping" technique can be played by using the stick on the first hi-hat note. Then immediately play the second note by stepping on the hi-hat footboard with an open hi-hat stroke.

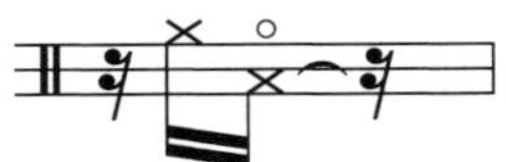

Section 8: Samba de Prato/Ensemble Samba (Part 1)

The expression Samba de Prato in Portuguese means "Cymbal Samba." It indicates that the hi-hat and/or the ride cymbal executes the sixteenth-note flow or similar patterns. The feet play hi-hat and bass-drum ostinatos. The left hand moves around the drum kit.

Samba de Prato is ideal for ensemble performance. It has a thinner orchestration than an Afro-Samba style. It makes more room for other instruments to play along. It also provides the hi-hat and/or ride cymbal drive that other musicians are accustomed to hearing in other music styles.

One of the most important elements of a good Samba groove is the constant sixteenth notes (in $\frac{4}{4}$) or eighth notes (in $\frac{2}{4}$ or cut time) played by snare drum or shakers. These constant ostinatos establish a note rate for everything else to lock into. They become the reference points, if you will.

When you play Samba de Prato, it is crucial to have a basic understanding of how to use different levels of dynamics to create a great feel. There are many dynamic levels played simultaneously by the Samba percussion section. Some instruments play very loud, while others play medium volume. Some instruments will play very softly in contrast to what might be expected from the tamborim, the caixa, or repinique.

Soft parts fill sound gaps from rests left by other percussion instruments. They continue the rhythm flow so it does not feel "chopped off." The shaker, ganza or reco-reco continues a nice, rhythmic flow that doesn't sound "cluttered" by playing soft notes. Those notes they play can be compared to "ghost notes" used by great Jazz and Funk drummers.

Earlier in the book we demonstrated examples of Afro-Samba. The snare drum played consecutive sixteenth notes. We also saw sixteenth-note phrasing distributed among the snare and tom-toms. Next we discussed the Samba Cruzado, where the right hand assumed the sixteenth-note-ostinato function. The left hand moved around the kit. In all of those examples, the snare drum usually played the role of the shaker in constant sixteenth notes. This continues to be a major role in the Samba de Prato, but now the hi-hat and the ride cymbal will assume that role.

Slow To Medium Tempos

There are many ways to come up with ideas for the Samba de Prato. One of the most obvious is to borrow some of the rhythms played by the tamborim. Assign them to the left hand, and the right hand will play different ostinatos on the hi-hat or ride cymbal with bass-drum ostinatos.

This group of ostinatos can be used on the closed hi-hat or ride cymbal. They are suited to slow or medium tempos.

Closed hi-hat and bass drum ostinato

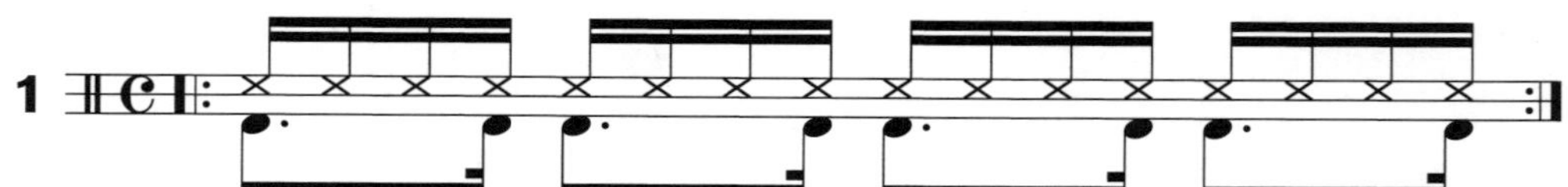

Ride-cymbal ostinatos

Practice procedures:

1. Play ostinato 1 from page 78. Memorize it. Turn to the tamborim examples shown earlier in the book on pages 35 to 36. Play these examples with the left hand using cross stick on the rim of the snare drum while playing ostinato 1.

2. Repeat the procedure above now with ostinato 2.

3. Repeat the procedure above now with ostinato 3.

4. Repeat the procedure above now with ostinato 4.

5. Repeat the procedure above now with ostinato 5.

6. Repeat steps 1 to 5. This time play the tamborim parts on the drumhead rather than the rim.

NOTE: Try to play the foot hi-hat part on the same ostinatos by opening the hi-hat with the foot.

Saudades on page 150 in the Play-along Section (Disk 2, Track 7 without drums on Track 14) incorporates the slow Samba feel presented in the text. Have fun playing this chart.

SECTION 9: SAMBA DE PRATO/ENSEMBLE SAMBA (PART 2)

Once you become comfortable with the exercises in Part One, the next step is to play ostinatos against the modified tamborim parts presented below. Play these new tamborim examples with your left hand. Simultaneously play one of the ostinatos from pages 78-79.

The following examples are tamborim parts with added buzz rolls.

Section 10: Samba de Prato/Ensemble Samba (Part 3)

If you have successfully practiced playing tamborim rhythms on the rim and with the buzz rolls on the snare drum, the next step is to go back to the tamborim examples on pages 35 to 36. This time practice the parts moving the left hand around the snare drum and tom-toms.

Notation Key:

Practice playing these left-hand examples against feet and right-hand ostinatos 1,2,3,4 and 5 from pages 78-79.

Here it is an example of what it will sound like.

Note: Agogo and samba whistle parts can be another source of rhythmic ideas to play among the toms.

An Agogo-based example:

A Whistle-based example:

Section 11: Samba de Prato/Ensemble Samba (Part 4)

Tamborim parts can be played all around the kit, including the hi-hat, with the left hand. Take a look at the examples below. Try to come up with our own interpretations by exploring more possibilities.

Slow- to Medium-Tempo Groove Ideas

Play ostinatos 2, 3, 4 and 5 from page 79, while the left hand plays these examples.

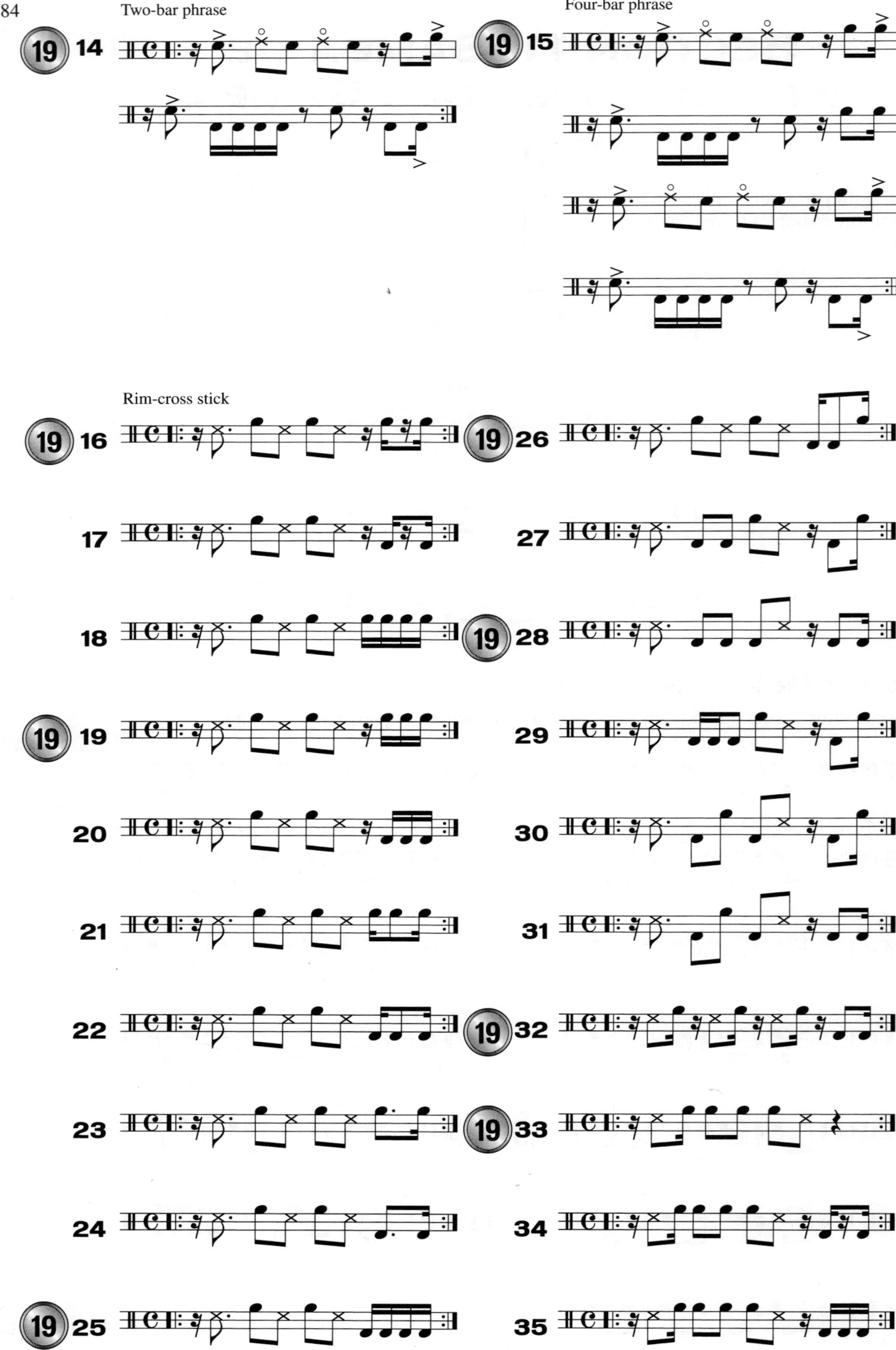

Two-bar phrase
Four-bar phrase
Rim-cross stick

Fast-tempo Examples

It can be difficult to play Samba de Prato at faster tempos on the ride cymbal or hi-hat, because you are playing straight sixteenth-note patterns. Breaking up the patterns into smaller units can be one way to make it easier on your wrist. This allows your wrist to relax between strokes.

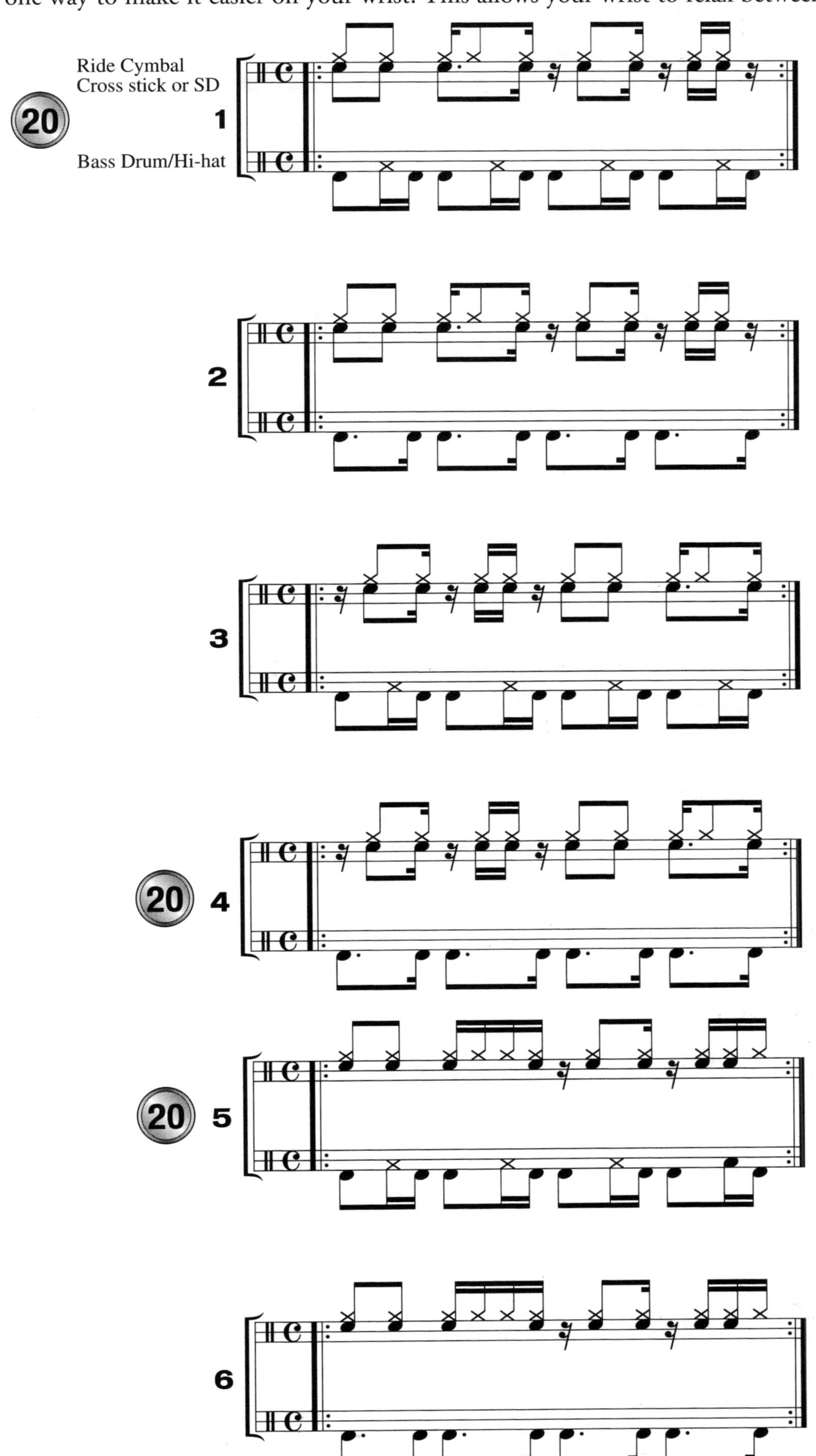

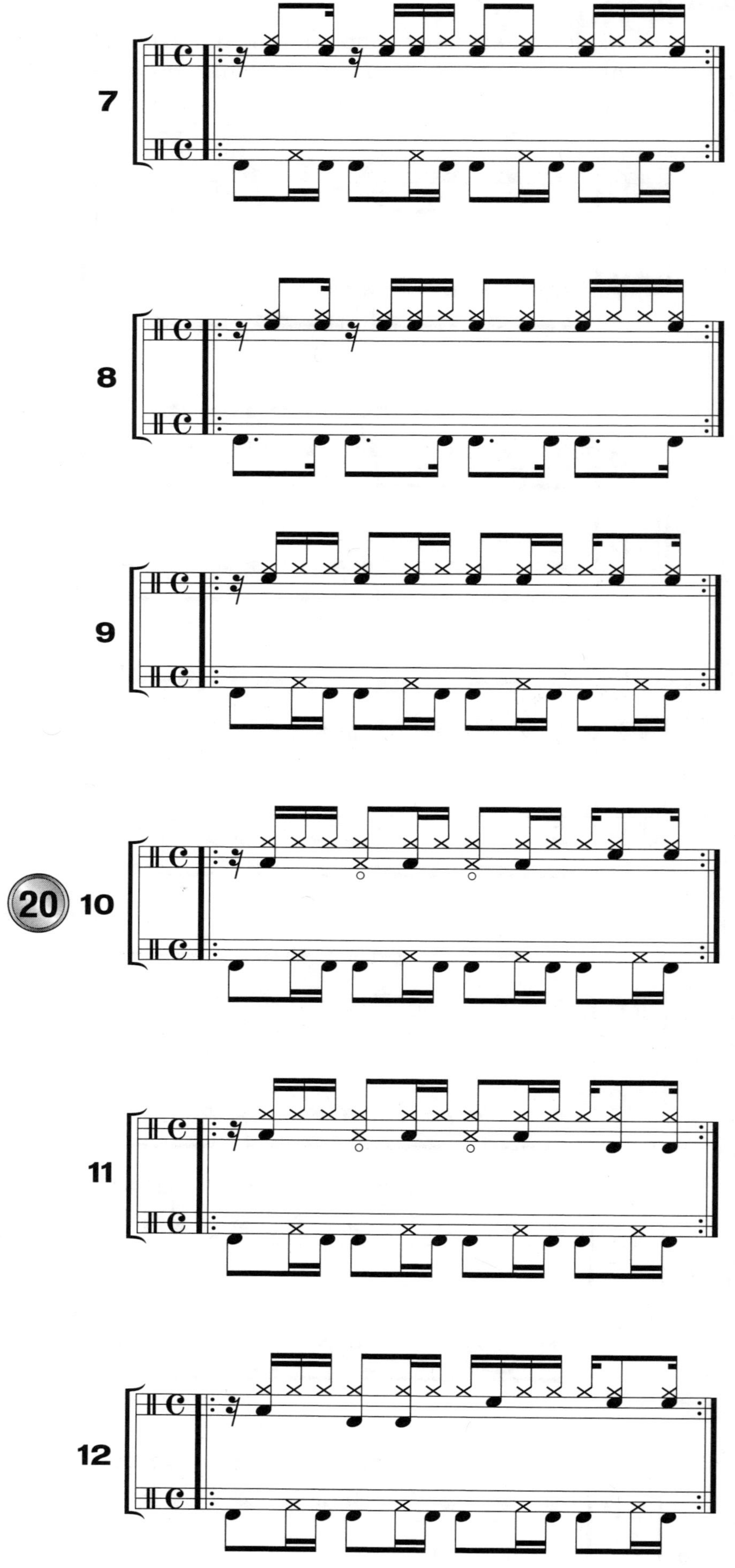

SECTION 12: SAMBA-FUNK

Samba-Funk is a contemporary term referring to the way an electronic group plays Samba and incorporates elements of Funk.

Brazilian music in general is heavily influenced by music from other countries. Blended musical styles quickly develop in larger cities such as Rio de Janeiro and Sao Paulo, where there is constant cross-cultural exchange, especially with the United States. For example, James Brown is very popular in Brazil.

Rock bands permeate Brazil's musical culture. Many of them adopt Jazz and Funk styles. Of course, Samba finds its way into many of today's modern popular genres and performance venues. Samba-Funk is popular among Rock groups performing dance music, although instrumental Pop and Jazz groups also incorporate Samba-Funk.

Here are some elements common to Samba-Funk:

- Electric bass plays bass lines that incorporate the "slap technique".
- Keyboards are often preferred as opposed to acoustic piano.
- Electric guitar plays Funk styles more frequently than Samba rhythms.
- Percussion instruments play Samba patterns.
- Drumset patterns that have a strong back-beat accent (not always on the "2" and "4").

Samba-Funk compositions will frequently incorporate very simple song forms such as AABA. More often than not, the B section, as the bridge of an instrumental tune or the chorus of a song, will have a straight Samba de Prato feel. In other words, the form will be:

A: Samba-Funk

A: Samba-Funk

B: Samba de Prato

A: Samba-Funk

Because Samba-Funk is a blend of two styles, we may hear the tamborim, cuica, pandeiro, ganza, and surdo playing authentic Samba rhythms at the same time a drumset plays a Funk style. The drummer will sometimes play a bass-drum ostinato in a straight Samba style.

It is essential to understand that different musical ingredients contribute to what the music industry recognizes as Samba-Funk. If we isolated some parts by themselves, each would be classified as either "Samba" or "Funk." But when we put them together, they enhance each other. We can create an exciting combination when we bring together all the parts, for example, a Funk guitar riff complementing a Samba percussion section. Played together, they are transformed into Samba-Funk.

Drumset Performance

There are small subtle differences between a straight Samba de Prato and Samba-Funk. One in particular is the left-hand rhythm on the snare drum. When Brazilian drummers play Samba on the drumset, they usually play cross stick on the snare drum, or they tap on the drumhead using tamborim-like rhythms such as these:

Drummers playing in the Samba-Funk style will modify tamborim rhythms such as the one above to create a new style feel. If we isolate accented rhythms that are inherent in the rhythm shown above, the result would be this:

Rhythms such as these are commonly played on snare-drum Samba-Funk patterns.

Remaining, non-accented rhythms of the pattern are usually played with the bass drum.

Samba-Funk Pattern

Play the accented notes from a tamborim part on the snare drum and some of the non-accented rhythms with the bass drum will create a nice Samba-Funk rhythm.

Let's take a look at some common Samba-Funk drumset patterns.

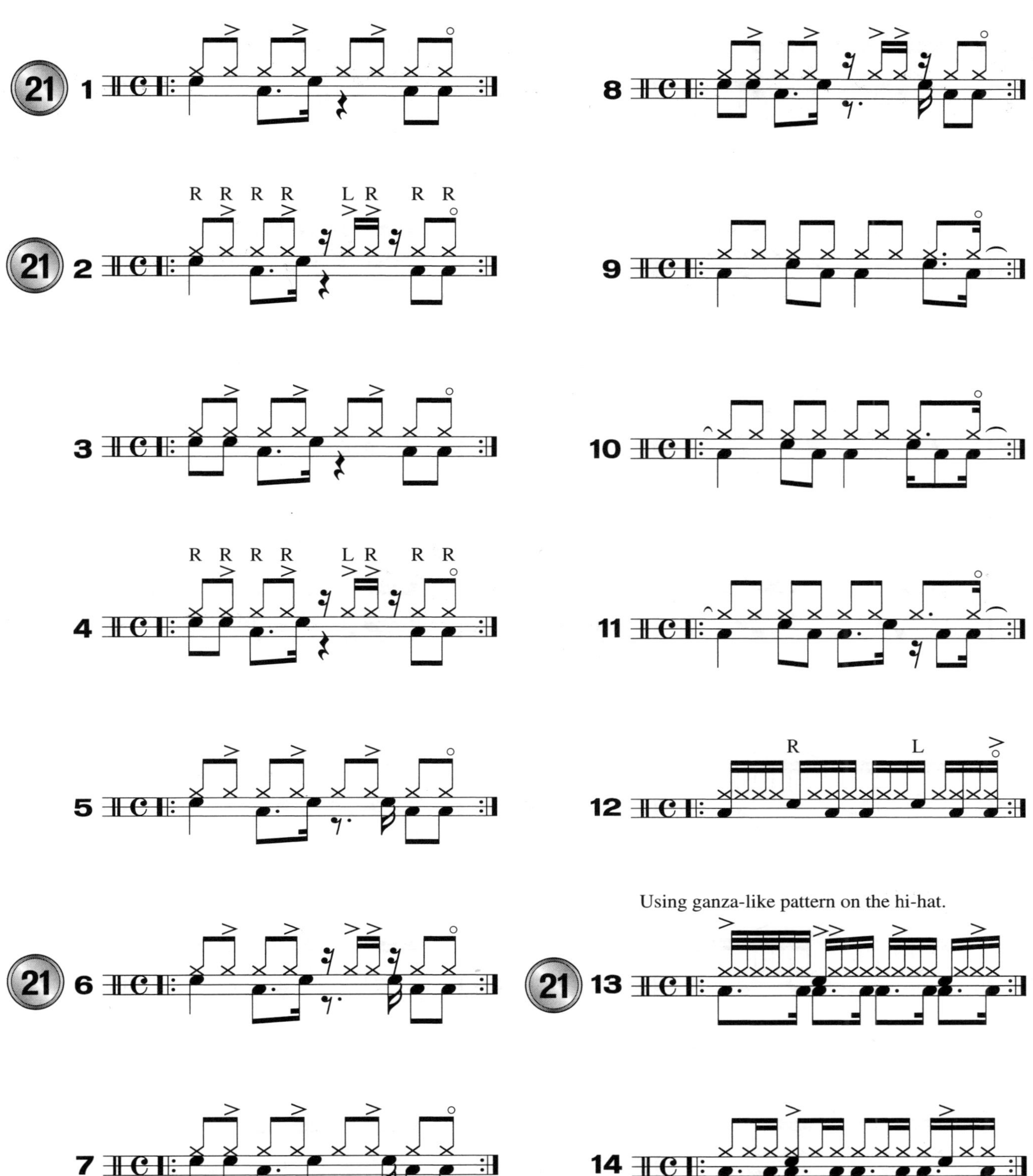

Using ganza-like pattern on the hi-hat.

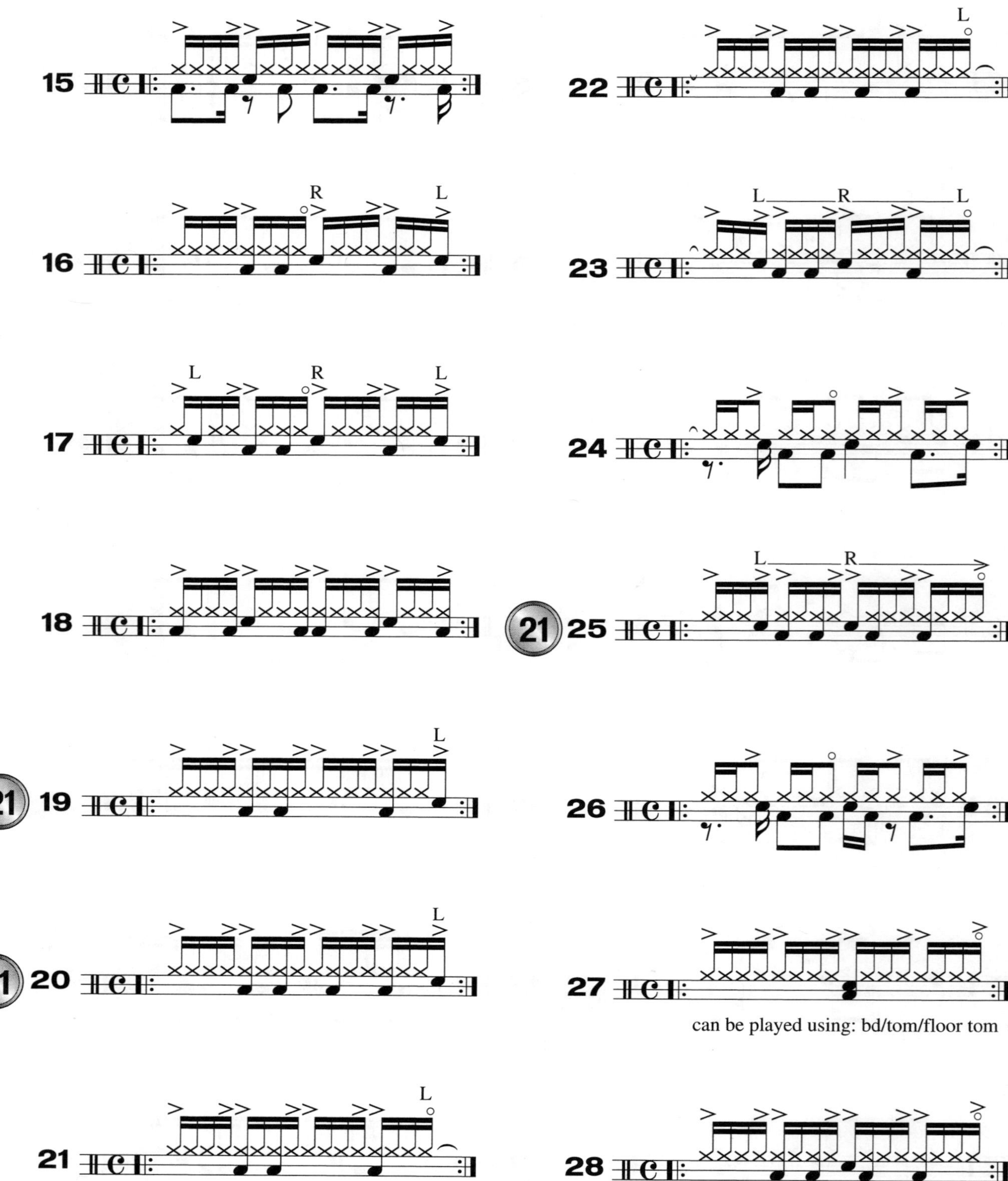
can be played using: bd/tom/floor tom

Two-measure Phrase Examples

NOTE: Play quarter notes with the left foot on the hi-hat with the examples above.

Performance Concepts

The drumset can reproduce a Samba percussion ensemble's inner dynamics to create a Samba-Funk combination. "Ghosted-notes" become essential to the rhythmic flow of a smooth groove. They fill in the spaces with softer notes on the snare drum or hi-hat/ride cymbal. By doing so, two important effects are achieved: constant motion and note flow.

Fill the time and space between each note played by keeping hands moving in a constantly relaxed manner. This helps to keep the tempo and time feel. "Ghosted notes" create a multi-dynamic rhythm flow that dramatically changes the feel of a groove.

Here is how to use those concepts when playing earlier-demonstrated examples.

When patterns are notated such as this one:

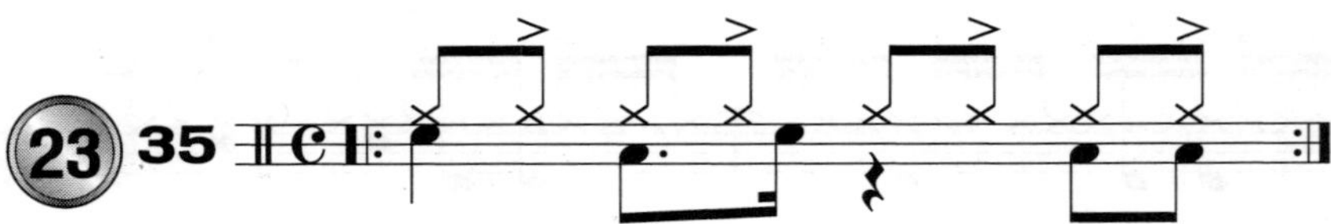

Implement ghost notes, filling up the space:

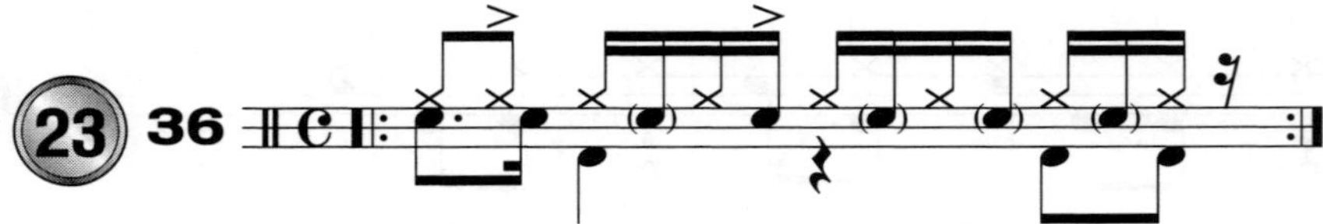

SECTION 13: PARTIDO ALTO

In a traditional Samba group, Partido Alto can be played with acoustic string instruments such as the cavaquinho or the seven-string guitar. The traditional Samba percussion instrumentation omits the drumset. Partido Alto played on a drumset becomes a type of Samba-Funk performance.

The Partido Alto is played with a constant, unique, clave-like rhythm. This distinctive rhythm sets it apart from Samba-Funk styles discussed previously. While the drummer sets the clave, the entire rhythm section embellishes it by phrasing around the beat. The main accents are reference points for the feel of the music, especially the bass, electric guitar, or keyboards.

There is one pattern that is considered the signature of the Partido Alto. Its origins come from a pandeiro rhythm. This main accented rhythm dominates an entire Partido Alto performance.

Pandeiro rhythm:

Sometimes the tamborim plays a variation of the rhythm:

The cuica will also play the rhythm very effectively, using high and low pitch bends such as this:

Note: The rhythm can be introduced at different parts of a phrase:

Partido Alto Ghost-notes Interpretation

Basic figure of Partido Alto:

Suggested interpretation: Remember the main accent dominates the Partido Alto "clave". After you become comfortable with simpler versions of some Partido Alto grooves, try to incorporate "ghost-notes" in between the main accents.

Here are some of the most common Partido Alto grooves for the drumset:

cross stick
cross stick

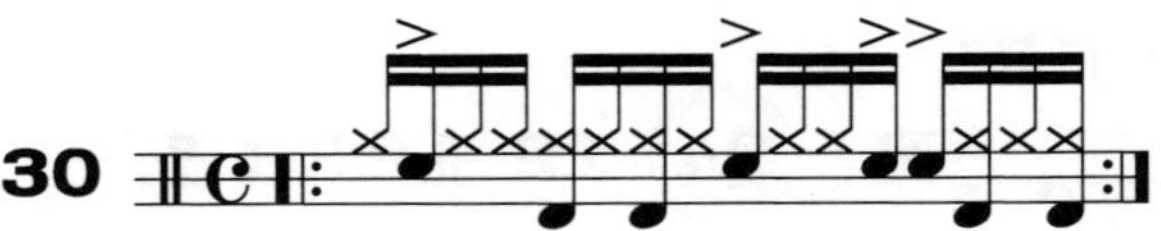

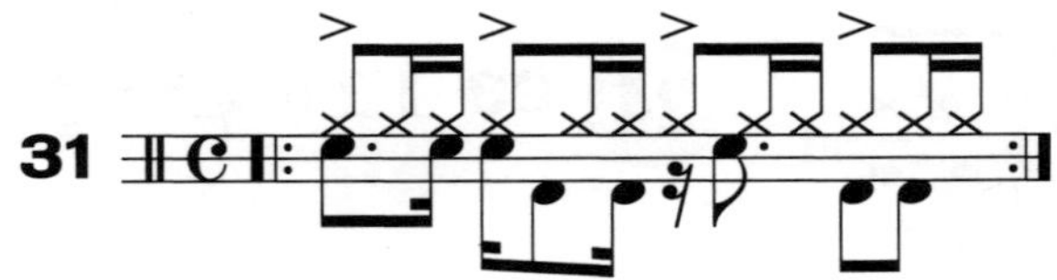

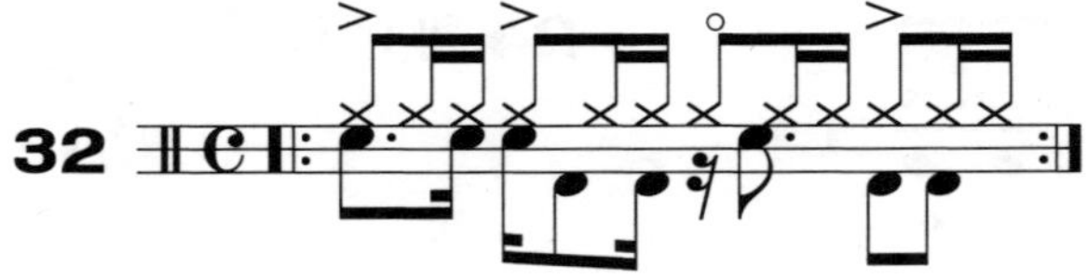

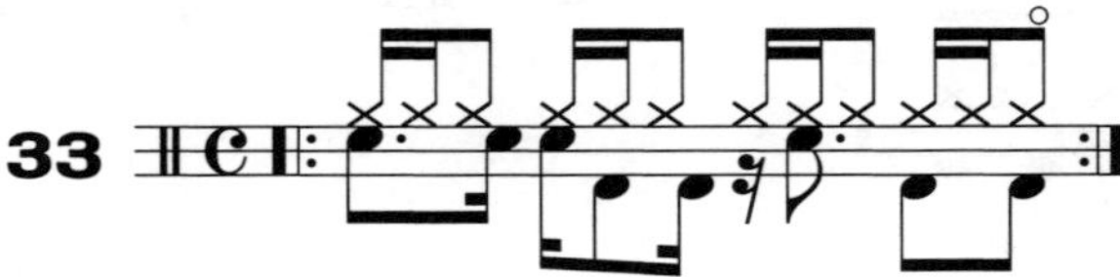

After practicing the examples above, go back and experiment by playing ride-cymbal ostinatos and hi-hat ostinatos with the foot. Here are a couple of ideas using this concept.

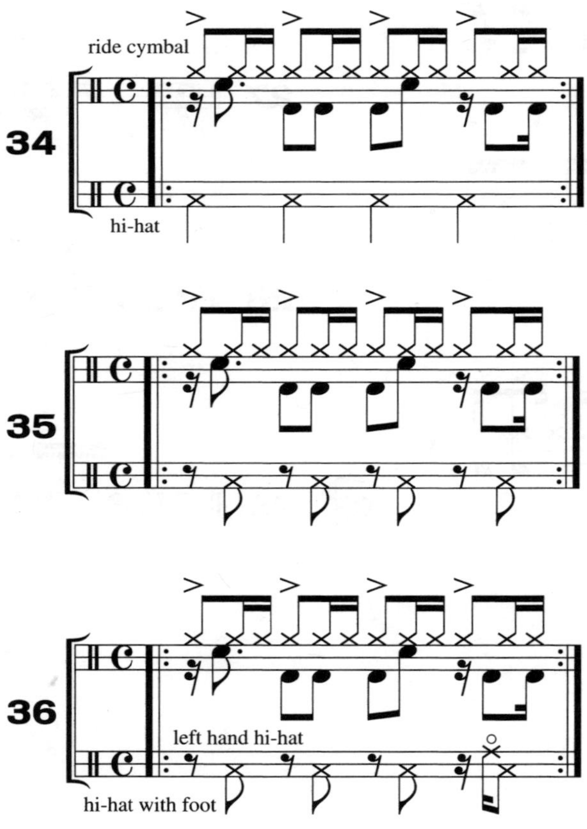

Create and expand your own grooves by experimenting with the examples above, using the ride-cymbal and hi-hat ostinatos with the foot. It's also a good idea to try moving the left hand from the snare drum to perhaps the tom-toms.

Use your imagination, and develop your own Partido Alto expressions. There will be places when you will want to use them in certain sections of songs, such as bridges.

Here it is a different approach to playing a Partido Alto style. The groove is based on a caixa pattern:

This orchestrated version uses the hi-hat, snare drum, bass drum and floor tom.

NOTATION KEY:

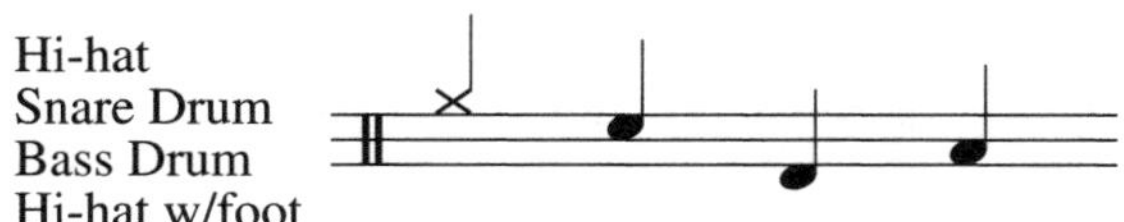

SECTION 14: JONGO

Jongo is a variation of Samba style that Brazilian composers and arrangers quite often use. It usually acts as a "bridge" to release tension between the verse and chorus.

The Jongo groove is similar to some Samba-Funk and Partido Alto grooves demonstrated in previous pages. But it has a slightly different feel. The Jongo has a little more emphasis on the straight eighth- note figure; it is not based on the Partido Alto clave.

It's possible to find a wide variety of music from many of Brazil's regions that incorporate special accents functioning as clave rhythms. This is particularly true of music from the Northeast region. Here are two examples that demonstrate how to find a reference point for the Jongo rhythms that will follow.

Jongo Grooves

Here are a few examples of Jongo grooves on the drumset.

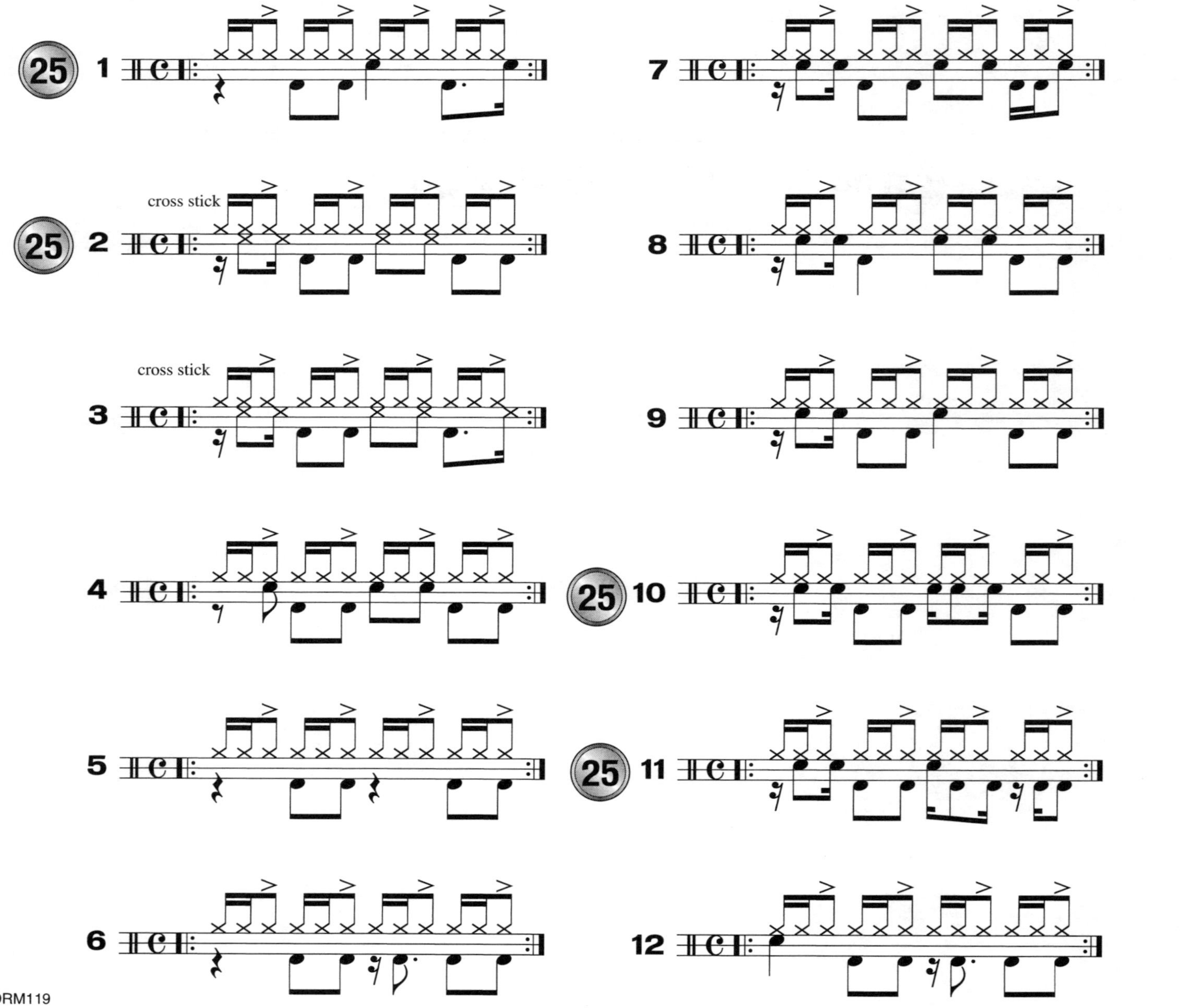

SECTION 15: SAMBA PATTERNS WITH BRUSHES

There are so many ways to play Samba with brushes that the possibilities are endless. There are five examples below and on the following page. Use them as a starting point for practice. Then improvise to develop your own style.

Here the left hand plays eighth notes by sliding the brushes across the drumhead in a side-to-side motion (Sliding Staccato Sweep). Do not lift the brush off the drumhead.

The right hand plays a tamborim-like rhythm by tapping on the drumhead. Meanwhile, the bass drum and hi-hat play a Samba ostinato on the bottom.

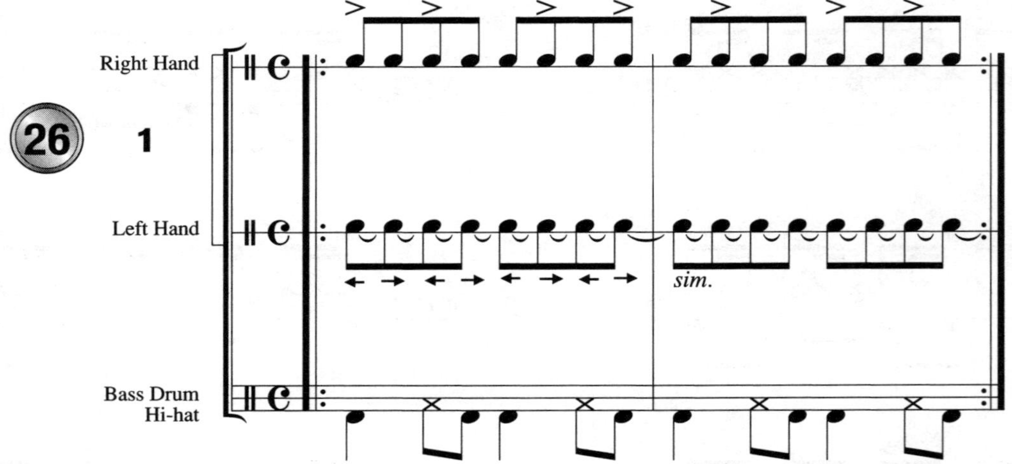

Diagram for the hands:

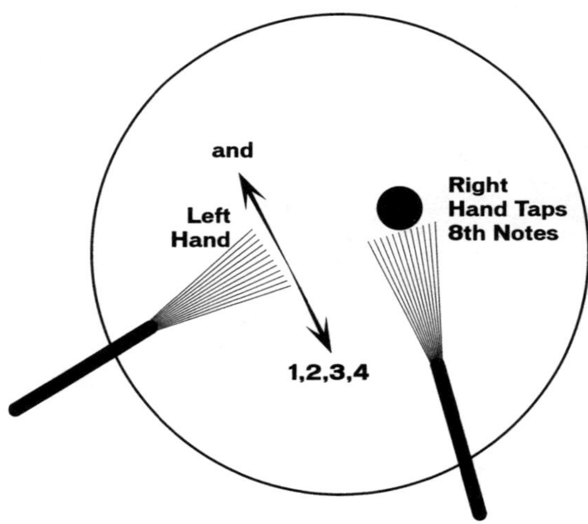

Here the left hand plays quarter notes by sliding the brushes on the drumhead in a circular motion, either clockwise or counter-clockwise (Quarter-Note Legato Sweeps). The brush does not come off the drumhead. The right hand plays a Samba tamborim-rhythm Samba ostinato on the bottom.

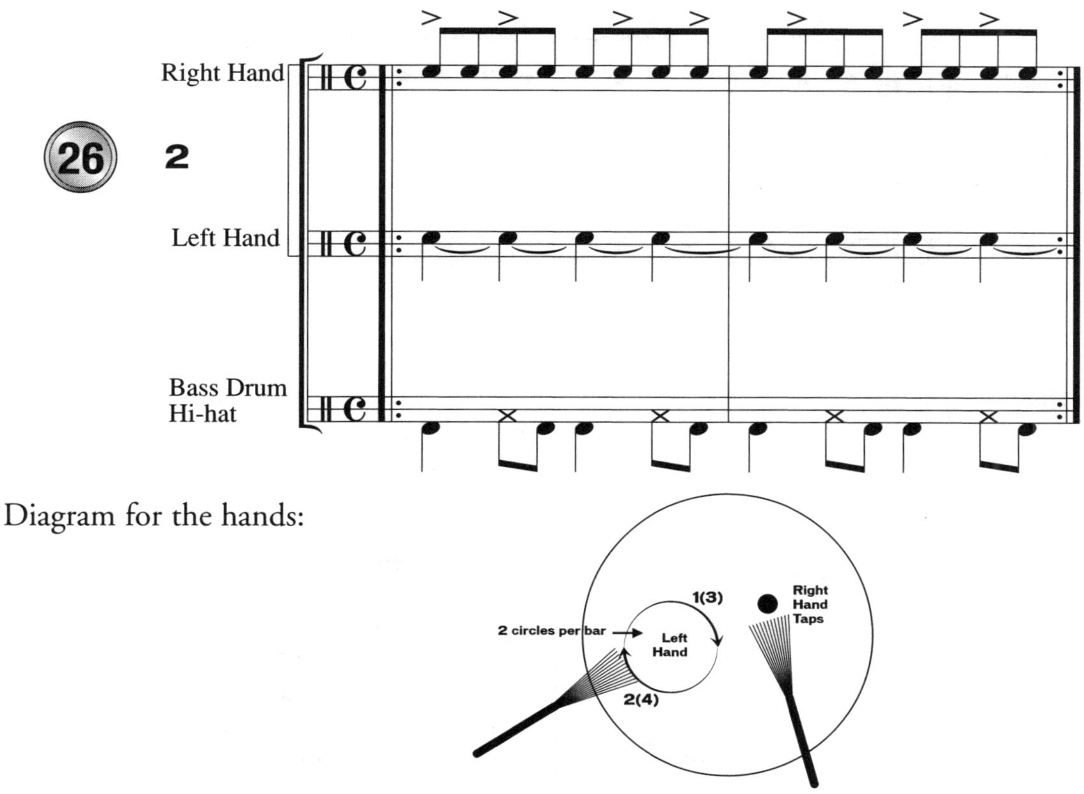

Diagram for the hands:

In this example the right hand combines the swish sound and tap sound. The right hand swishes the "1" and the "and" (Broken Heart Sweep) while the rest of the measure is played in a side-to-side tapping motion.

The left hand plays quarter notes by sliding the brushes across the drumhead in a circular motion, (Quarter-Note Legato Sweeps) clockwise or counter-clockwise. Bass drum and hi-hat play a Samba ostinato.

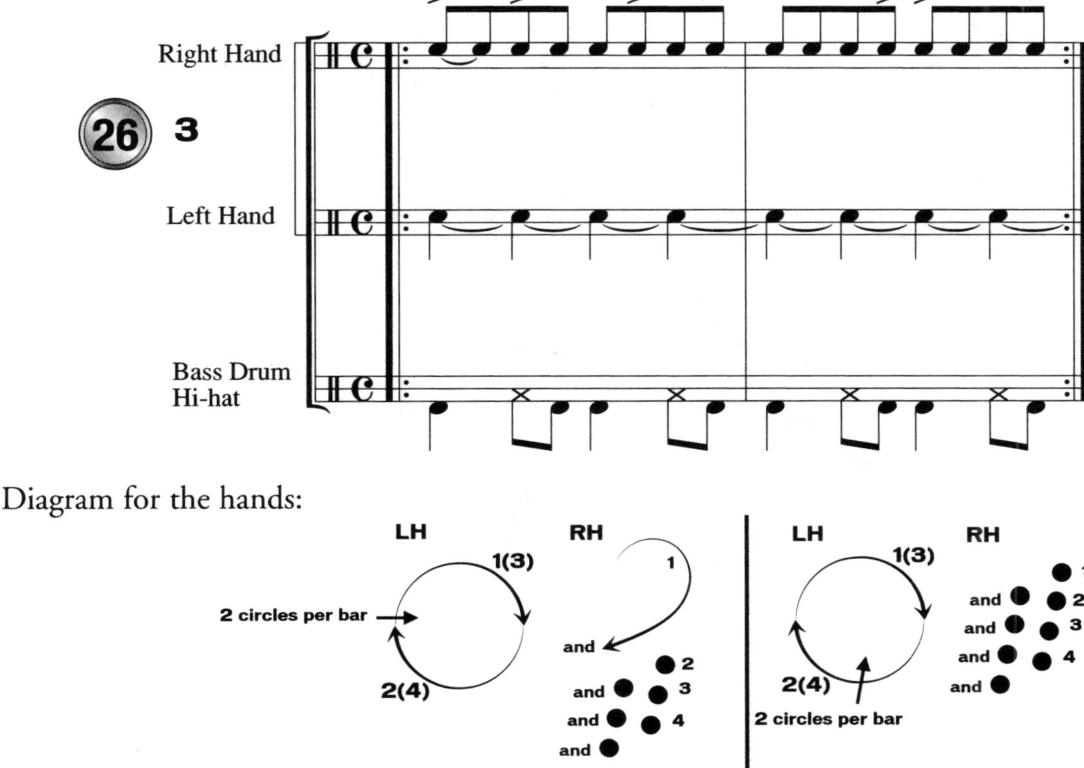

Diagram for the hands:

Here, the left hand plays quarter notes by sliding the brushes across the drumhead in a circular motion, clockwise or counter-clockwise. The right hand taps and swishes the drumhead on the "1" and "and" on every measure (Broken Heart Sweep). Bass drum and hi-hat play a Samba ostinato.

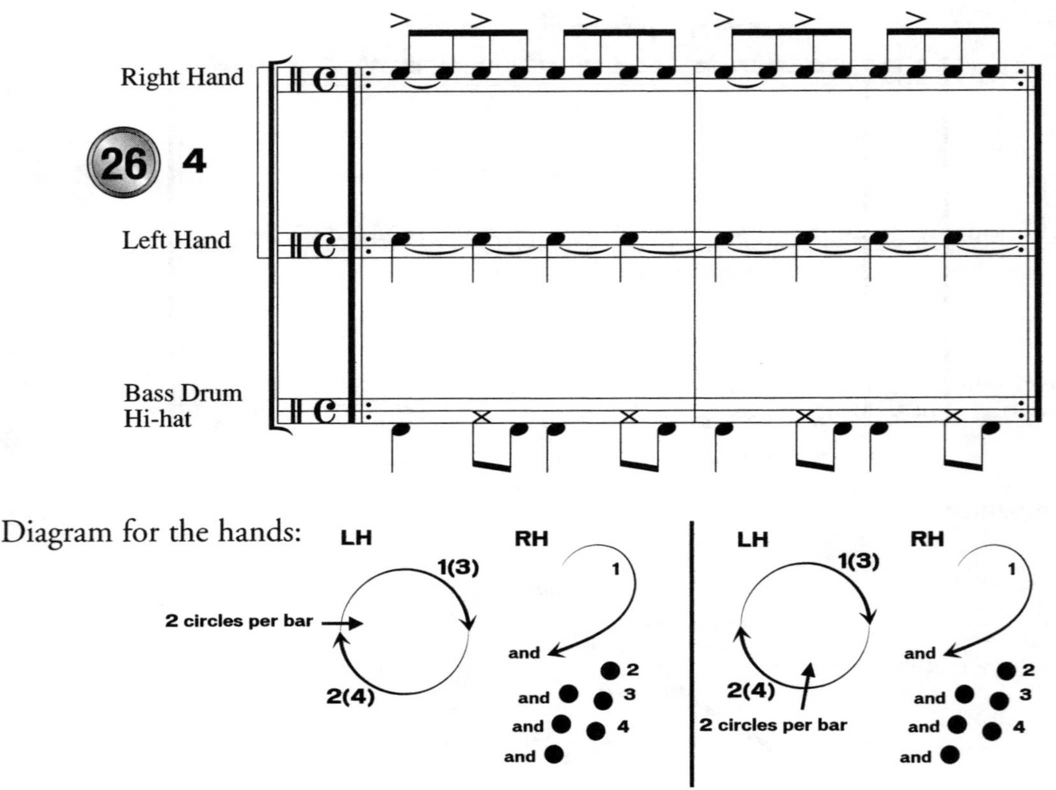

Diagram for the hands:

In this example, the right hand plays the tamborim rhythm by tapping the notes. The left hand fills up the sixteenth-note rests by swishing in a side-to-side motion. Bass drum and hi-hat play a Samba ostinato.

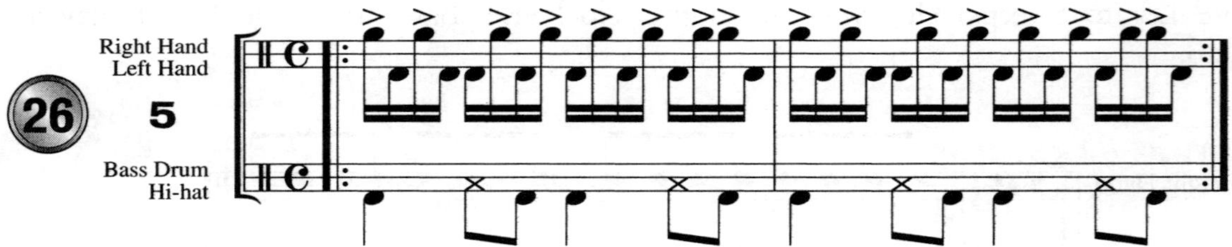

Diagram for the hands:

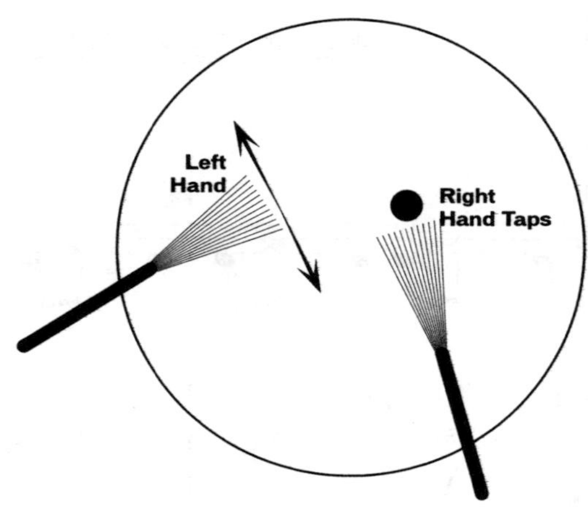

SECTION 16: SAMBA FUSION

The term Samba Fusion is used in this book to identify a drumset interpretation of Samba style that blends Afo-Samba and Samba De Prato. It excludes hi-hat or ride-cymbal ostinatos as leading voices in the orchestration on the drumset. Instead, hi-hat and ride-cymbal rhythms are interpreted and integrated as equal voices.

In the section highlighting Samba De Prato, the hi-hat and ride cymbal focus on rhythms originating from shakers, ganza, snare drum or chucalho parts. In Samba Fusion, however, the hi-hat and different cymbals (played with sticks) will not be used as leading voices. Instead, they will complement, accent and embellish rhythms that are typically distributed among tom-toms, snare drum, cymbals, floor toms and hi-hat.

In Samba Fusion, the bass drum and hi-hat played with the feet become the ideal drumset voice to carry on constant ostinato rhythms on the bottom. This leaves the hands free to play rhythms on several of the kit's sound sources.

Let's take a look at some concepts, patterns, styles and examples of Samba Fusion techniques that we will play on the drumset.

Samba Fusion Concepts

One of the most practical ways of using this material is to find the rhythmic structure you want to work from. An example of where to find such rhythms would be from the many percussion parts listed in the previous sections, especially from the caixa, tamborim, agogo, and cuica patterns. A good source of rhythmic ideas would be the Partido Alto claves and the Samba Funk rhythms, etc. So use your imagination.

When playing with a band, listening to the rhythm section will give you direction on where to go as far as the type of rhythm, clave-motif to construct a groove upon. For example, if the band is playing a Partido Alto you have a good chance to succeed with a groove that is based on that style of rhythmic motif; if the band is playing a straight Samba, chances are that tamborim or caixa patterns would work well and so forth.

Once you find a rhythm that you like follow those procedures as guidelines.

Performance Concepts

1. Find a rhythm that you like. Let's use this Partido-Alto clave as an example.

2. Play the rhythm with the right hand (or your leading hand).

3. While playing the rhythm with the leading hand try to play a flow of sixteenth notes by filling the rests with the other hand. If you play the rhythm with your right hand, the left hand will fill it up with sixteenth notes.

4. Find a basic hi-hat and bass-drum Samba ostinato for the feet.

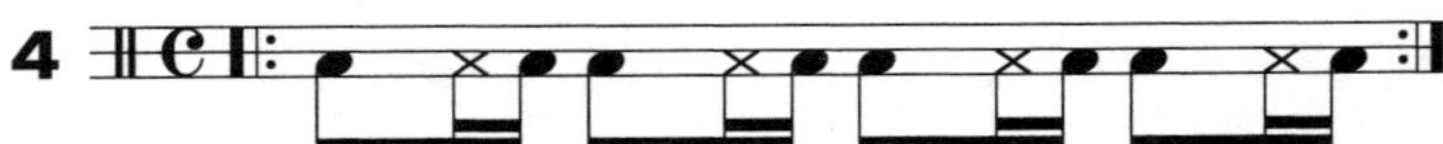

5. Now we have what sound likes an Afro Samba with the snare and bass drum/hi-hat ostinato.

6. The next step is to orchestrate the stickings among the tom-toms, snare drum, hi-hat, cymbals etc. while the feet play a flowing bass drum and hi-hat Samba ostinato. Keep in mind that to make the rhythm and sticking of your choice sound somewhat like a Samba, you must have the "surdo" part, usually played by a low tom or floor tom on the set on the "2" or "4" if in $\frac{4}{4}$, or very close to it. If displaced, try if you can, placing it somewhere inside the four sixteenth notes located in each beat on the "2" or the "4." For example:

7. The high tom could function as the counter-surdo by playing on the "1" or "3" of the measure or both; it could also be placed as a pickup to the surdo part. The middle tom, if available, could be placed in many different parts of the measure to imitate the "third surdo" part.

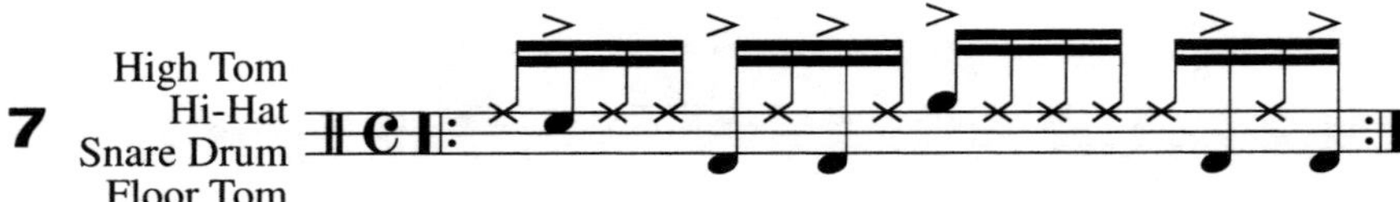

Here it is an example of this whole process. Play the bass-drum ostinato with all the following examples.

Experiment opening the hi-hat in different places.

Moving the left hand to the small tom-tom.

Moving the right hand to the floor tom.

Moving both right and left hands to the tom-toms.

Shift some right-hand movements over to the hi-hat.

Creating New Rhythms Using Fused Samba Concepts

Combine Fused Samba concepts discussed earlier to create new rhythms. Play the same bass-drum Samba ostinato used in previous examples.

NOTATION KEY:

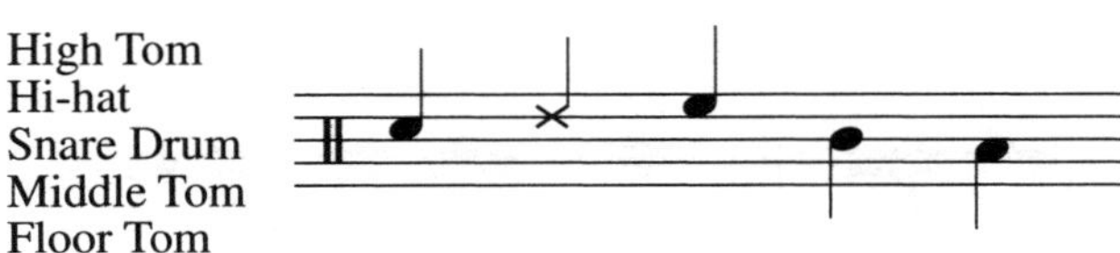

Remember, you can achieve a reversed accent placement by turning the clave around. This can be useful when creating Samba Fusion grooves based on rhythms such as the Partido-Alto clave. The following examples are of Samba Fusion grooves based on the Partido-Alto reversed clave.

Opening the hi-hat.

Moving the left hand over to the small tom-tom.

Moving some of the right-hand notes to the floor tom.

Moving right- and left-hand notes to the toms.

Moving some of the right-hand notes to the hi-hat.

Recommended Practice Routines

Note that on all previous examples the sticking was as follows: LRLL RLRL RLRLLRLR. Try to use other stickings for Samba Fusion performances. The section in the book dedicated to the caixa patterns (pages 43-44) and tamborim patterns (pages 35-36) is a good source for this material.

Here are a few examples of new stickings to be played using the same procedures demonstrated earlier in this section.

1. L R L R   L R L R   R L R L   R L L R
2. L R L R   L R L R   R L R L   R R L R
3. L R L L   R L R L   R L R L   R R L R
4. L R L L   R L R L   R L R L   R L L R
5. L R L L   R L R L   R L R L   R L R L

Suggestions To Supplement Performances

Previous examples of Fused Samba gave ideas about how to combine the hi-hat, tom-toms, and snare drums with a common Samba bass-drum ostinato. Use your imagination to experiment. Think of what is available to you: ride cymbal, drum rims, drum shells, cowbells, etc.

Here are a few groove examples demonstrating this concept:

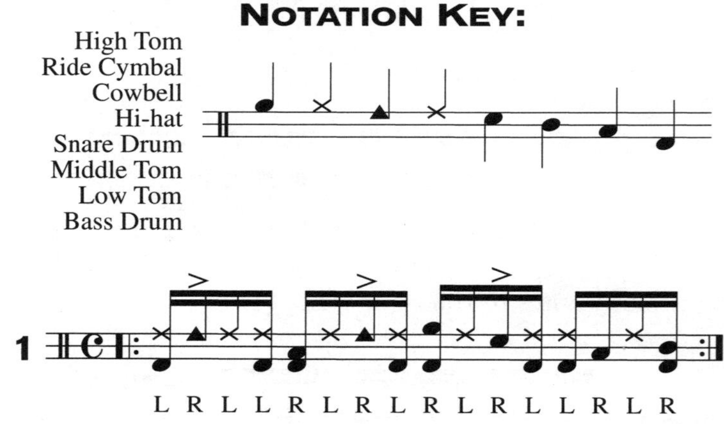

Samba de Macumba

Fused Samba techniques can be successfully applied to other Samba styles. One is the Samba de Macumba, also known as Samba de Batuque.

Samba de Macumba is a style heavily influenced by rhythms played in Afro-Brazilian religious ceremonies. The rhythms are usually played by hand drums very similar to conga drums or Afro-Brazilian drums such as the atabaque.

There are many different songs and rhythms heard in today's Afro-Brazilian religious ceremonies. These will be explored in another volume of *Brazilian Rhythms for the Drumset*. For now, this brief illustration shows how to use one of them with Fused Samba techniques presented earlier in this section.

Here is an example of one rhythm heard in Afro-Brazilian rituals:

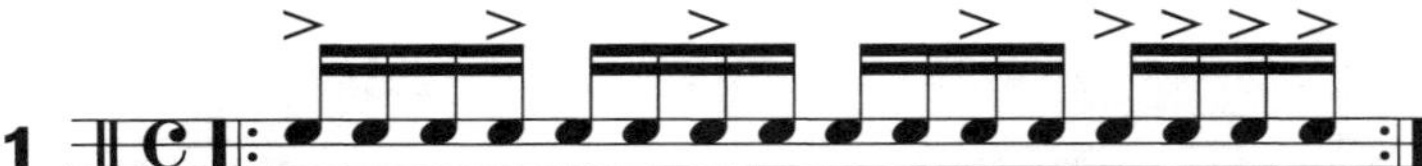

Here is its drum set adaptation:

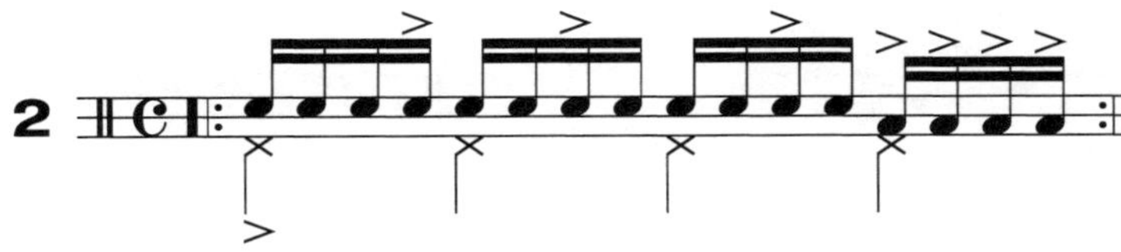

Here are inherent accents or "claves":

In this particular example, there is a very strong accent after the three first beats. The entire beat is accented in the fourth beat of the measure.

Keep the rhythm of the first three notes. Then, by alternating the last part of the measure, you have more choices.

Using the same procedures used in the Fused Samba grooves based on the Partido Alto, let's go on to explore some Samba de Macumba possibilities.

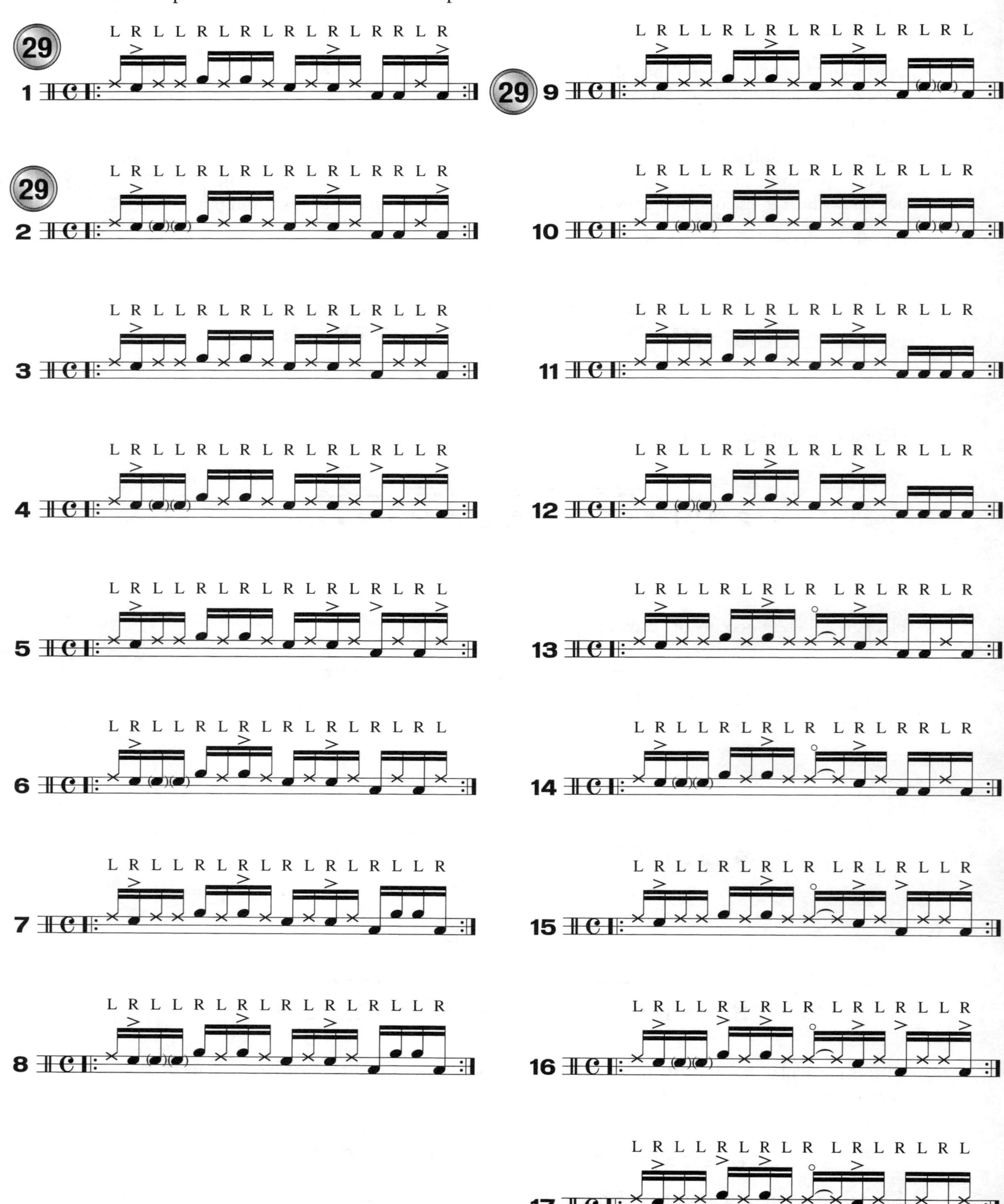

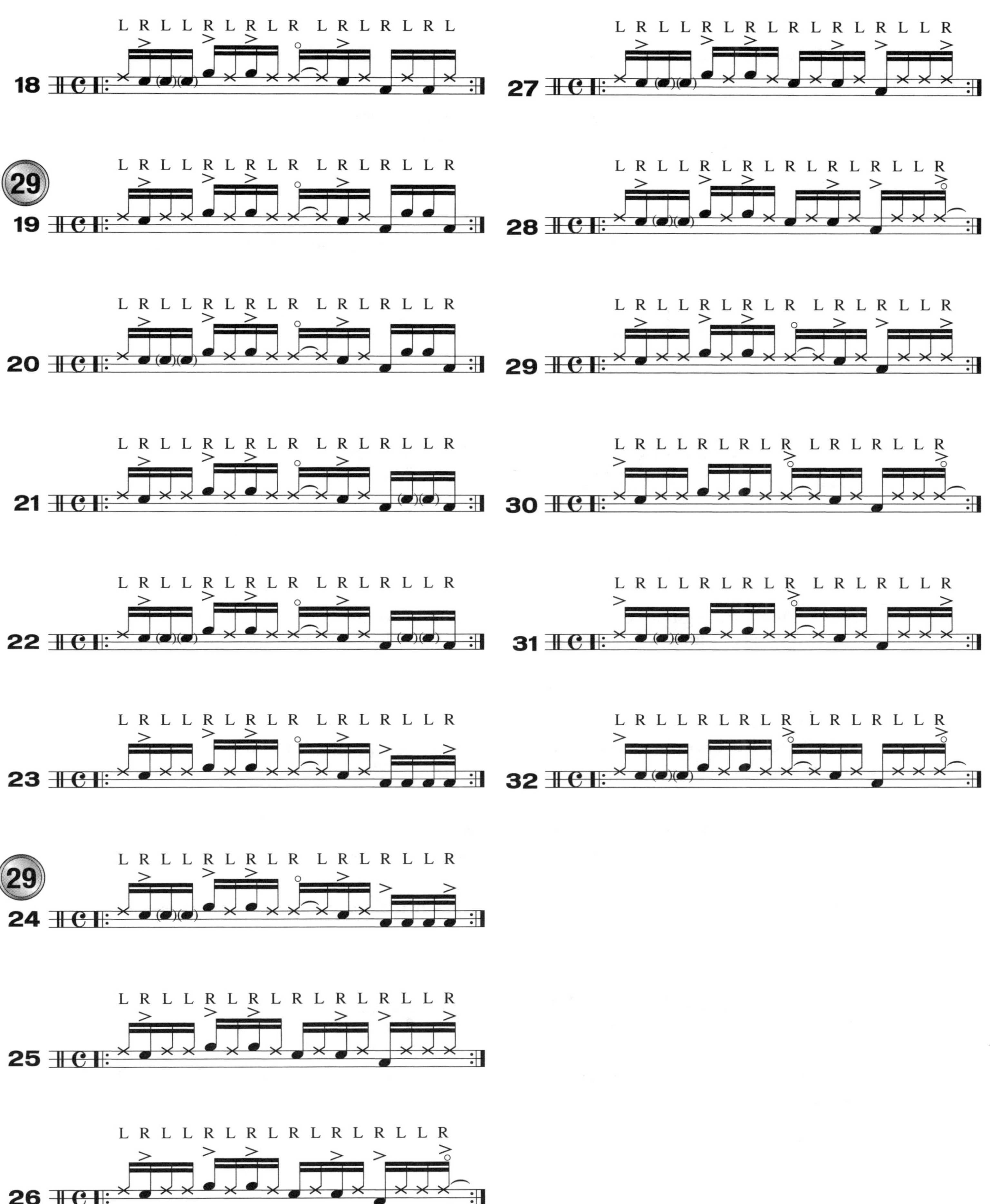

Samba de Roda

Samba de Roda is a style that has a different syncopation. Although it is still in the Samba family, it is not based on regular sixteenth-note patterns from the caixa, shakers, or tamborim figures:

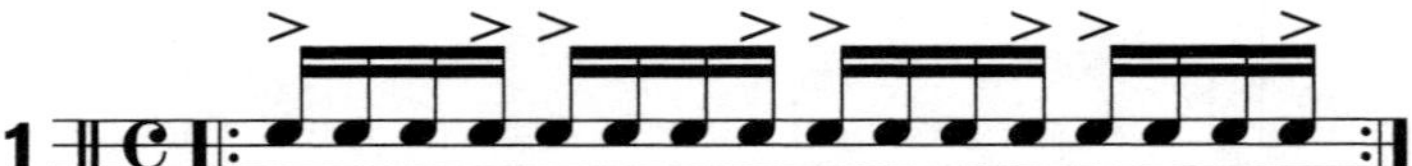

Instead, it is constructed around rhythms originating from hand-clapping patterns such as these:

The Samba de Roda, like the Partido Alto, can be used in various contemporary musical situations. But its roots are found in small gatherings of Sambistas in religious, social, and holiday festivities.

A very small four-string guitar, the cavaquinho, plays an important role by centering the groove, playing its rhythms in unison with whatever clave is used. The cavaquino role can be compared with the Salsa montunos played on the piano, or the rhythm guitar in the Funk style, playing strong repetitive rhythms that hold the whole arrangement together.

The pattern played by a Samba school's bateria is rich in sixteenth notes. Its rich sixteenth notes flow in a somewhat horizontal fashion. Its strong accents are predictable and stationary on the comping parts.

By contrast, the Samba de Roda is more vertical. Its main accents move more often between the beats.

The original Samba de Roda instruments were made to be easily carried to someone's backyard as small hand drums or string instruments. Samba de Roda shares similarities with Partido Alto and Samba de Pagode.

Clave Examples

Remember, Samba de Roda is heavily influenced by various Afro-Brazilian rhythms and claves. Here is a group of commonly used claves. They can be the basis of some interesting drumset Samba grooves.

Groove Examples

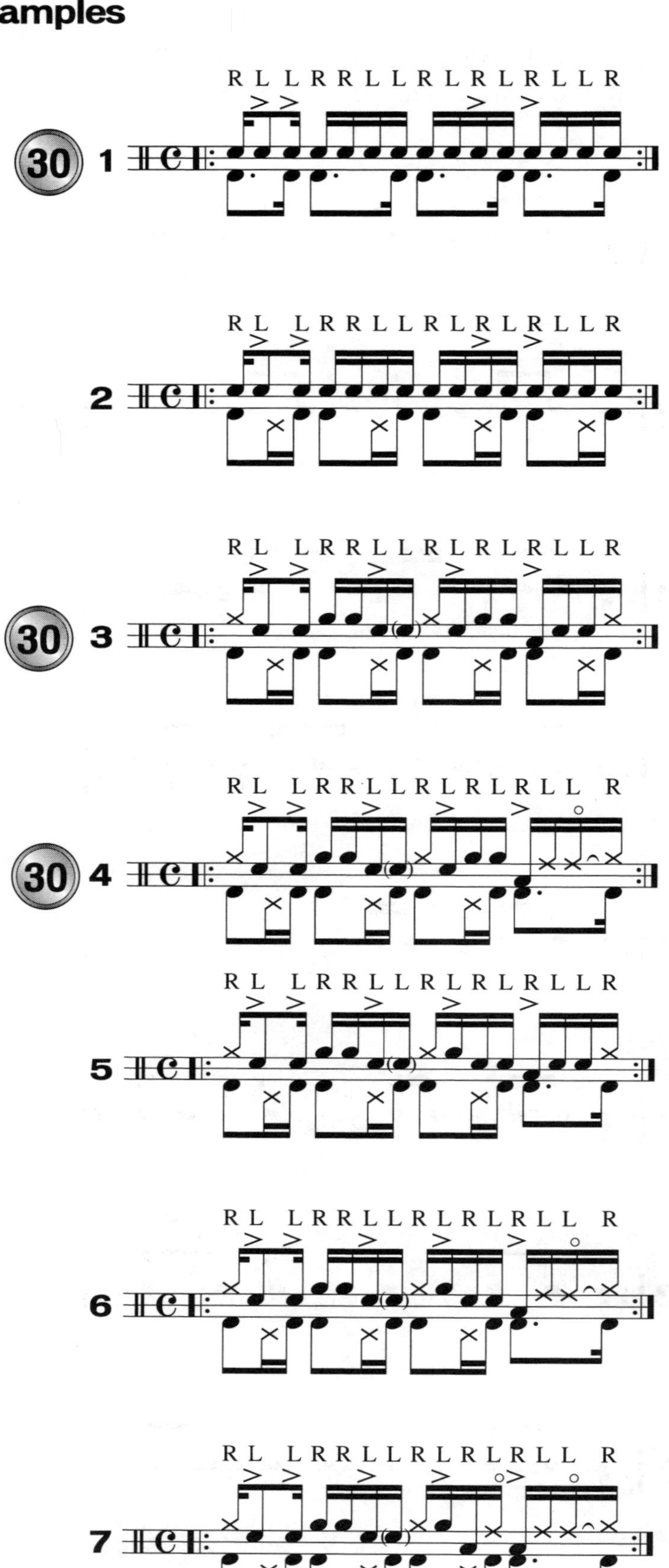

Here are some sticking possibilities to apply to the Samba de Roda, applying Samba Fusion concepts.

Sticking variation on the fourth beat.

Sticking variation on the fourth beat.

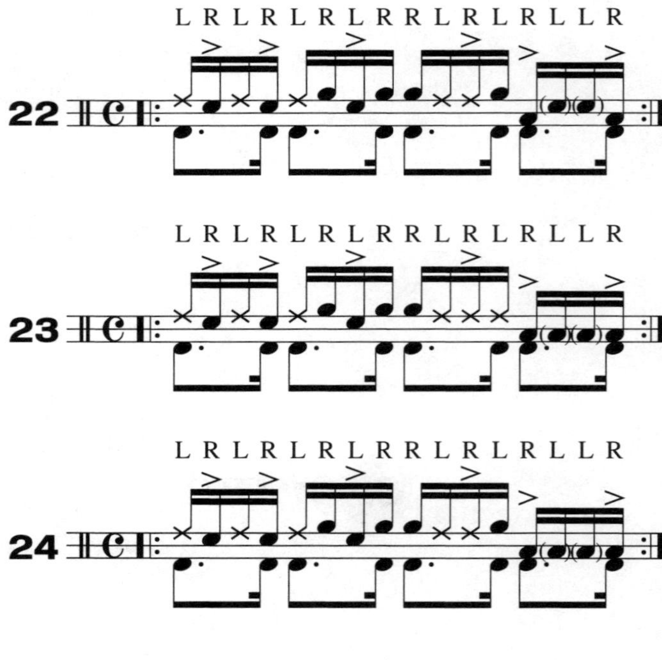

Samba de Trio Electrico

Samba de Trio Electrico is a type of Samba played in northeastern Brazil, especially in the states of Bahia and Pernambuco. This unique Samba style that inspires thousands of people to jump up and down in excitement. Samba de Trio Electrico gains power by combining carnival styles from Brazil's northeastern and southern regions with a strong Rock attitude.

The term "Trio Electrico" was first used to describe an easy-going group from Bahia organized by two performers known as Dodo and Osmar. They set up a speaker or two on a wagon to carry three musicians. The popularity of the style spread so today's popular Trio Electricos play on the tops of truck trailers equipped with state-of-the-art engineering, with powerful lighting and sound systems.

Modern carnival, truck-type floats are set up with electric bands on top. They usually consist of a drumset, electric bass, electric guitars, keyboards, additional percussion instruments, and may have some horns. They move from street to street to wherever they find huge crowds. These open-air performances require drummers to play with the same energy as you would expect from any large, outdoor Rock concert. They mobilize enthusiastic audiences with very strong, loud, and clean pulsating rhythms.

Concepts applied to Fused Samba in earlier sections can be successfully applied here. The way the hand plays the ride cymbal is especially useful. You won't find the examples to be as complex as earlier examples. But it is important to pay particular attention to how the same hand that plays the ride/china cymbal also comes over to tom-toms.

Samba de Trio Electrico Examples

The right hand plays the ride cymbal and floor-tom ostinato. The left hand reads the snare-drum exercises. The feet play the bass-drum/hi-hat ostinato.

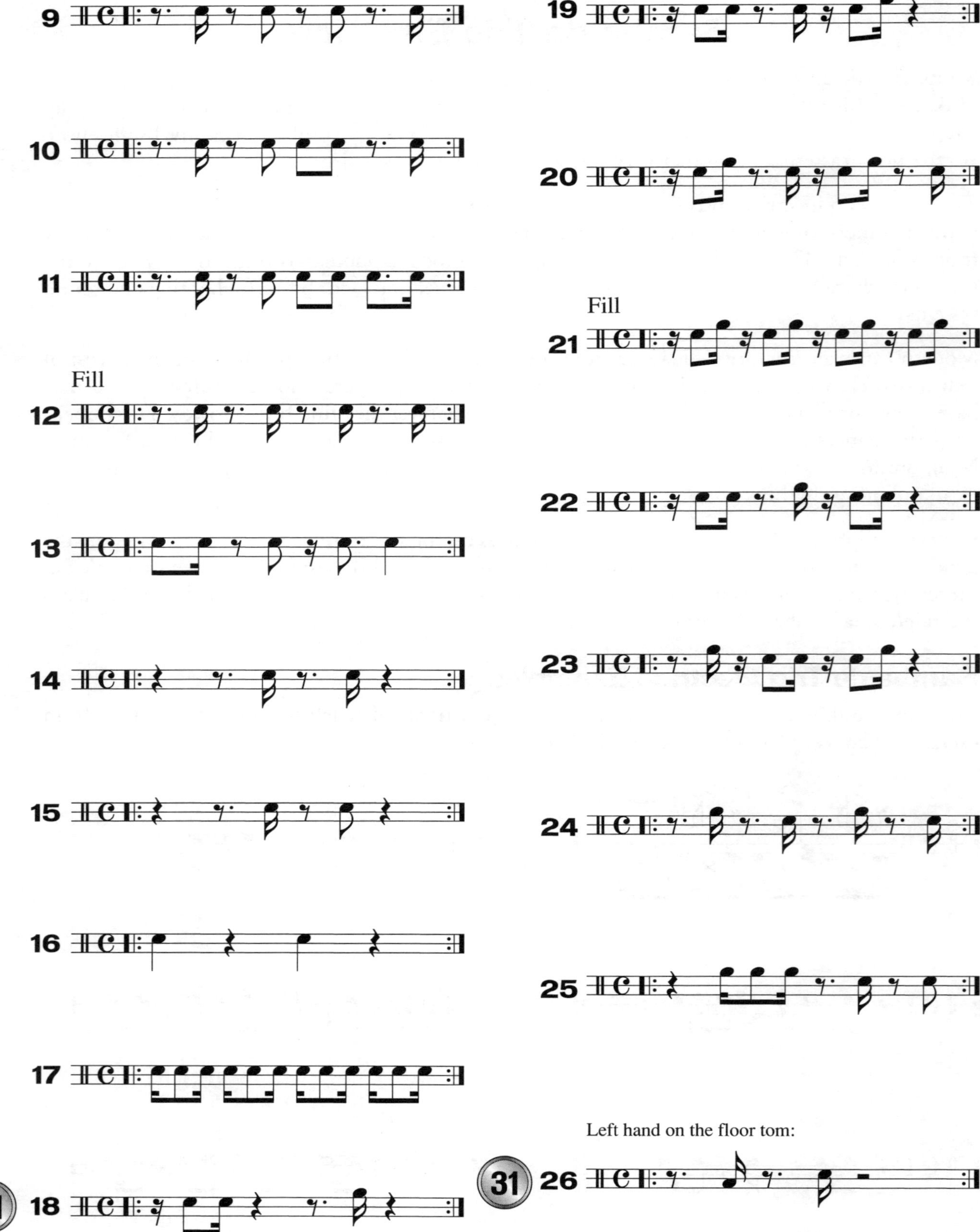
9
10
11
Fill
12
13
14
15
16
17
31
18
19
20
Fill
21
22
23
24
25
Left hand on the floor tom:
31
26

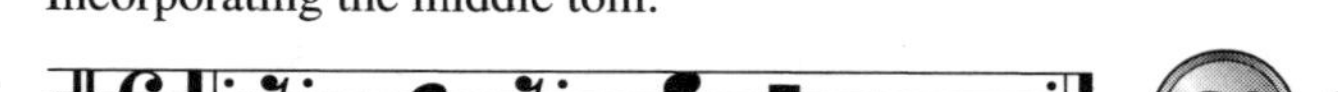
Incorporating the middle tom:

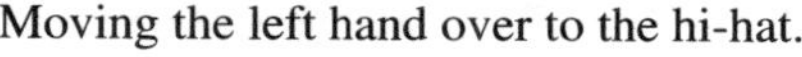
Moving the left hand over to the hi-hat.

Fill

Supplementary Practice Procedures

1. Try playing some of the examples above by adding the middle tom to the comping ostinato.

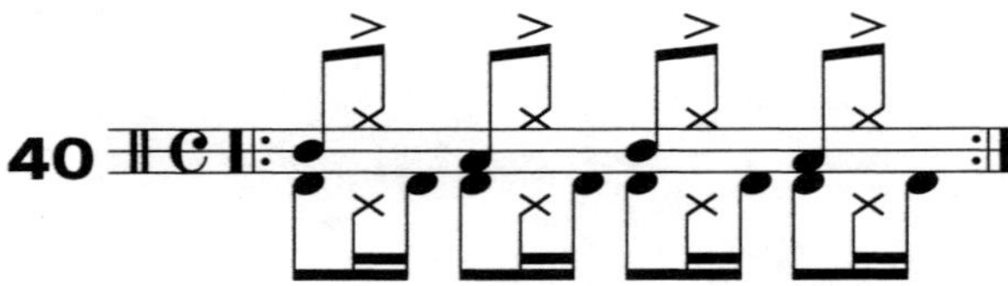

2. Play rhythms from the tamborim section of this book. The left hand plays the snare drum while the right hand and the feet play the Samba de Trio Electrico ostinatos.

Deixa Falar on page 151 in the Play-along Section (Disk 2, Track 1, without drums on Track 8) incorporates Samba Funk and Samba de Prato grooves presented in the text. *Contigo* on page 152 in the Play-along Section (Disk 2, Track 4, without drums on Track 11) incorporates Partido Alto, Samba de Prato, Caixa Samba patterns and Jongo grooves presented in the text.

SECTION 17: ODD-TIME PHRASING: AFRO-SAMBA, SAMBA DE PRATO AND SAMBA-FUSION EXAMPLES

There are many ways to play Samba in odd meters. Samba has become popular with Jazz musicians and their groups. In fact, it's more common for them to play Samba styles with $\frac{3}{4}$, $\frac{7}{8}$, and 5/8 meters than once was the case. This makes it useful to practice these meters in the following Samba styles: Afro-Samba, Samba de Prato, and Fused Samba.

Try this suggestion to make phrasing go a little more smoothly. Phrase the hi-hat in two-measure phrases instead of one-measure phrases. This should create a steady pulse across the two measures. The constant hi-hat sound creates a more settled feeling. It makes the groove flow much better.

Each of the various meters on the following pages has been grouped in the order of Afro-Samba, Samba de Prato, and Fused Samba examples. After you have practiced them go back to earlier sections where those styles were first demonstrated. You should be able to modify the grooves to fit the meter you need.

After you have practiced all of the following examples, follow up with your own versions of odd-time Samba grooves. The first set of examples begins with $\frac{3}{4}$ meter.

Afro-Samba in $\frac{3}{4}$

NOTATION KEY

All $\frac{3}{4}$ Afro-Samba examples have the feet playing this same bass-drum/hi-hat ostinato.

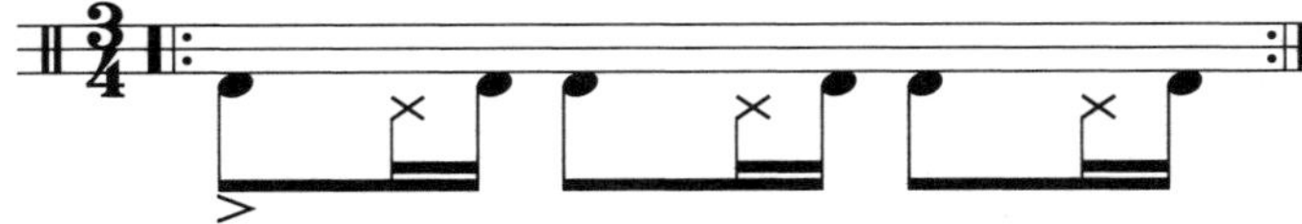

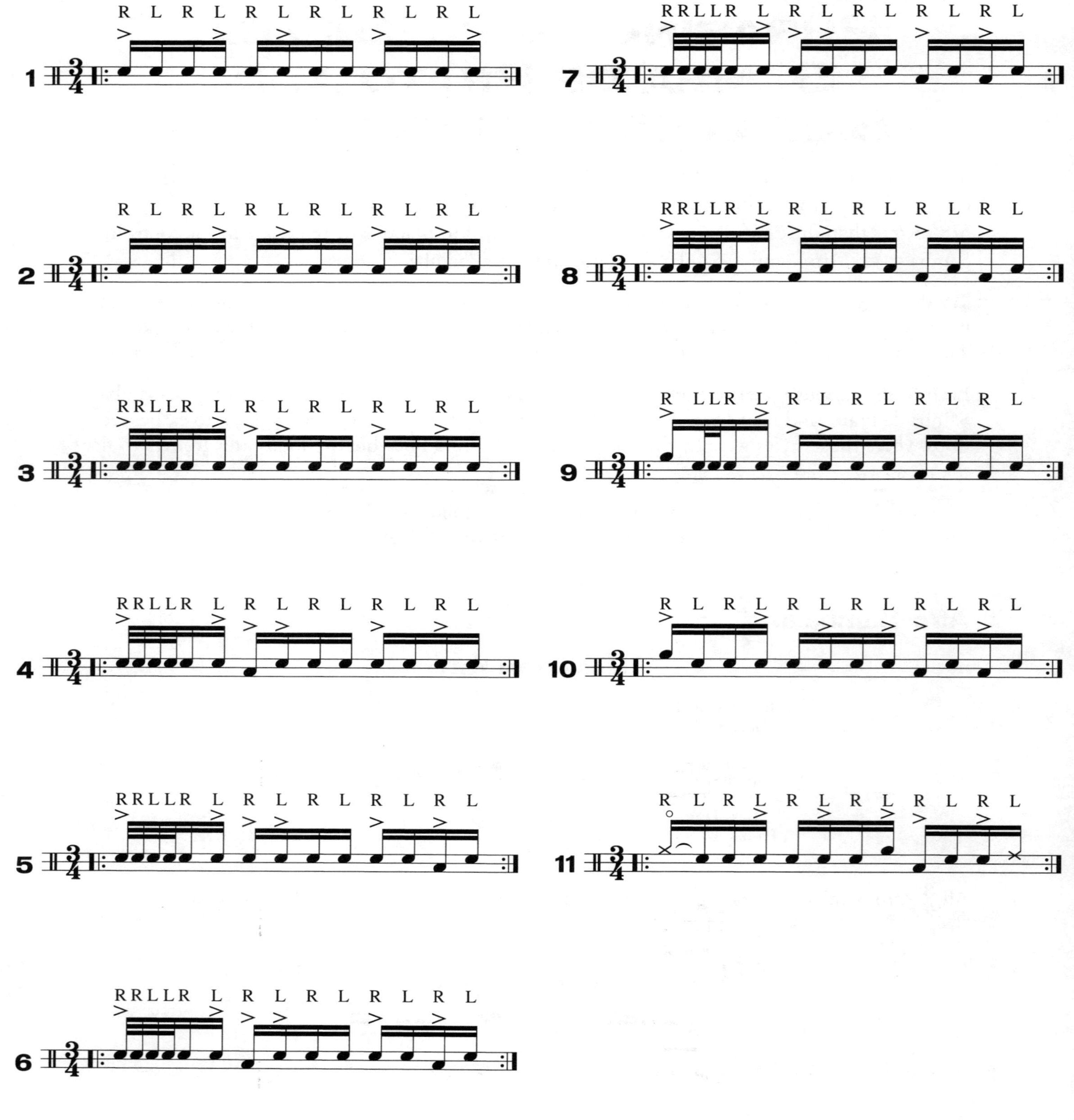

Samba de Prato in 3/4

Refer to the same notation key used in the previous examples. Perform the examples below with the left hand while playing this ride-cymbal and bass-drum/hi-hat ostinato.

Note: "X" means play cross stick on the snare-drum rim.

1 

7 

2 

8 

3 

9 

4 

10 

5

11 

6

12 

13

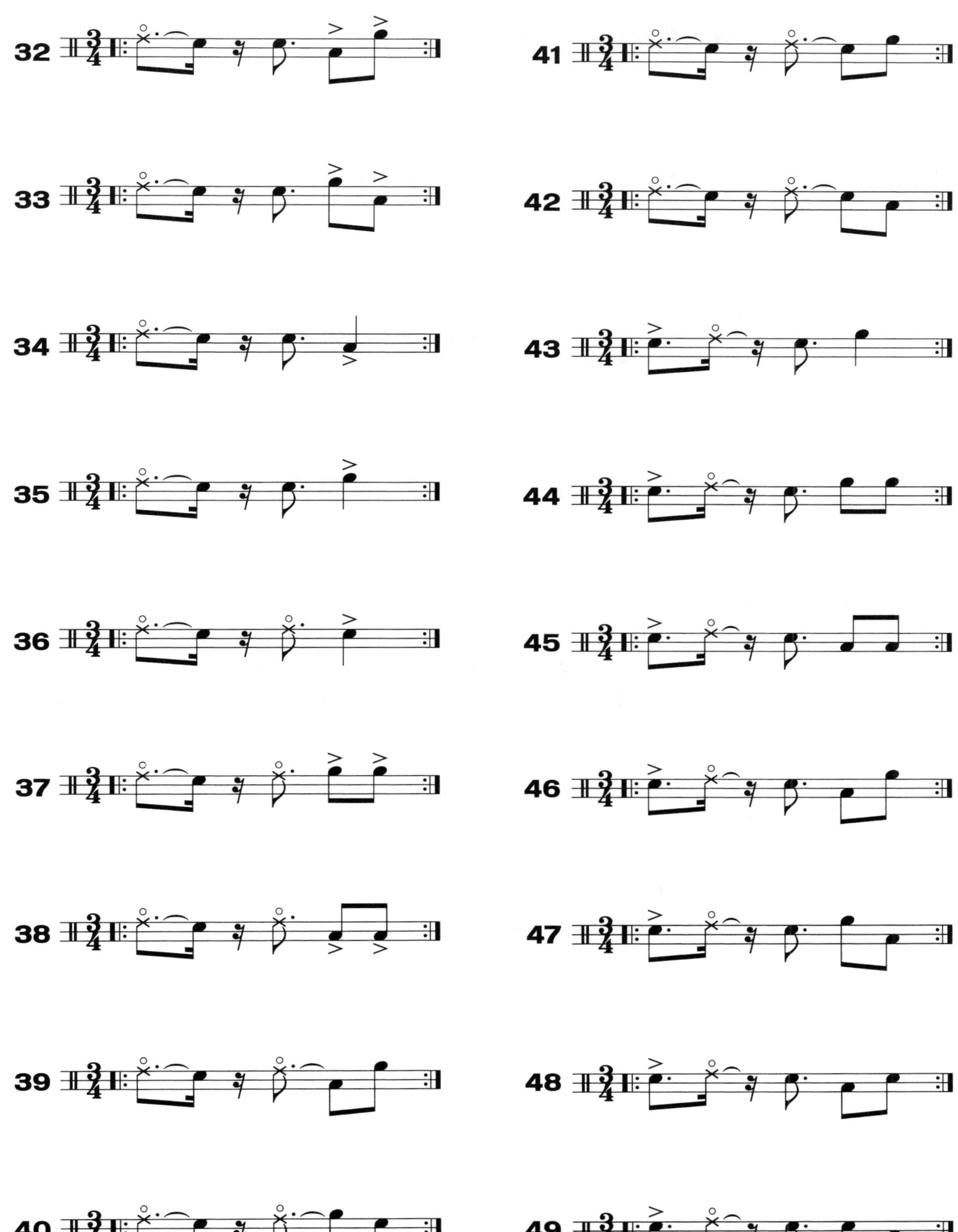

Samba Fusion in 3/4

We can build grooves in 3/4 meter by using the same concepts and practice procedures found in the Samba Fusion section. Practice this group of Samba Fusion grooves in 3/4, and try to come up with your own versions.

Use the same notation key given in Samba de Prato on page 82. Use this bass drum ostinato with all the examples below.

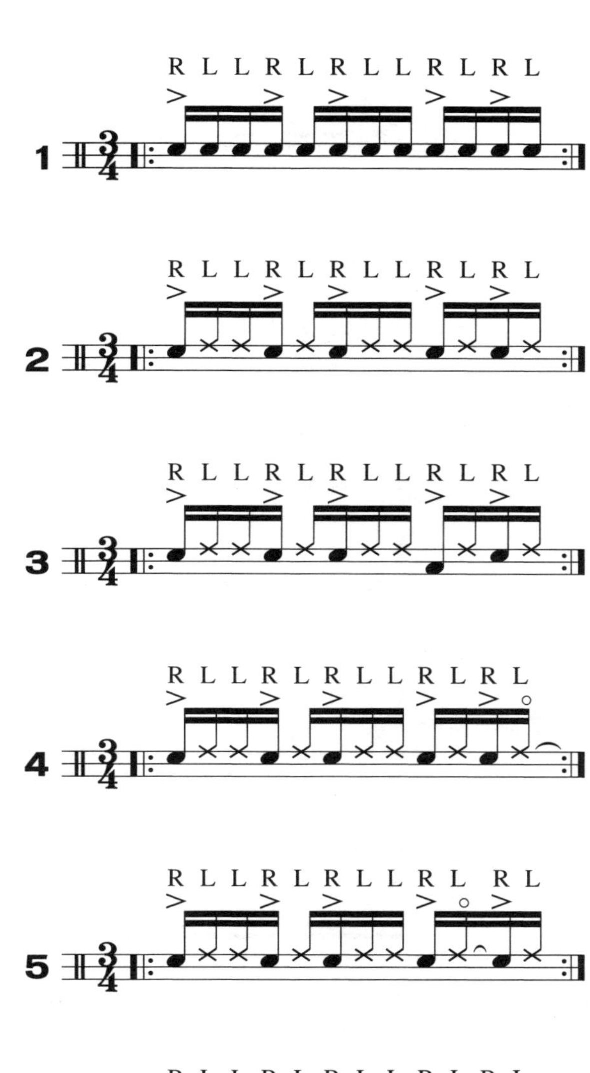

Using the ride cymbal:

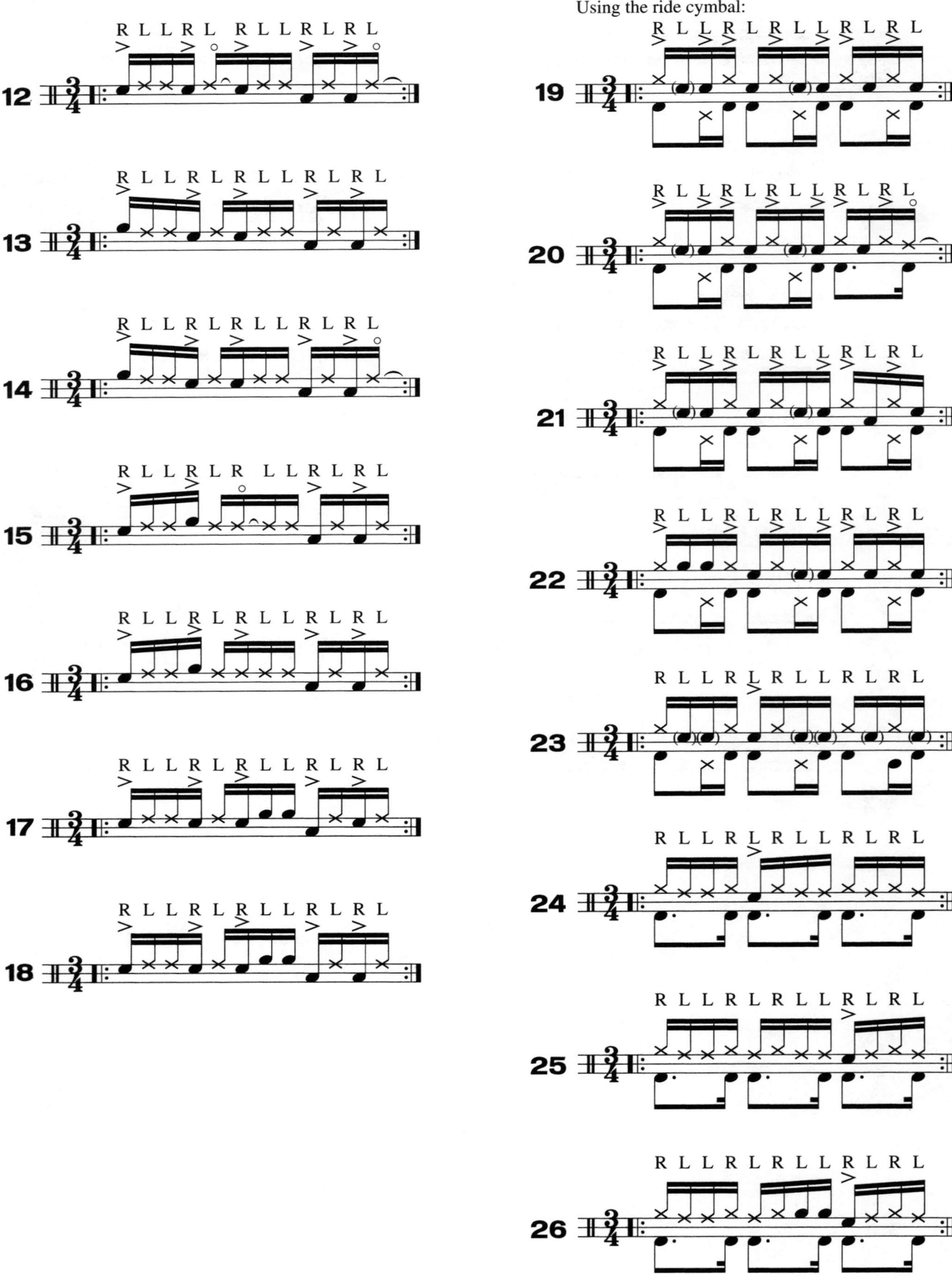

Milton on page 154 in the Play-along Section (Disk 2, Track 5 without drums on Track 12) incorporates Samba Fusion in 3/4 grooves.

Afro-Samba in $\frac{5}{8}$

1

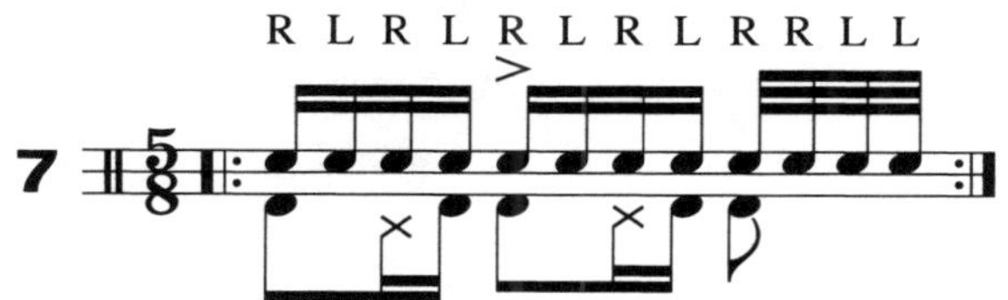

7

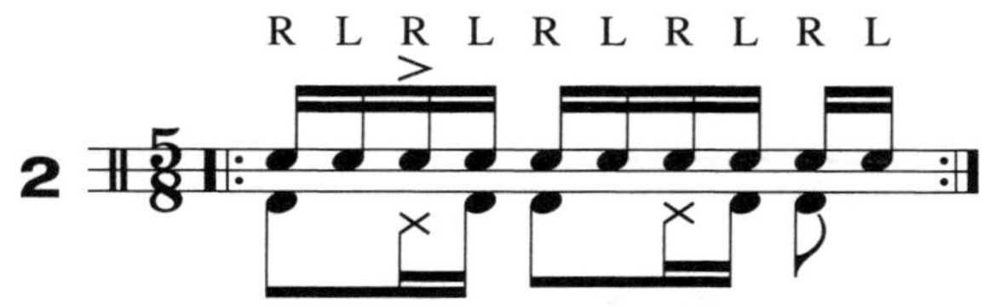

2

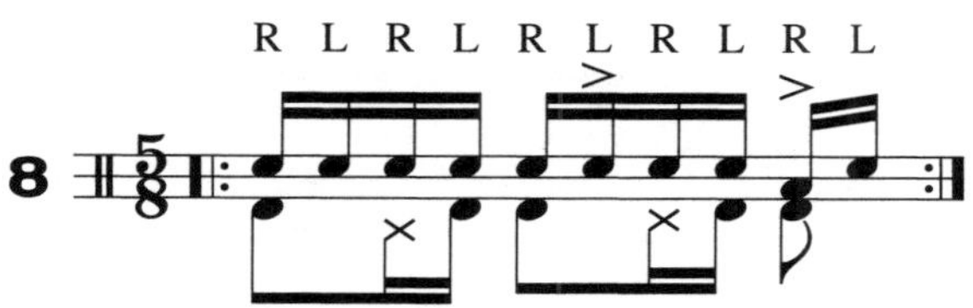

8

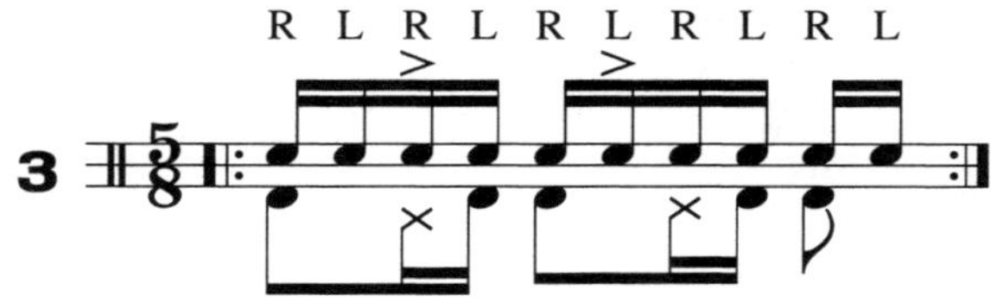

3

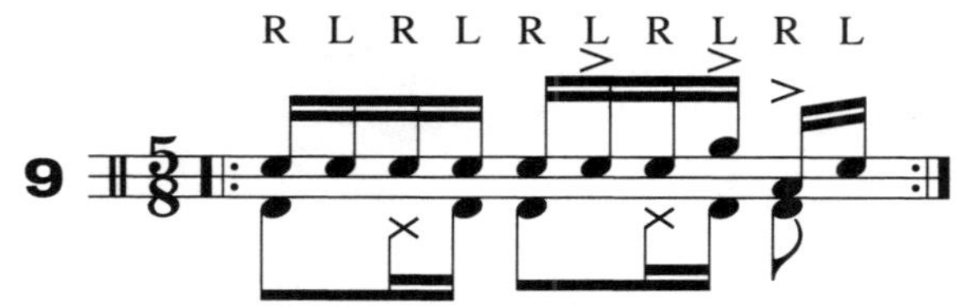

9

4

10

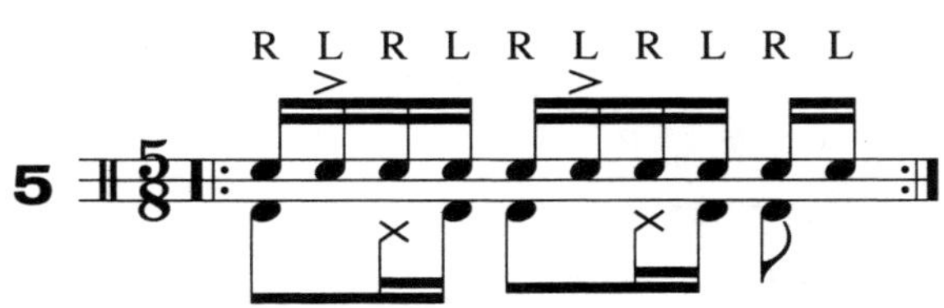

5

11

6

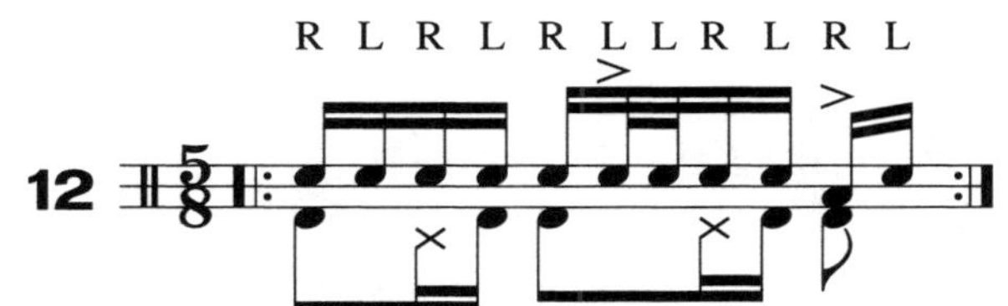

12

TWO-MEASURE PHRASES IN $\frac{5}{8}$

Here is the second example of an Afro-Samba groove. The hi-hat overlaps for two measures. Phrasing the hi-hat in two-measure phrases makes your groove flow.

Practice this exercise, then go back to the original Afro-Samba section beginning on page 63 and play the patterns with this new hi-hat exercise.

Samba de Prato in $\frac{5}{8}$

Play the following examples with the left hand. Practice them with ride-cymbal and bass-drum/hi-hat ostinatos.

Ostinato One

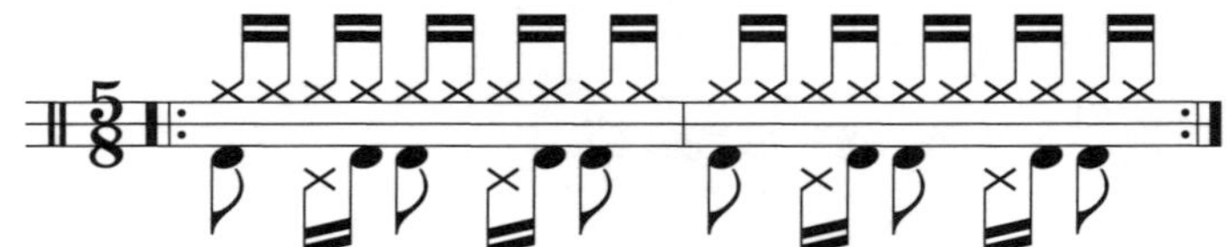

Ostinato Two.

Play with left hand:

1 

9 

2 

10 

3 

11 

4 

12

5

13

6

14

7

15

8

16

Samba Fusion in 5/8

Using the ride cymbal:

Afro-Samba in $\frac{5}{4}$

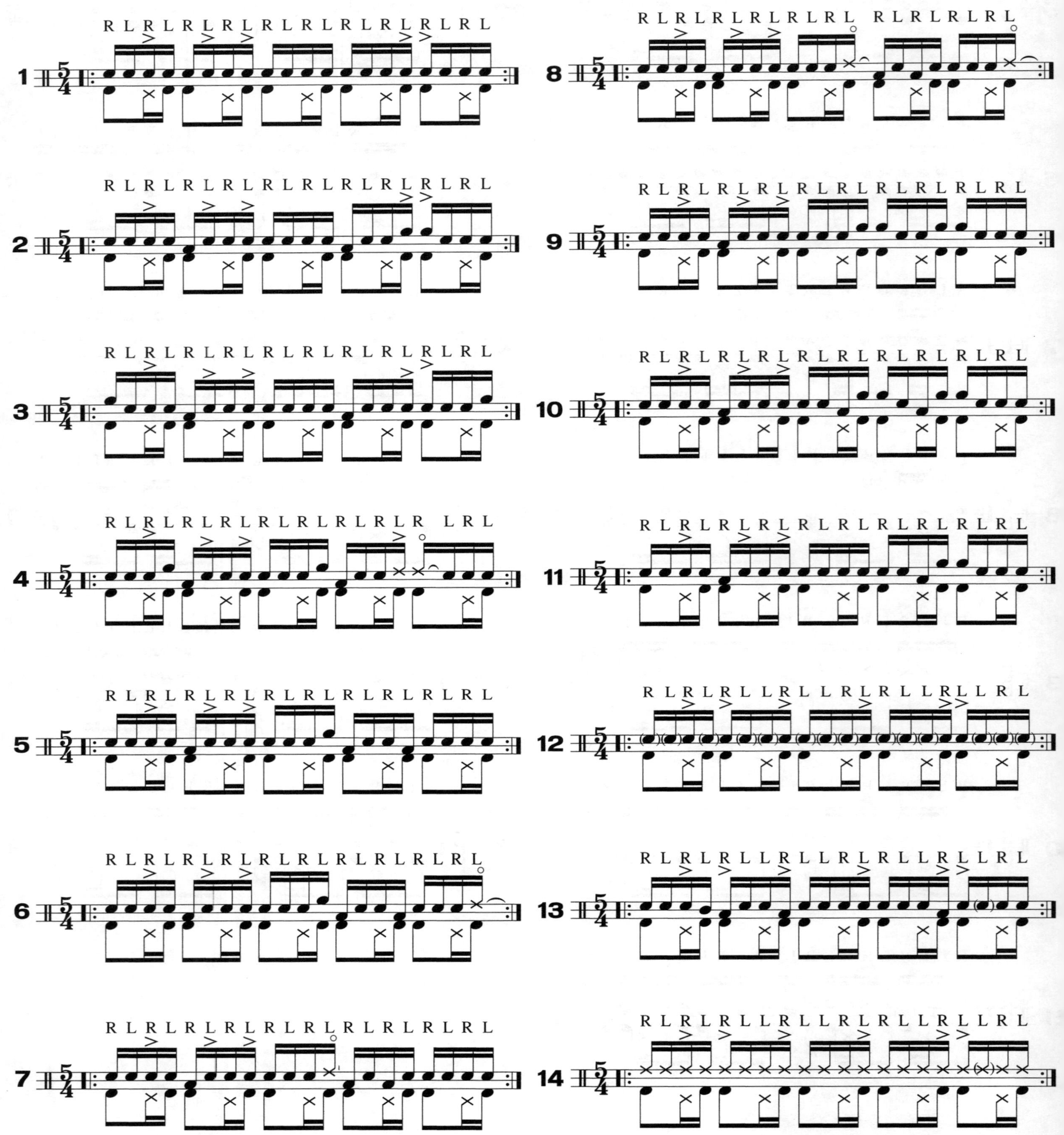

15

16

17

Samba de Prato in $\frac{5}{4}$ (Medium tempo)

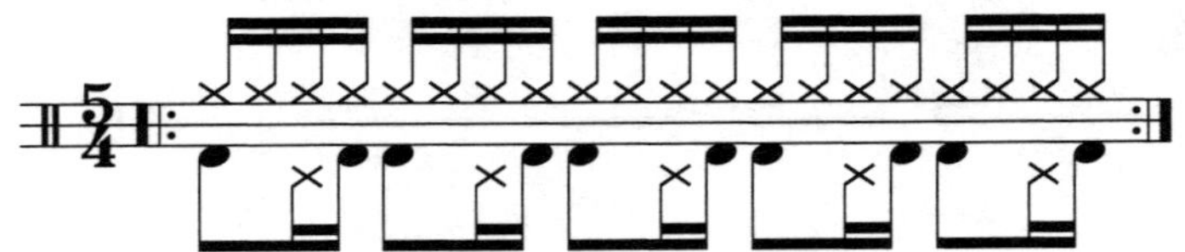

Play the following examples with the left hand:

Samba de Prato in $\frac{5}{4}$ (Fast tempo)

Open hi-hat with left hand:

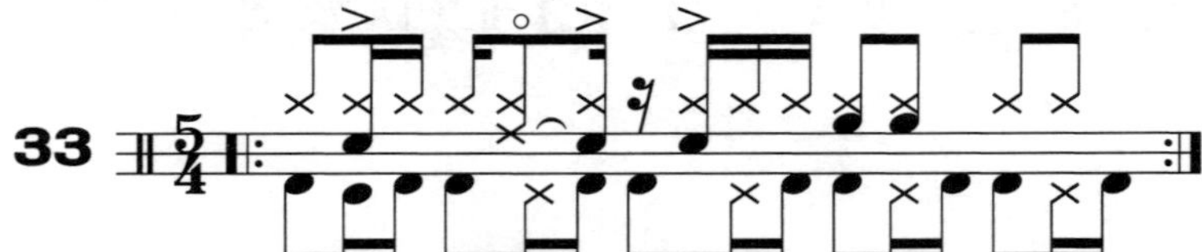

Open hi-hat with left hand:

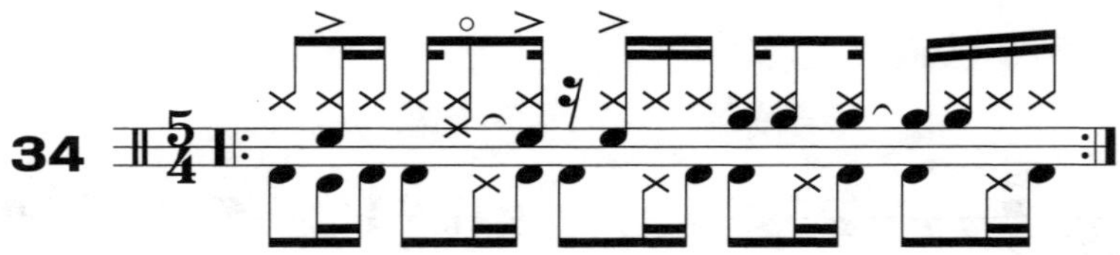

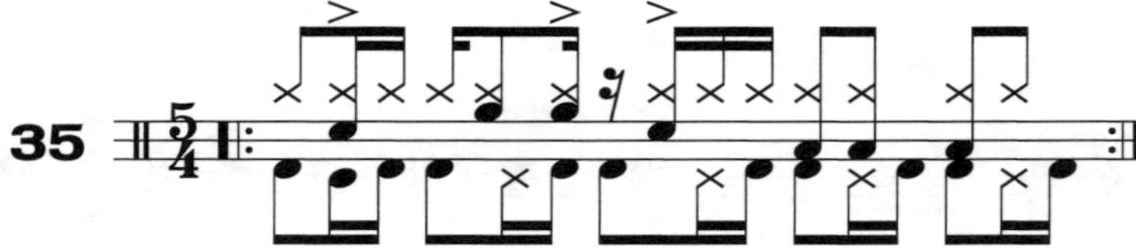

Open hi-hat with left hand:

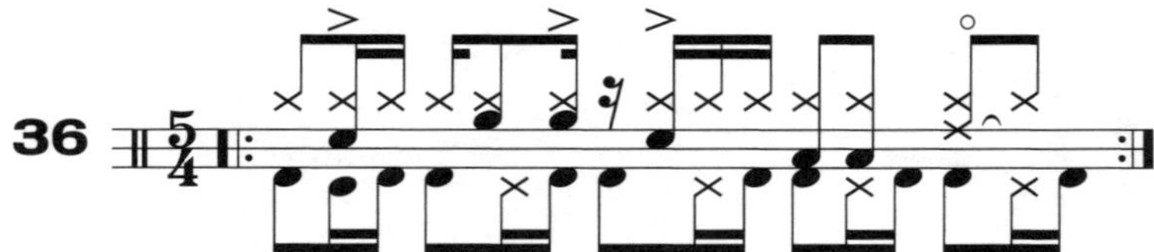

Samba Fusion in $\frac{5}{4}$

Playing the high tom.

Playing the high tom

R L R L L R L R L R L L R L L R L R R L

9

R L R L L R L R L R L L R L L R L R R L

10

Right hand plays the ride cymbal:

11

12

13

14

15

16

17

18

19

20

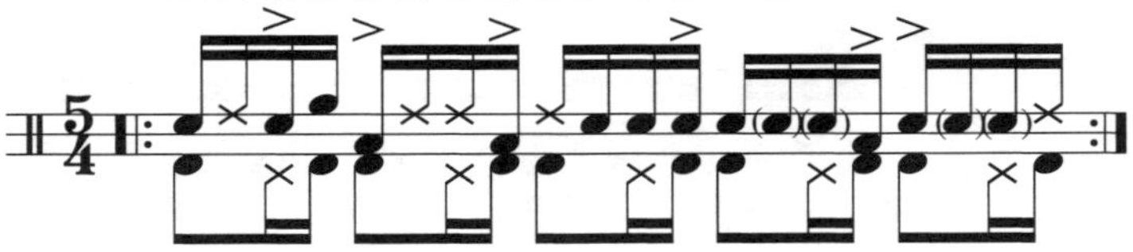

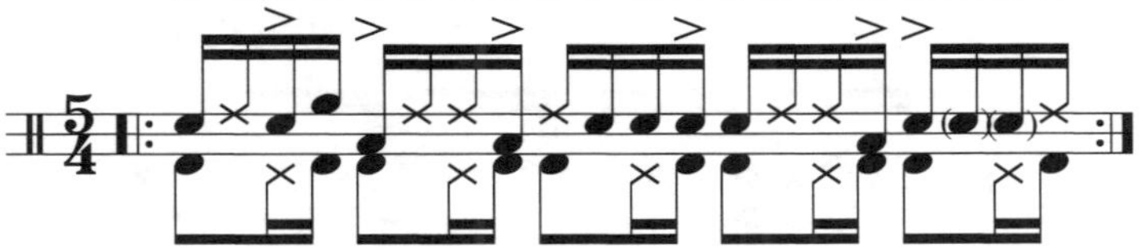

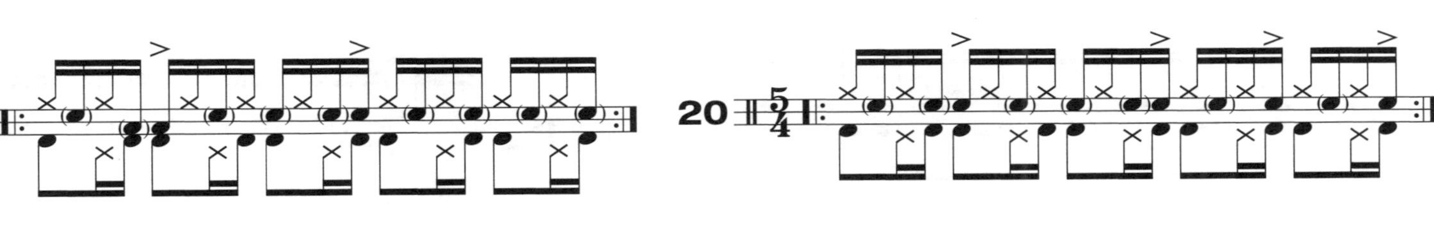

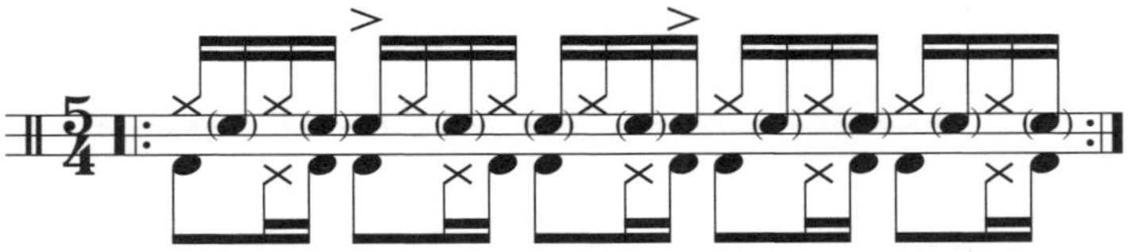

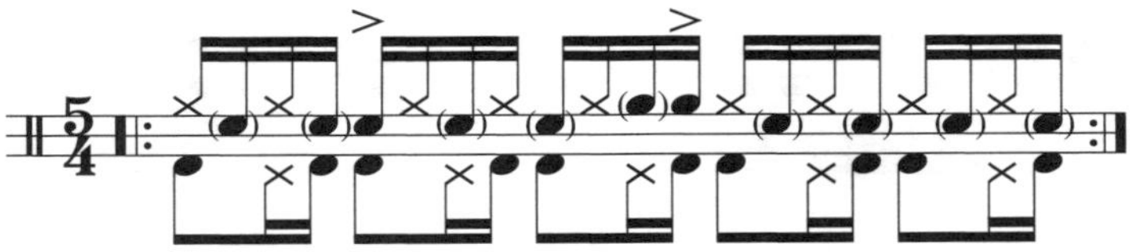

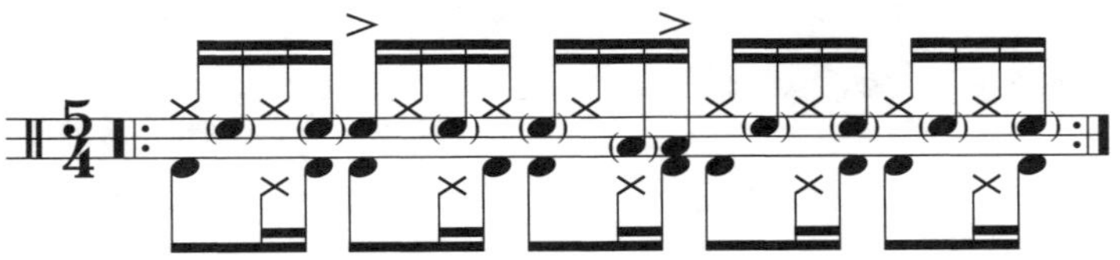

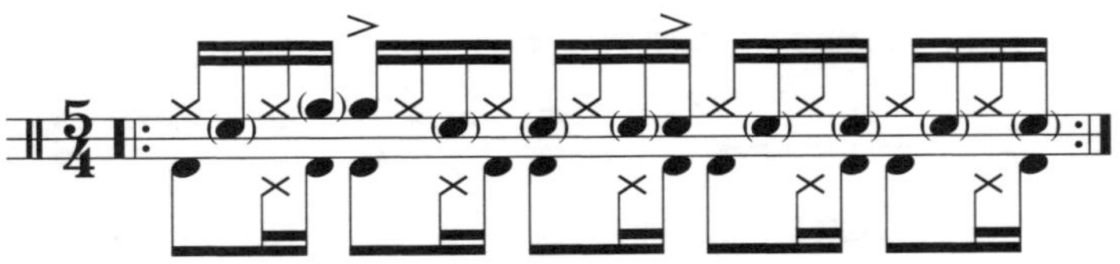

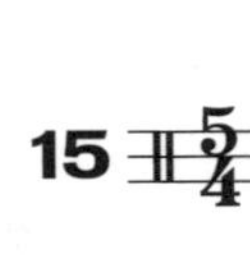

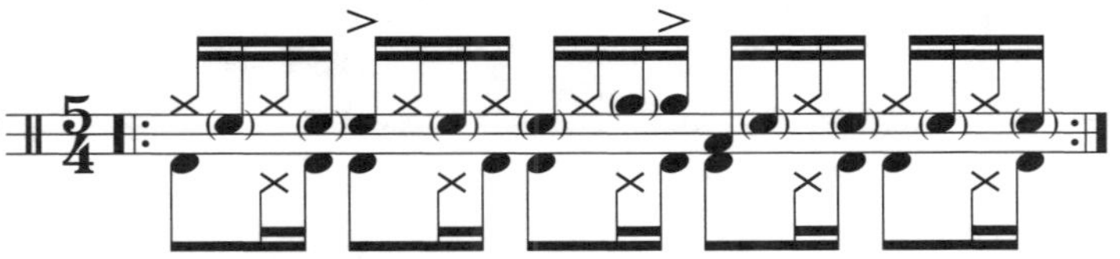

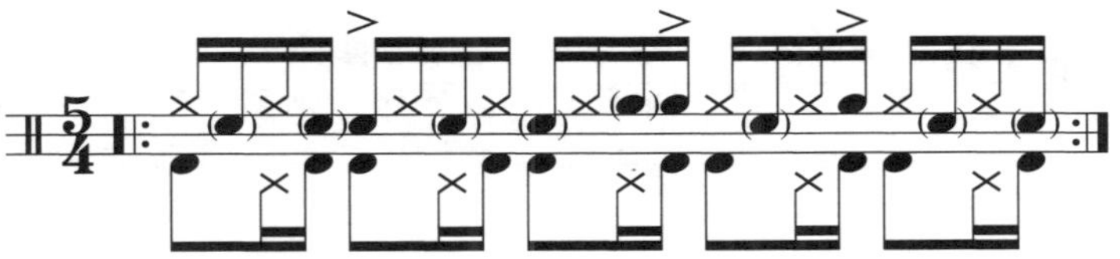

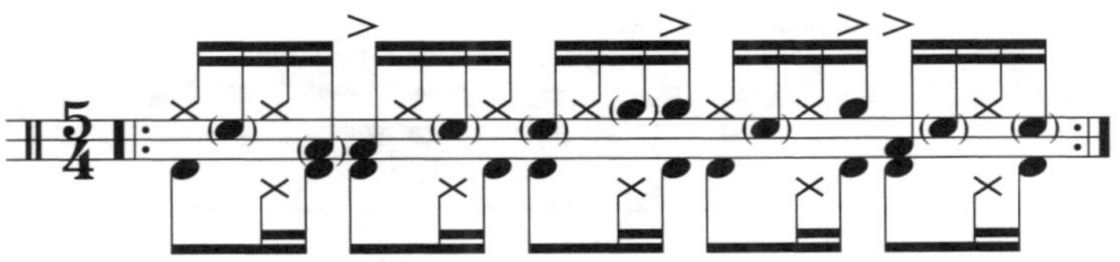

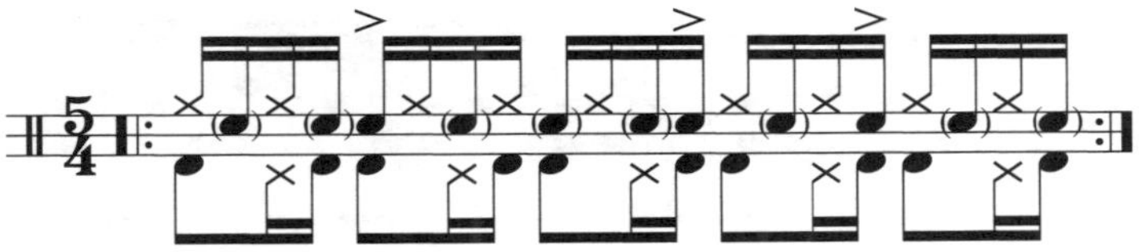

Dori on page 156 in the Play-along Section (Disk 2, Track 6, without drums on Track 13) incorporates Samba in $\frac{5}{8}$ grooves.

Samba in 7/8

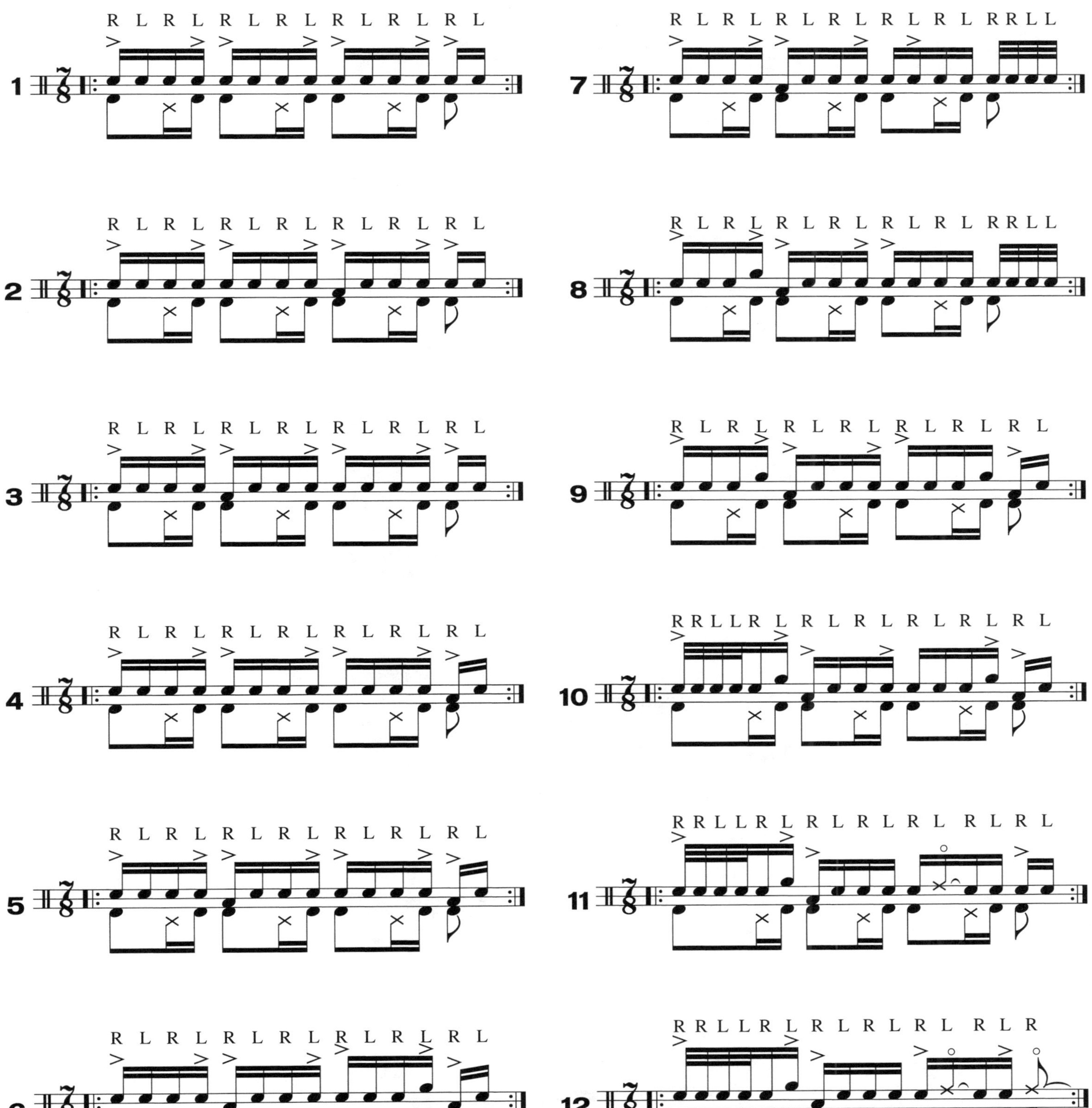

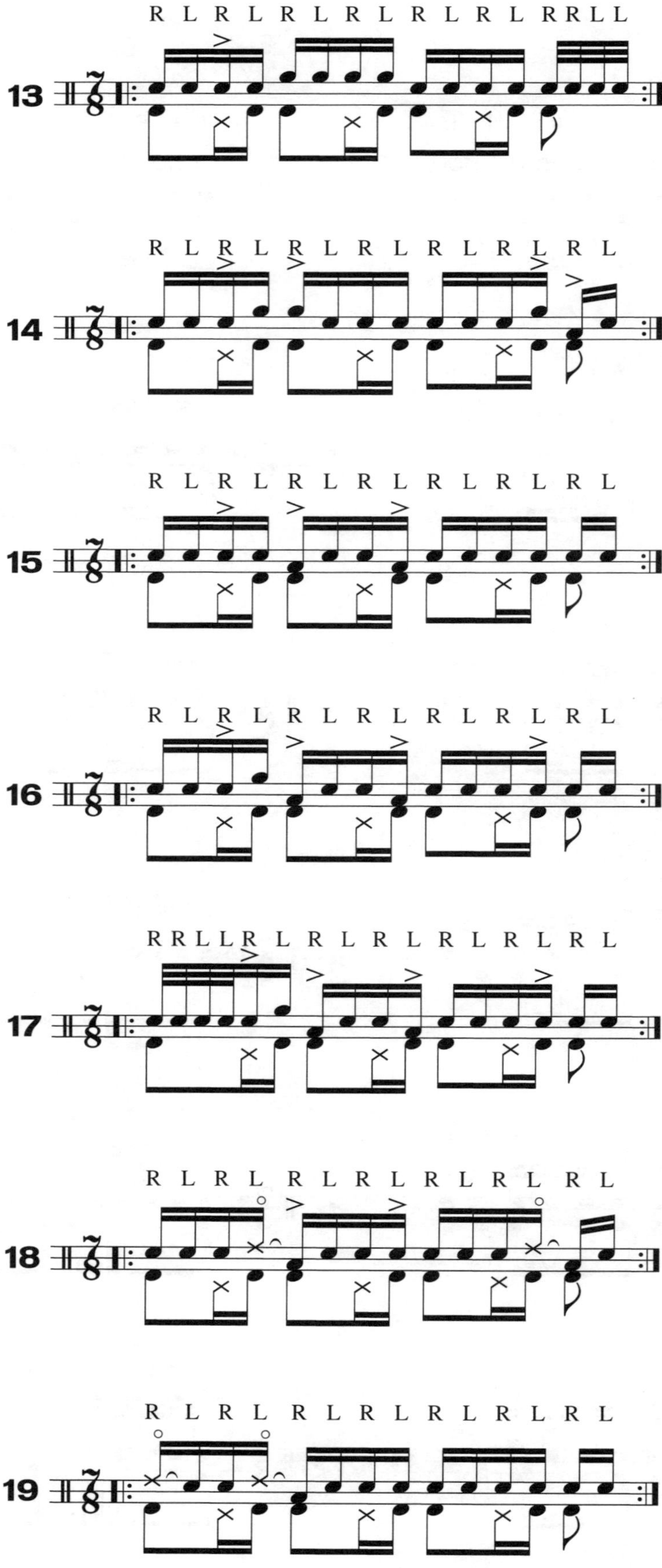
R L R L R L R L R L R L R R L L
13
R L R L R L R L R L R L R L
14
R L R L R L R L R L R L R L
15
R L R L R L R L R L R L R L
16
R R L L R L R L R L R L R L
17
R L R L R L R L R L R L R L
18
R L R L R L R L R L R L R L
19

Samba de Prato in 7/8

Perform the following examples with the left hand while playing this ride-cymbal, bass-drum and hi-hat ostinato.

DRM119

20 

21 

22

23

24

25

26

27

28

29

Samba de Prato (Fast-tempo Examples)

Ride Cymbal patterns:

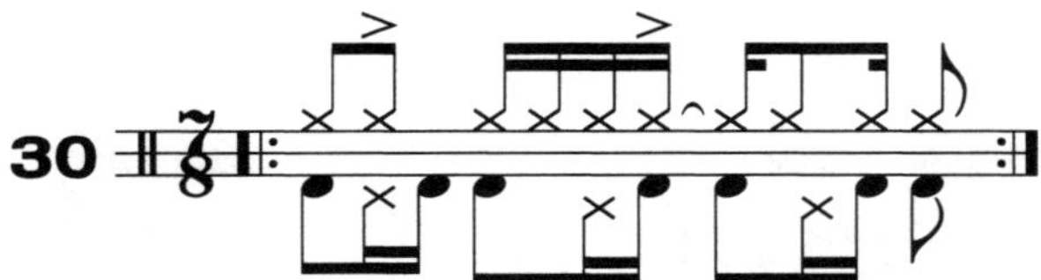

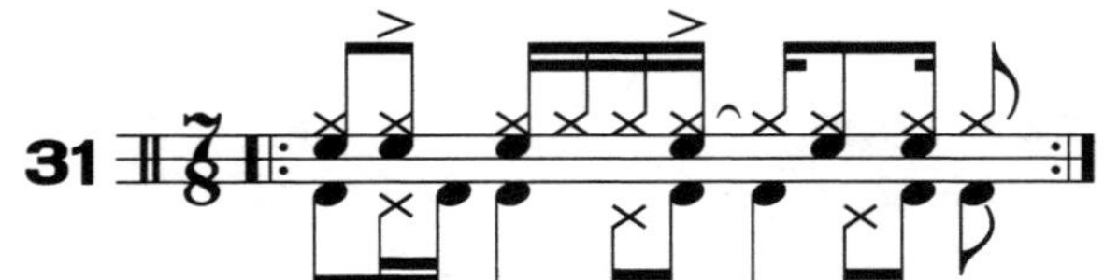

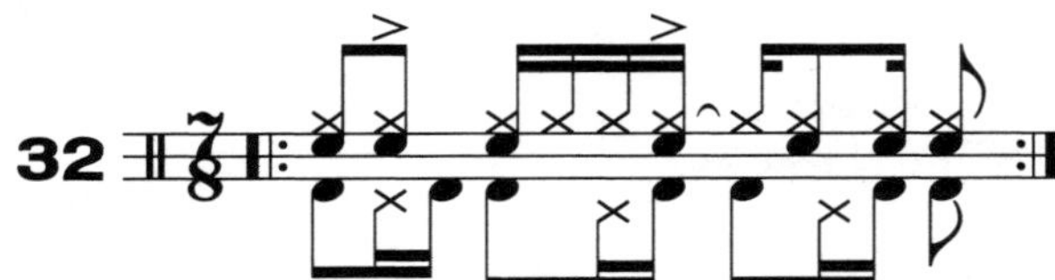

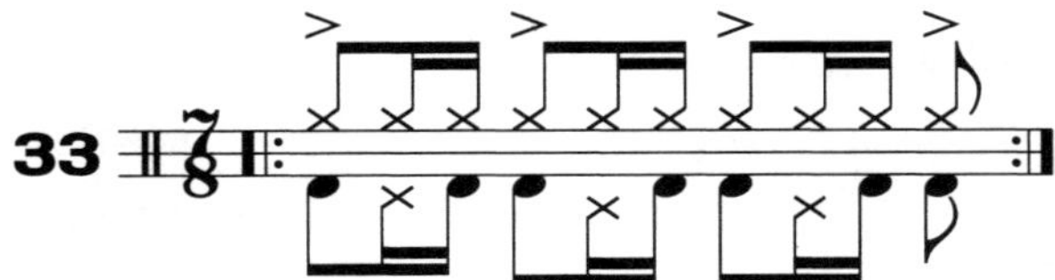

146

Samba Fusion in 7/8

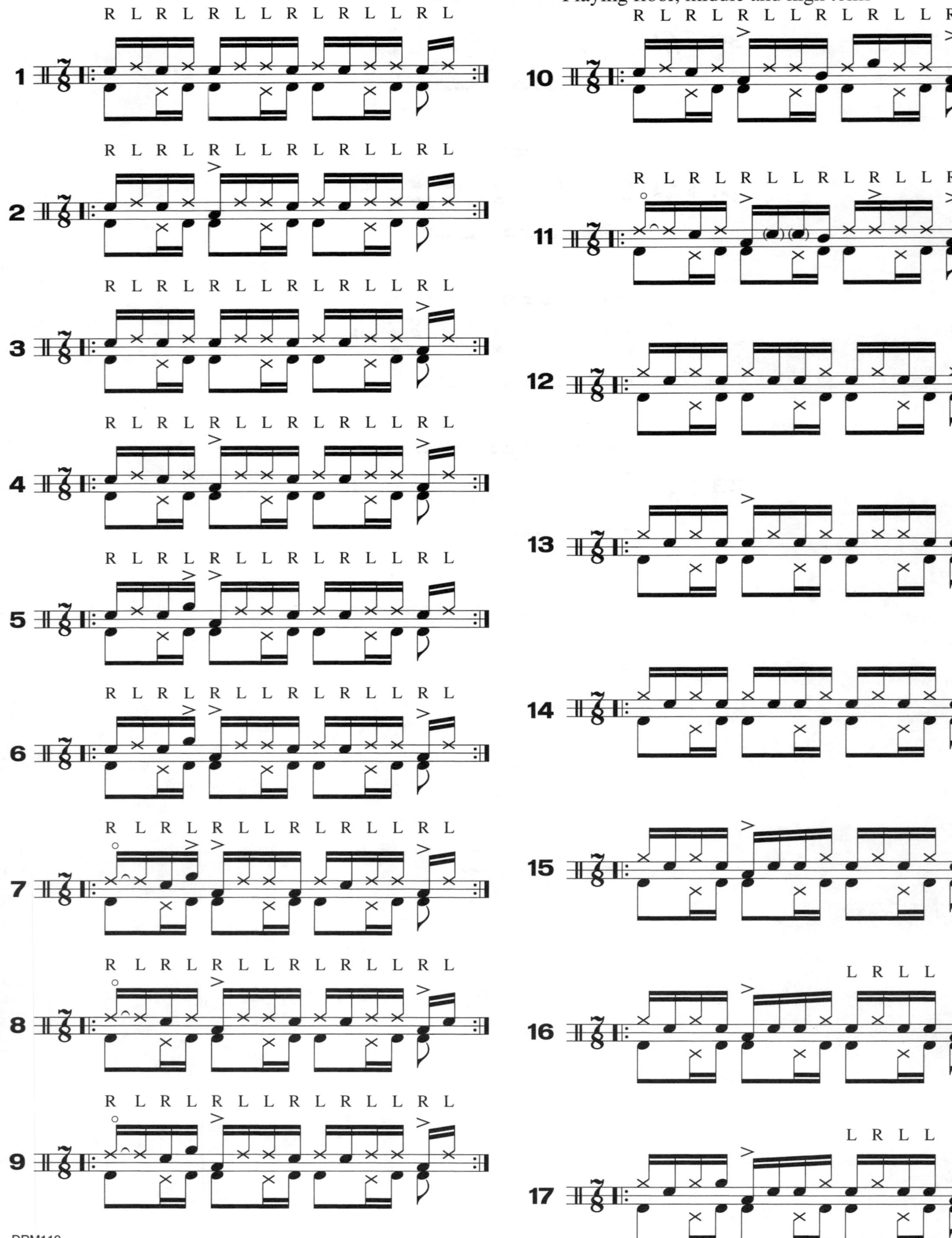

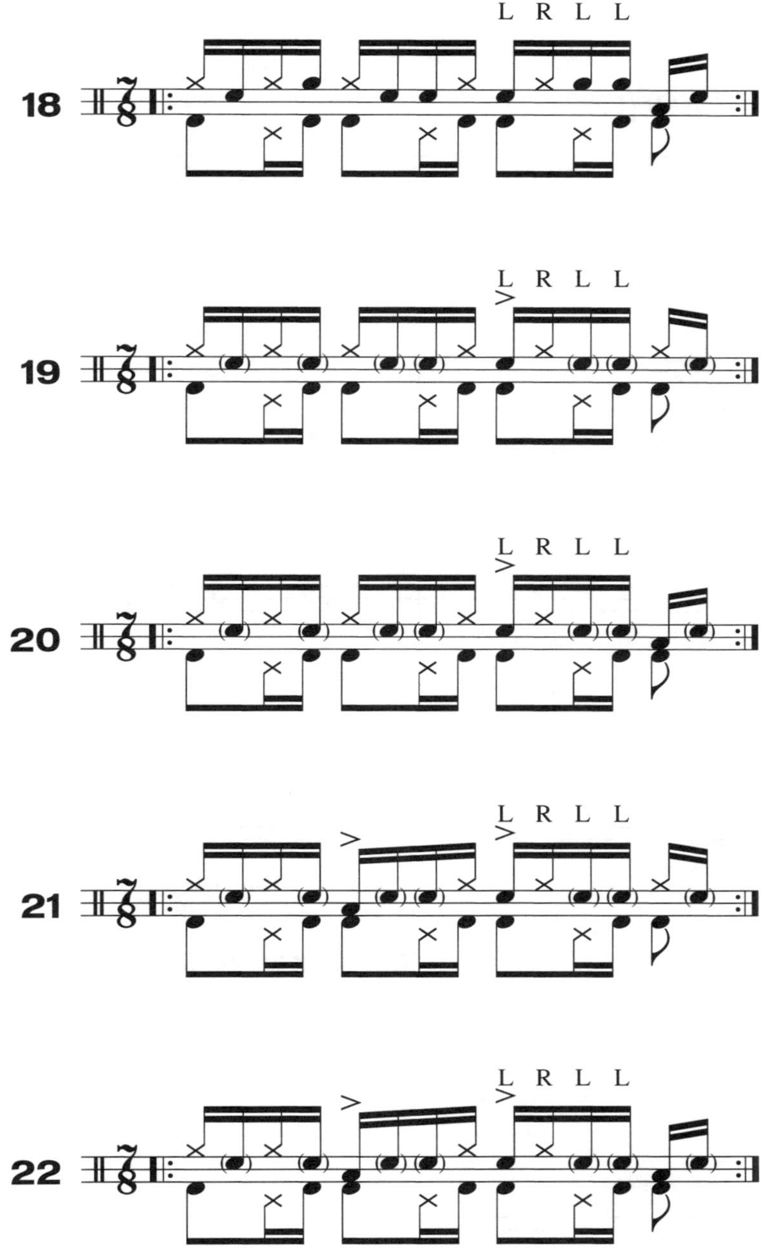

7 Days on page 157 in the Play-along Section (Disk 2, Track 3 without drums on Track 10) incorporates Samba in 7/8 and Samba de Roda in 4/4 grooves.

Play-along Section
Autumn Tale

Drum Set

Henrique C. De Almeida

Intro Contemporary Bossa Groove (Ride)

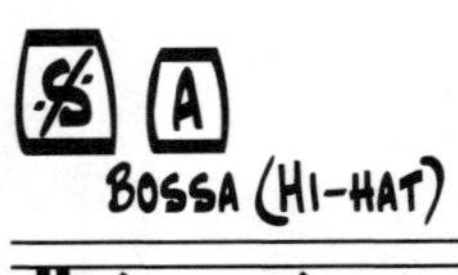

(Ride)

Contemporary Bossa Groove

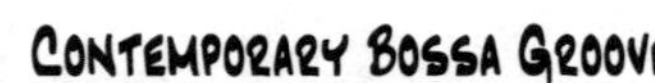

B Bossa

Cymbal Fills

DRM119

C BOSSA (HI-HAT)
D RIDE CYMBAL
FILL
TO CODA
(TO A)
D.S. AL CODA
CODA
FINE
33 34 35 36 37 38 39 40 41 42 43 44 45 46 47 48 49 50 51 52 53 54 55 56 57 58 59 60 61 62 63 64 65

Drum Set

Saudades

Henrique C. De Almeida

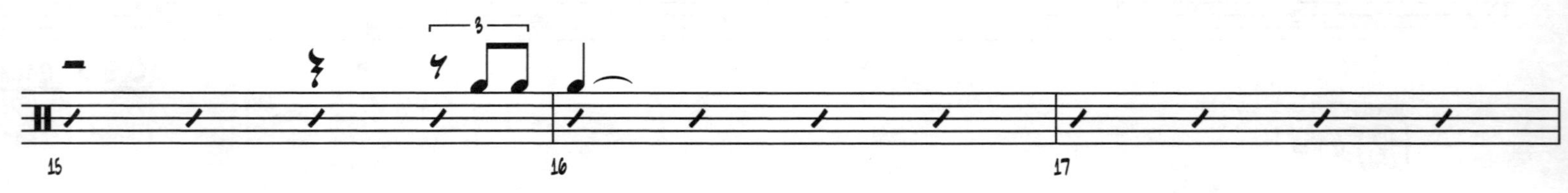

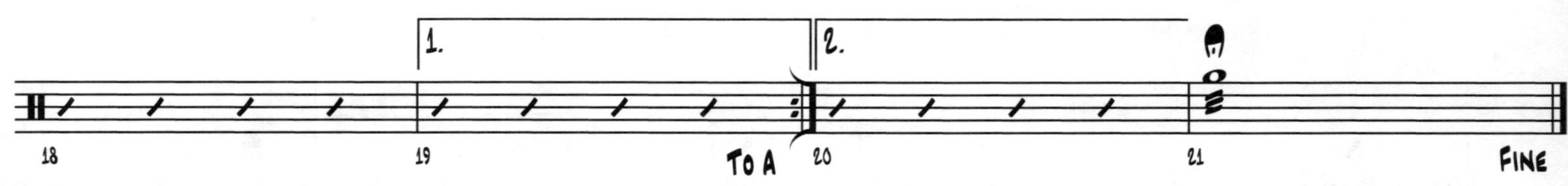

Drum Set

Deixa Falar

Henrique C. De Almeida

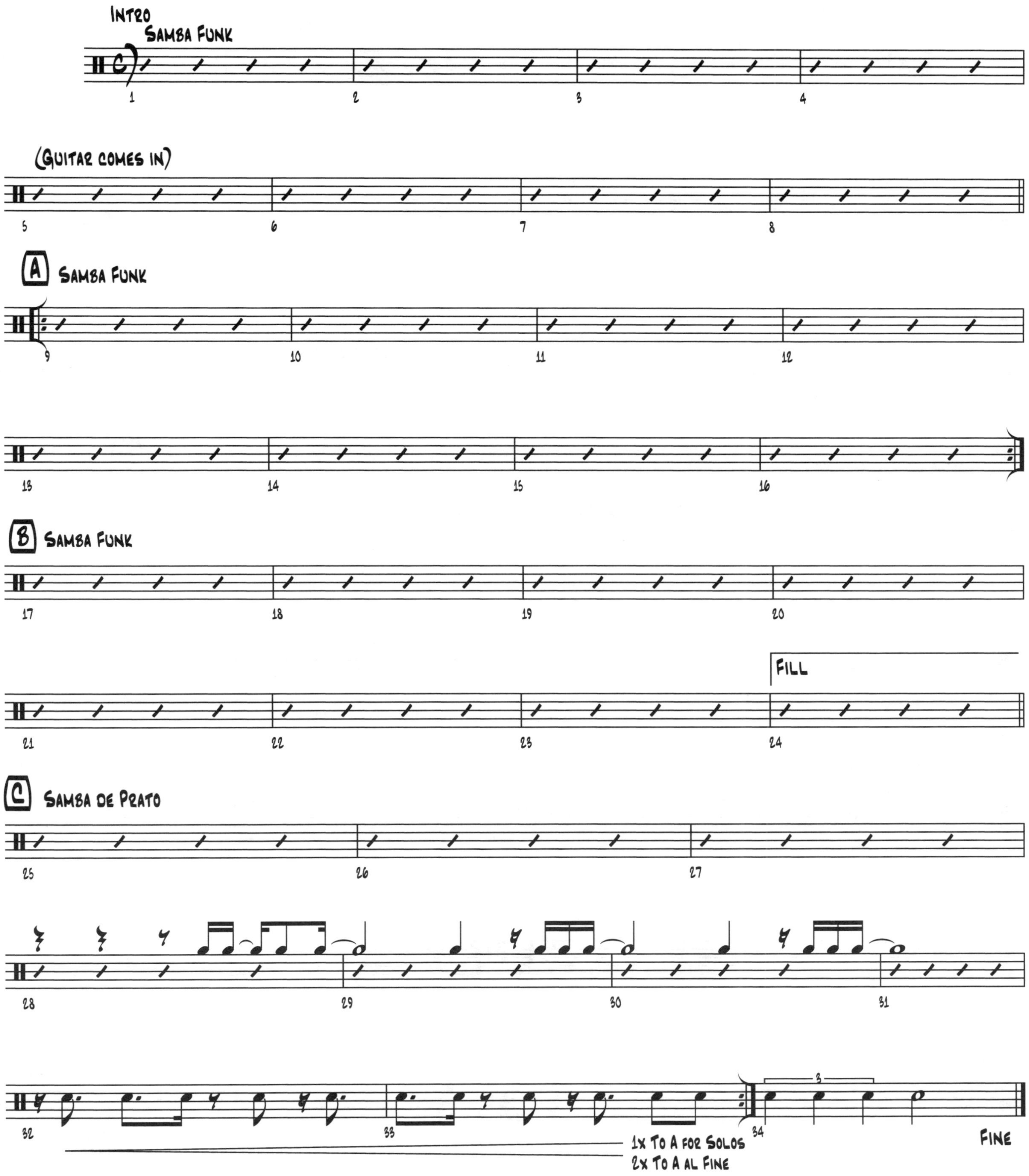

Drum Set

Contigo

Henrique C. De Almeida

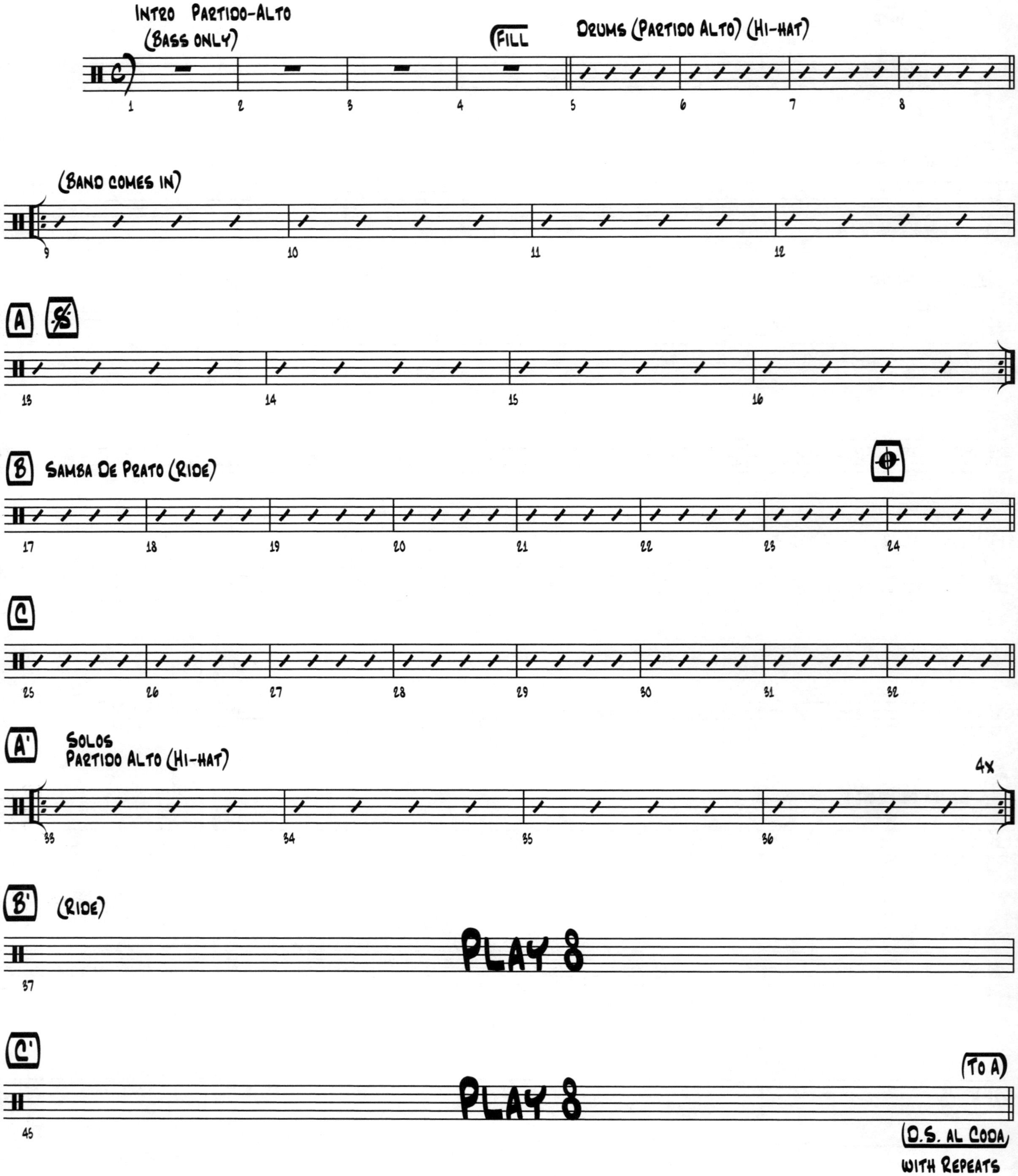

DRM119

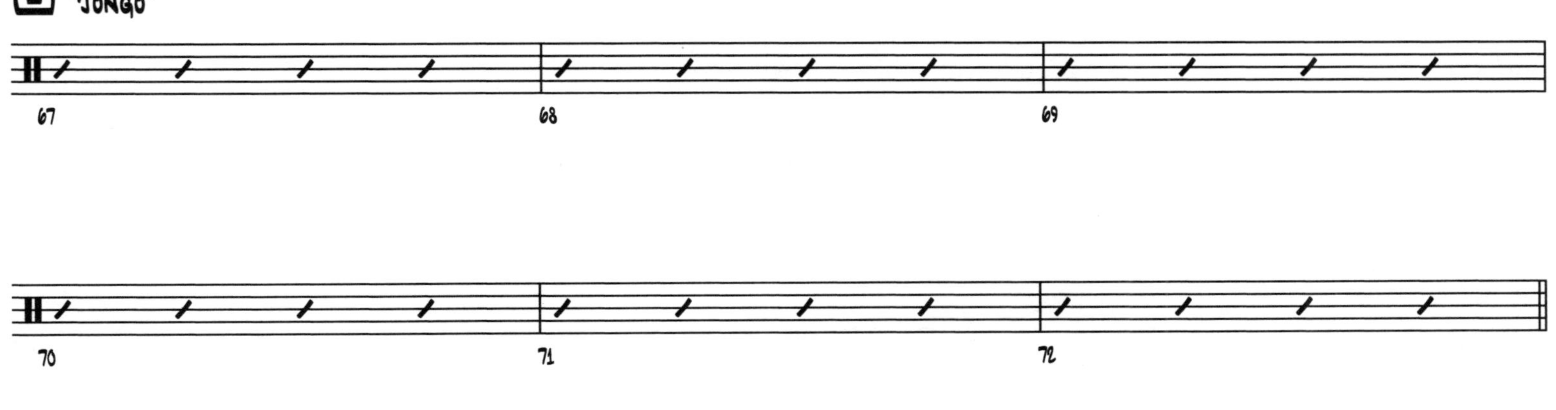
CODA
CAIXA SAMBA PATTERNS
DRUM SOLO
8x

E "JONGO"

FINE

MILTON

Henrique C. De Almeida

Copyright © 2004 by Henrique C. De Almeida

155
D7
4:3
4:3
61
62
63
64
Db7
4:3
4:3
65
66
67
68
4:3
4:3
69
70
71
72
(FILL
73
74
75
76
[77]
PIANO SOLO WITH DRUMS/PERCUSSION
PLAY 16
77
[E]
GUITAR SOLO
Db sus4
D7sus4
TO A
4x
PLAY 4
PLAY 4
93
97
D.S. AL CODA
CODA
4:3
4:3
101
102
103
104
105
4:3
4:3
4:3
106
107
108
109
110
FINE
DRM119

6 13
Play-along Disk

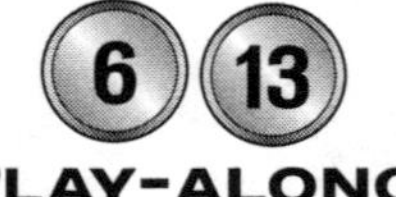

Dori

Henrique C. De Almeida

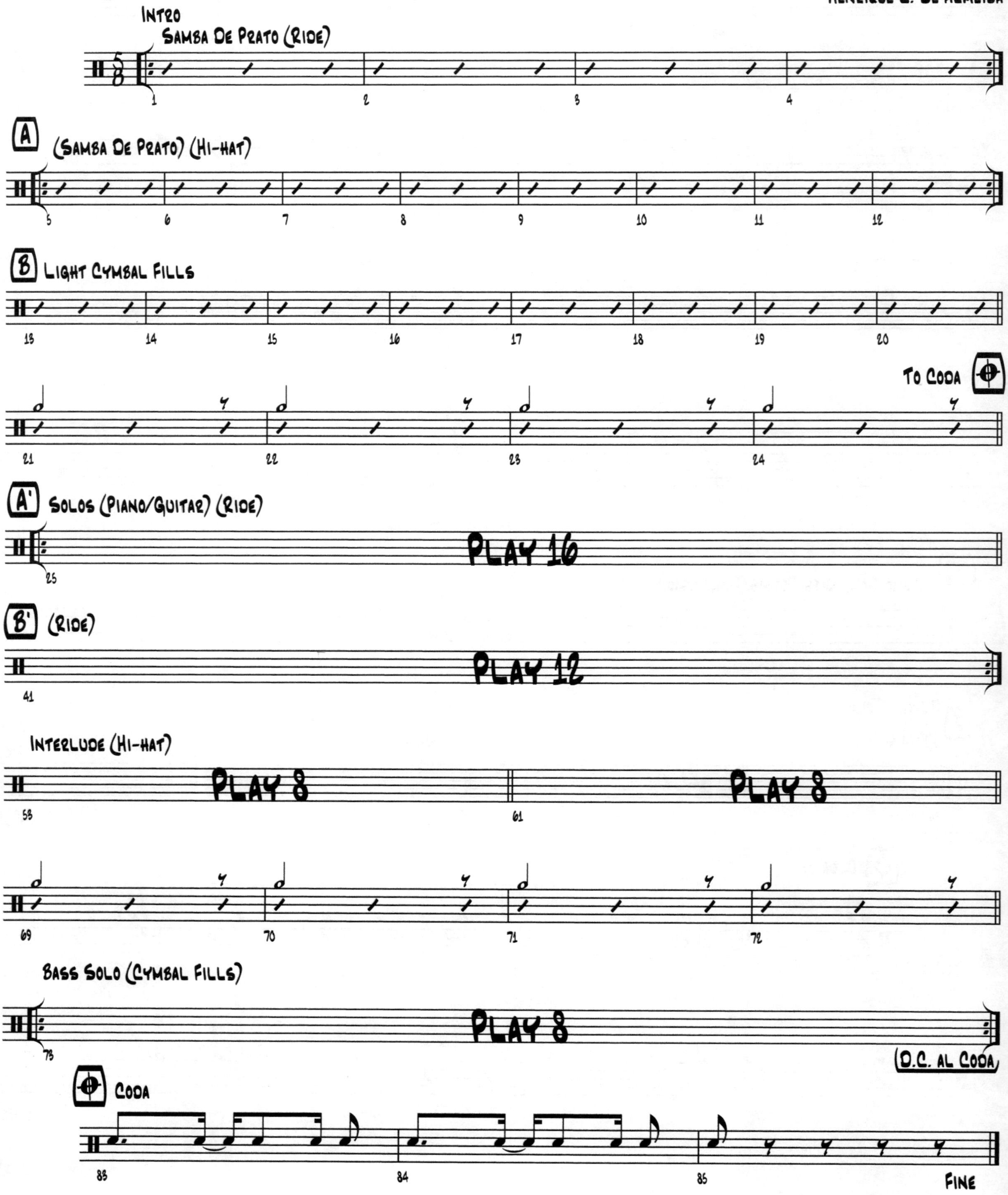

Drum Set

7 Days

Henrique C. De Almeida

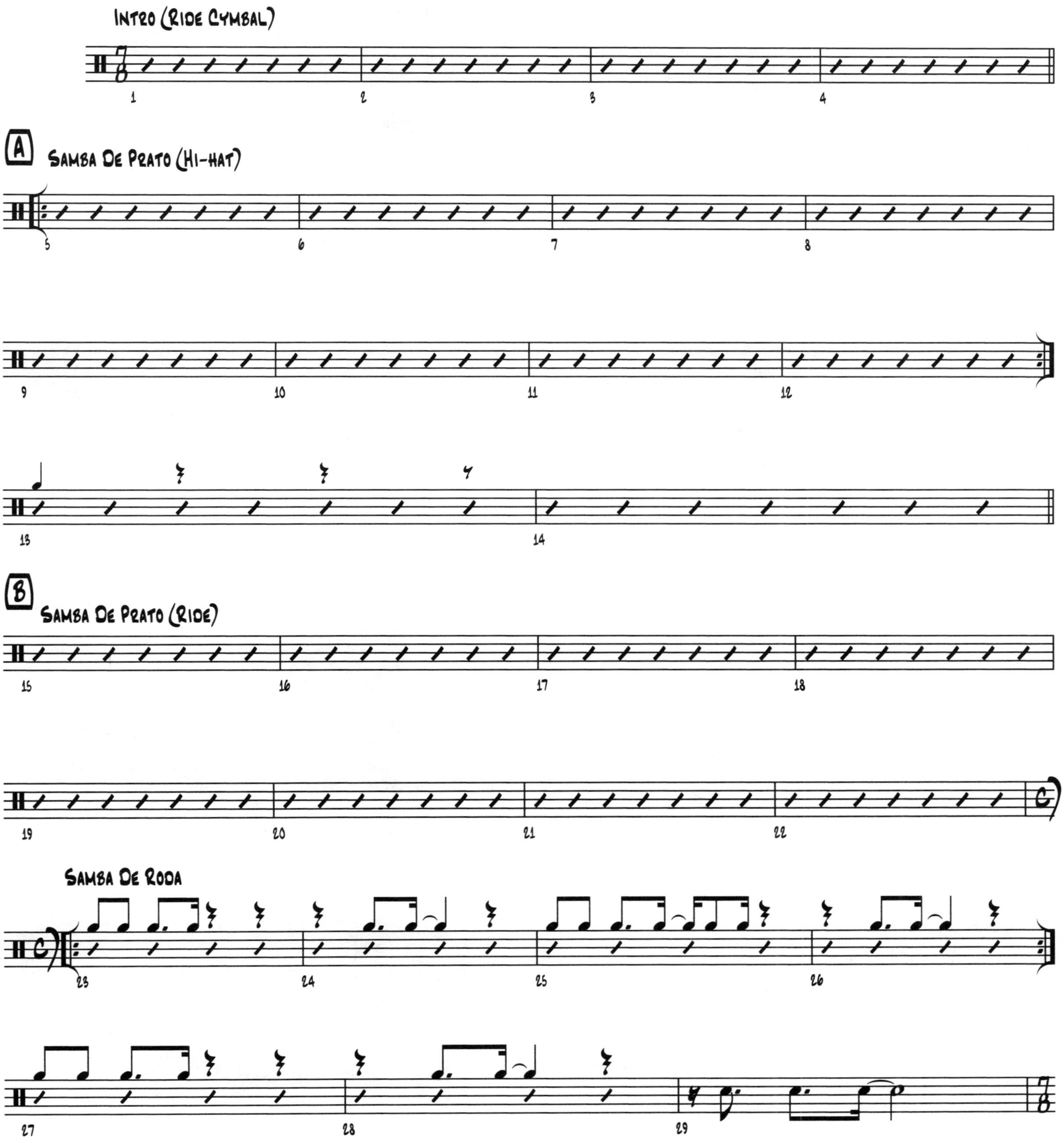

Intro (Ride Cymbal)

A Samba De Prato (Hi-hat)

B Samba De Prato (Ride)

Samba De Roda

DRM119

TAKE IT TO THE NEXT LEVEL!

AKIRA JIMBO

Fujiyama – Combining Acoustic and Electronic Drums - Book w/ CD (DRM108)
Fujiyama (DVD7)

Wasabi – Adding Spice to Your Groove - Book w/CD (DRM107)
Wasabi (DVD1)

In *Fujiyama*, Akira reveals his concepts on the use of acoustic and electronic drums and how they can be integrated into a unique playing style. Major topics of discussion include location of trigger pickups, trigger function modes and programming drum patterns. *Wasabi* helps drummers add spice to their groove and tells of his personal journey into the discovery of his drumming personality. DVDs are in English, Spanish and Japanese.

DAVE WECKL

Exercises for Natural Playing - Book w/CD (DRM110)

How to Develop Technique (DVD8)
How to Practice (DVD9)

In *How to Develop Technique*, Weckl explains his natural approach to the drums in clear language and with careful demonstrations. In this DVD, he focuses on wrist technique, stick grip, finger technique and the rebound approach to both hands and feet. *How to Practice* centers on hand and foot development, independent practice, Swiss triplets and his own warm-ups. In *Exercises for Natural Playing*, Weckl offers the reader exciting new exercises and concepts not covered in the DVDs including insight into hand positioning, the Moeller technique, bass drum pedal work, time and motion and playing without losing time. DVDs are in English, Spanish and Japanese.

STANTON MOORE

Take It To The Street - Book w/ CD (DRM115)
A Study in New Orleans Street Beats and Second-line Rhythms As Applied to Funk

A Traditional Approach to New Orleans Drumming (DVD15)
A Modern Approach to New Orleans Drumming (DVD16)

❖ **Rated 5 stars by Modern Drummer** ❖

Mix it up New Orleans Style and *Take It To The Street!* in this comprehensive book and two DVDs by one of the Crescent City's hottest drummers. In this series, Stanton focuses on street beats, funk, clave and second-line drumming along with his personal insight into becoming a truly gifted and musical drummer.

RICK LATHAM

Advanced Funk Studies - Book w/2 CDs (RLP1)
Contemporary Drumset Techniques - Book w/4 CDs (RLP2)

Advanced Funk Studies 25th Anniversary (DVD18)

Drummers have considered Latham's best selling books *Advanced Funk Studies*, which Modern Drummer calls one of the 25 greatest drum books ever published, and *Contemporary Drumset Techniques* as 'must have' publications for decades. Latham also celebrates 25 years with this Anniversary DVD that includes material from both books focusing on linear playing and includes exclusive interviews legendary drummers Ed Shaughnessy and Louie Bellson.

These publications are available at your local print music dealer.

For more information about Carl Fischer Music log on to:
www.carlfischer.com

GLOBAL RHYTHMS

Vodou Drumset
Drumset Applications of Traditional Afro-Haitian Rhythms
by James Armstrong and Travis Knepper forward by John Amira

Learn to apply Afro-Haitian rhythms (including traditional styles such as Ibo, Nago and Yanvalou) to drum set. This enormously rich but often neglected tradition will add a new, nearly endless range of possibilities for the creative drummer. This book features a play-along CD that will help you incorporate the Haitian sound into your playing.

DRM103

Afro Caribbean and Brazilian Rhythms for the Drumset

Derived from the courses developed at the famed Drummers Collective in New York, this comprehensive introduction to Afro- Caribbean and Brazilian drumming styles is sure to add some spice to your playing. The two CD set included with this publication lets the user hear examples and performance tracks by The Collective faculty. Also included are play-along tracks where the drummer can join in. This workbook features explanations on style and derivatives, historical background, notated examples and playing tips.

CO1

The ABCs of Brazilian Percussion
Ney Rosauro

Learn to play with the right feel and the correct technique in this comprehensive guide to Brazilian percussion. This book with DVD focuses on the 12 most important percussion instruments in Brazilian music and concentrates on teaching the viewer the right "groove" to become proficient with samba, samba reggae, baião, frevo and maracatú. In addition, the viewer will learn basic patterns and the importance of Brazilian clave. The DVD is included because Brazilian percussion is best learned though visual examples. A beautiful way to start delving into the world of Brazilian percussion!

DRM118

The Quick Guide to Djembe Drumming
NOW AVAILABLE ON DVD!
Featuring Steve Leicach

This DVD brings you a concise and comprehensive look at the techniques that a player will need when learning to play the African Djembe drum. Topics covered include essential drum tones, diverse assortment of African rhythms, improvisation, soloing, cultural contexts and much more.

DVD13

The Quick Guide to Playing Doumbek
NOW AVAILABLE ON DVD!
Featuring Todd Roach

The Quick Guide to Playing Doumbek offers a preliminary approach to learning to play Doumbek, the popular Middle Eastern drum. The lessons are taught progressively where the viewer will learn proper tone and rhythmic combinations that are directly integrated into playing traditional Middle Eastern Music.

DVD14